THE LAND OF ISRAEL

Its Theological Dimensions

A Study of a Promise and of a Land's "Holiness"

Jack Shechter

University Press of America,® Inc.
Lanham · Boulder · New York · Toronto · Plymouth, UK

Copyright © 2010 by
University Press of America,® Inc.
4501 Forbes Boulevard
Suite 200
Lanham, Maryland 20706
UPA Acquisitions Department (301) 459-3366

Estover Road
Plymouth PL6 7PY
United Kingdom

Library of Congress Control Number: 2010924019
ISBN: 978-0-7618-5127-1 (clothbound : alk. paper)
ISBN: 978-0-7618-5128-8 (paperback : alk. paper)
eISBN: 978-0-7618-5129-5

⊖™The paper used in this publication meets the minimum
requirements of American National Standard for Information
Sciences—Permanence of Paper for Printed Library Materials,
ANSI Z39.48-1992

To Leah...

For her indispensable help, inexhaustible patience –
and abiding love.

The selection of Israel, the indestructibility of God's covenant with Israel, the immortality of Israel as a nation, and the final restoration of Israel to Palestine, where the nation will live a holy life, on holy ground, with all the wide-reaching consequences of the conversion of humanity, and the establishment of the Kingdom of God on earth—all these are the common ideals and the common ideas that permeate the whole of Jewish literature extending over nearly four thousand years.

Solomon Schechter,
Seminary Addresses

When the people of a land adopt holiness as an ideal, the land is also touched with sanctity. In the case of Israel, the entire land of Canaan became a holy place because it was the physical setting for Israel's effort to build a holy nation in the image of the ideals set forth in the covenant...The land was an integral part of the culture created in it, and because holiness was the dominant ideal of that culture, the land itself became tinged with that holiness.

Ben Zion Bokser,
Jews, Judaism and the State of Israel

TABLE OF CONTENTS

PREFACE

The Land of Israel has been a phenomenon in the annals of the Jewish people for four millennia. The religious dimensions of this phenomenon have always been at its heart. To trace these dimensions is a daunting task indeed, but it is one that needs to be undertaken because of the huge consequences the land has wrought in the life of the Jewish people as well as people of the Muslim and Christian worlds.

My study of this subject began in earnest with doctoral studies at the University of Pittsburgh and the Pittsburgh Theological Seminary. The focus was on the theology of the land as it appeared in the biblical book of Deuteronomy. The dissertation on the subject that culminated in my doctorate has been adapted to constitute the core of this book. Because of its compelling nature, I decided to add to the first findings of the Deuteronomic perspective—the nature of the promise—an exploration of the prophets on the matter. This is then followed by a description of Israel's land phenomenon in the rabbinic, medieval and modern periods. Its theological dimension is the focus.

I have also added to the second findings of the Deuteronomic perspective—the meaning of "holiness"—studies that amplify that notion as depicted in the original dissertation.

The fruits of these studies constitute the contents of this work.

Acknowledgments

In the initial research and writing there were and are now a number of people to thank in a personal way.

While serving my congregation in Pittsburgh as its rabbi, I knew I had to continue to study. The Pittsburgh Theological Seminary was nearby. I enrolled in its doctoral program in conjunction with the University of Pittsburgh. There I met Dr. Eberhard von Waldow, Professor of Old Testament—excellent scholar, warm human being, and peerless pedagogue. He was my guide throughout the years of my doctoral studies. He supervised these studies with such discernment, patience and goodwill that it is difficult to find the appropriate words with which to thank him.

At the seminary I met another special man, Dr. Markus Barth, then Professor of Bible and subsequently at the University of Basel in Switzerland. Son of the renowned theologian Karl Barth, Professor Barth was particularly interested in the biblical perspectives on the land and their pertinence to the contemporary situation. His personal passion for this subject combined with a penetrating intelligence stimulated me to pursue this research. Ours was a friendly and intense "dialogical" association in Pittsburgh and during a memorable visit in Switzerland that was highlighted by his incredibly luminous demeanor. I owe him much.

When I left for California to serve as Dean of Continuing Education at the University of Judaism and teach in its Bible Department, Dr. von Waldow asked his colleague Dr. Rolf Knierim, Professor of Old Testament at the Claremont Graduate School, to help oversee the dissertation work there. In him I encountered scholarly brilliance, methodological meticulousness and rigorous standards for study. To him I owe much in helping develop the plan and method of the dissertation.

Professors von Waldow, Barth and Knierim shared in common not only profound scholarship, but another basic lifetime preoccupation: each was deeply committed to a constructive rapprochement between Christian and Jew. They were profoundly sensitive to the traumatic aftershocks of the Holocaust and to the condition of the State of Israel today. As faithful religionists they sought guidance on these issues from scripture. That is why they encouraged my work. But most significantly, they allowed me to pursue this research in a way that respected and affirmed my own particular orientation as a Jew. They helped me find my own way. This respect for the integrity of one of another faith stemmed from gifts of heart and mind they possessed in such abundance.

When I began at Pittsburgh Seminary I also came under the tutelage of Dr. Paul Lapp, who had just come to the seminary as Professor of Archaeology after eight years as Director of the American Schools of Oriental Research in Jerusalem. He was profoundly interested in the subject, 'The Holy Land," and in numerous personal discussions in the ambience of his home and at the seminary, he stimulated me to pursue this work. His was a combative and controversial approach on the matter, but suffused with the profound insight derived from wide-ranging scholarship. His tragic drowning during an archaeological expedition in Cyprus was a great loss to so many in the field of biblical scholarship throughout the world.

Nahum Sarna

There is another person to whom I owe thanks for the seminal influence he had on me in the area of biblical studies. He is Dr. Nahum Sarna, who served for many years as Professor of Biblical Studies at Brandeis University outside of Boston. At the time I was Director of the New England Region of the United Synagogue of America headquartered in Brookline, Mass.

For five consecutive years we sat together as congregants in the pews of Congregation Kehillath Israel in Brookline. This was every Shabbat and holiday service, the consistency about which we both complained yet from which we rarely absented ourselves. Nahum was a warm and friendly and embracing persona and most especially a profoundly informed and creative biblical scholar. I had arranged a wide-ranging seminar program for rabbis and educators in Boston featuring Dr. Sarna and his path-breaking approach to Bible study which successfully reconciled biblical tradition with the new literary, historical and archaeological findings that have emerged from the studies of scholars of the ancient Near Eastern milieu. This helped cement a bond between us.

At each of the Shabbat and holiday services before, during and after the Torah reading (yes, we were a bit out of line on this score), Nahum would share with me his interpretations, replete with documented data, insights, bon mots that illumined for me fascinating traditional and modern approaches to the world of the Bible. The utter consistency and substantive content of these encounters constituted an education (tuition-free) in scripture of the first order.

Before leaving Boston for Pittsburgh to take up my post as a pulpit rabbi, Nahum gifted me with a 14th century illuminated manuscript reproduced from the original. It was a prayer from an Ashkenazic Yom Kippur prayerbook. Framed by an *Aron Kodesh* (holy ark), towers, birds and figures in various praying postures was the text:

בָּרוּךְ אַתָּה ה׳ אֱלֹהֵינוּ מֶלֶךְ הָעוֹלָם הַפּוֹתֵחַ לָנוּ שַׁעַר

Blessed are You O God, King of the universe, who opens for
us the gates."

Nahum reminded me that this, of course, meant the gates to heaven asking for forgiveness; but also, he said, it meant the "gates to learning" as I proceed to my new task.

Nahum also took me with him to the Andover Theological Seminary library in Newton to study the collection of biblical books and made sure that I had the latest comprehensive publication containing the standard resources for intensive biblical study.

I've long since been persuaded that the five-year encounter with Nahum Sarna laid the groundwork for the kind of work a book of this nature required. Yet more: When I applied for admission to the doctoral program in biblical studies at the University of Pittsburgh/Pittsburgh Theological Seminary, Nahum wrote a recommendation for me which helped in no small measure. Nahum has since passed away. The memory of him is, indeed, a blessing.

More Thanks

A number of Jewish scholars and friends have helped me considerably during the work on the original dissertation and especially on its updating for more general interest in the subject. I am grateful to them. Dr. Sarna's encouragement was constant. Dr. Bernard Goldstein, Professor of the History of Science at the University of Pittsburgh, was especially sensitive about the distinctively Jewish perspective on this work and did not allow me to be veered from it. Rabbi Arthur Hertzberg, author of the seminal volume *The Zionist Idea* from which I learned so much, favored me with his characteristically incisive insights about the modern Zion/Israel period. Dr. Marvin Sweeney (a classmate of my wife, Leah, at Claremont decades ago), a consummate biblical scholar, Professor of Old Testament Studies at the Claremont School of Theology in California, read the manuscript and made numerous extremely valuable and helpful comments. To be sure, whatever errors are discovered in this work (I hope not too many) are to be exclusively attributed to me.

Thanks to John McDonough, whose passion for the religious enterprise, entrepreneurial acumen and, with his Pat, capacity for friendship, make for a potent combination indeed.

I must offer much appreciation to Terri Nigro for typing, and retyping—and retyping—the manuscript of this work and for preparing it for publication. Her skill and patience were ever present.

Thanks, as well, are due to Samantha Kirk, acquisitions editor of the University Press of America, for her proactive role in bringing this book onto the roster of the press's scholarly works, and to Brian DeRocco, UPA's editorial administrator, for managing the work through the publication process. Both have been very helpful in practical ways as well as encouraging and gracious along the way.

I am grateful to my sons, Reuven, David and Judah, for their patience and understanding through the years when so much of my time was consumed with pulpit and administrative responsibilities, as well as with research and writing. All three are quite familiar with the living reality of the Land of Israel, having spent considerable time there in their adult years. I hope that through their experience with this work they'll have additional reasons to understand why they did.

Finally, I wish to thank my wife, Leah, for her encouragement, support and active involvement in this work. Her extraordinary linguistic capacity, research skills and mastery of the Hebrew biblical text helped me lay the groundwork for the original dissertation as well as for this revision. She listened critically and offered valuable insights. Above all, her steadfastness made it possible for me to bring the work to a conclusion. To her I express my profound appreciation.

INTRODUCTION AND "ROAD MAP"

The Land: In Search of Its Meaning

The emergence of the State of Israel and the physical reclamation of the land in our time have generated many questions. Beyond the practical and political meaning of this phenomenon, there looms in many minds the overarching issue of legitimacy, compounded by the theological considerations of the major monotheistic faiths of the world for whom this piece of territory partakes of varying degrees and kinds of "sanctity."

The resurrection of the land and the ingathering of Jews from all over the globe have stimulated anew serious theological reflection, especially on the part of the Christian and Muslim communities. Their different religious spokesmen have been guided by the particular perspectives and emphases within their own respective traditions regarding the meaning of the land.

This is especially true in the Jewish community, which has been nurtured by a tradition deeply attached to Israel's land. For the Jew, this profound, ever present, and all-pervading consciousness of the land has its sources in the Bible, in rabbinic literature, in Jewish history, in the ongoing practice of Jewish religious ritual, in the collective life and consciousness of the Jewish people—past and present.

In view of the many and often conflicting interests and claims, interpretations and theologies with respect to the "Holy Land," none of which are considered by all as "definitive," it is, we believe, appropriate for a student of the Bible to turn once again to the biblical tradition itself and have it speak with its own words, on its own terms, from its own perspective and *Weltanschauung* about the meaning of this land. Indeed, we seek here to elicit from the biblical text what *it* believes and says about the land in the context of its own time and clime and on the basis of its own presuppositions. Our concern is with the biblical tradition because it antedates all the views and interpretations alluded to above, and, at the same time, represents the authoritative background of them all.

The core text of this work is the biblical book of Deuteronomy; the reasons for choosing it will be explained presently. Based on the study of this text, amplified by various extra-biblical resources, two fundamental notions are explicated in detail: the nature of the promise of the land to Israel and the particular perspective that enables one to speak of it as the "Holy Land."

Why Deuteronomy?

Clearly the Bible is preoccupied throughout with the subject of the land. The Pentateuch, the historical writings, the prophetic books, the Writings (*Ketuvim*) all speak of it in one form or another. However, as our study shows, the theological perspective about the promise of the land in Deuteronomy, we believe, is a dominant biblical view; it informs the normative rabbinic outlook down through the ages, and is the grounding for the modern perspectives on the land as well.[1] There are additional reasons, to wit:

• There appears in Deuteronomy an all-pervading preoccupation with the idea of land. The sheer mass of texts dealing in one form or another with the subject is indicative of this. No other biblical book approaches this preoccupation.

• The very setting of the book places the people poised on the eastern side of the Jordan River, ready to take possession of the land and to proceed to inhabit it. Thus Deuteronomy's basic orientation is toward its capture and settlement. Indeed, its entire spirit is pervaded with the consciousness of this specific place as the central focus of Israel's national existence, as the centerpiece of the covenant between God and Israel.

• There is a striking literary and historical phenomenon in Deuteronomy that clearly invites interpretation. On the one hand, we have a book in which Moses is addressing his people immediately prior to their entrance into the land in the 13th century BCE. On the other hand, the scholarly consensus has long since been that the historical matrix of Deuteronomy is the era of King Josiah in the second half of the 7th century BCE. Historically then, following the initial possession of the land in the Mosaic period, the northern kingdom of Israel had been destroyed in 721 BCE by Assyria, and Judah had lost its independence in 701 BCE. Then, in the time of King Josiah, a changed political scene opened up the possibility of a new era of independence for Israel and the reunification of its northern and southern units. Thus Deuteronomy is actually talking about *re*-possessing the land, and its literary text is projecting this aspiration back into the time of Moses and portraying taking possession of the realm for the first time under Joshua, Moses' successor. Why is this so? The answer is rich in significance and implication for the concept of land that emerges from this biblical book.

• While, as we have indicated, there are various perspectives on the land in the Bible of which Deuteronomy is but one, the book has a uniqueness that renders it especially valuable for a study of land. Deuteronomy's uniqueness is in its being the only literary corpus to focus on reclaiming the territory *while Israel was still living on it*. By contrast, the books of Ezekiel and Second Isaiah, for example, are each concerned with the meaning of Israel's territory *after Israel had been exiled from it*, and express the idea of return from their particular vantage points. They speak through the prism of the experience of exile, and reflect the situation and state of mind of a people that had gone through the trauma of actual separation from its land. For Deuteronomy, by contrast, the cataclysmic events of Judah's destruction and exile had not yet occurred, with the result that the way the territory is spoken of in the book is more natural, more concrete, more immediate; it is less an abstract concept as it was for the exiles, but rather a more real and tangible, earthy and vital thing. It is a place where people function in their everyday lives aware of and influenced by the soil, the air, the sounds and smells of their natural environment. This too has much significance for Deuteronomy's perspective on the land.[2]

Thematic Focus

Scrutiny of the welter of passages about the territory in Deuteronomy reveals that the idea of "the land" emerges under a number of basic rubrics:

1. The Land as Gift

2. The Land as Oath

3. The Land and the Law

4. The Land as a Good Land

5. The Land as Possibility and as Peril

6. Israel's Relations with the "Nations" on the Land

Each of these themes is explicated based on its characteristic Hebrew terminology, on biblical land traditions prior to Deuteronomy, on land traditions of the wider Near Eastern cultural milieu, and on the historical setting of the book's 7th century BCE period. The themes are also examined with additional "listening tools" such as anthropological, sociological and theological studies about "place" and "space."

The Talmudic, Medieval and Modern Periods

As one studies the post-biblical literature on the subject of the land as promised, one discerns a striking consensus on the subject, in that the religious dimension adumbrates the perspectives of the biblical period. Though, of course, through time—and especially during the modern period—there developed much nuance, variation and some deviation about the subject, the dominating theological dimension remained in place. Indeed, it served as the "template" upon which the rabbis, liturgists and modernists grafted their views. This work seeks to show how this was so.

A "Road Map" For This Book

To help the reader navigate the highways and byways of this work, what follows is a "road map," which we trust will be useful. Our work is presented in several sections:

PART ONE: *The Nature of the Promise*. The overall purpose here is to explicate Deuteronomy's basic notion about the land, which is God's promise of it to Israel. We do so by examining the various characteristics of the first three themes of the book: "The Promise as Gift" (Chapter One), "The Promise as Oath" (Chapter Two), and "The Land and the Law" (Chapter Three). We then establish that Chapters One and Two view the land as an *unconditional* promise, *not* subject to Israel's behavior, but that Chapter Three views the promise as *conditional*, that it *is* subject to Israel's fulfillment of a set of stipulations. A contradiction?

We then proceed in Chapter Four to demonstrate that there is, in fact, no contradiction, that Deuteronomy integrated the two seemingly contradictory promises into a seamless thought line, to wit: the promise of the land to Israel is unconditional; however, its realization, Israel's actual possession of the land, is subject to her observance of the Law. What Deuteronomy succeeded in doing was to weave together the unconditional Abrahamic covenant and conditional Sinaitic covenant in a way that harmonized their seeming contradiction. Thus we are presented with an integrated, consistent theological concept concerning Israel's relationship to the land.

Chapter Five ("The Land in the Prophets and the Writings") continues with the biblical perspectives on our subject. We ask: is the connection between Israel's religo-moral behavior and loss of land as formulated in Deuteronomy to be found in the prophets and Writings as well? And, simultaneously, is the idea of hope and renewal after land loss similarly to be found in this literature? Our answer is in the affirmative, with the chapter seeking to demonstrate how this is so.

We then proceed to deal with the promise of the land in the post-biblical period when Israel was in exile. In Chapter Six ("The Land in Talmudic and Medieval Periods"), the era of the classical rabbis and the later liturgists and exegetes is dealt with; their perspectives give evidence of basic continuity of concept with Deuteronomy, the prophets and the Writings (i.e., sin/exile... hope/restoration). This is followed in Chapter Seven ("The Land in the Modern Period") with a depiction of the dual notion in the modern era; though deviating significantly from the biblical and post-biblical perspectives, we show that the modernists also manifest unmistakable strands of continuity with the traditional notion.

PART TWO: *The Meaning of "Holy" Land*. The overall purpose of this section is to examine the idea of Israel's land as a "holy" place. We do this by first examining the various characteristics of the book's next three themes: "The Land as a Good Land" (Chapter Eight), "The Land as Possibility and as Peril" (Chapter Nine), and "Israel's Relationship to the Nations on the Land" (Chapter Ten).

In Chapter Eleven we summarize the essence of the pertinent Deuteronomic themes (those in Parts One and Two). The summaries, taken together, point to the notion of the land as "holy." We show, along with additional evidence, that in the Deuteronomic perspective holiness is not inherent in the land but is rather conferred on it by virtue of the people of Israel charged to be a "holy people" who are to act out that role on the promised territory.

SUPPLEMENTS: *This section contains a set of materials that seeks to amplify various elements in the body of our text*. Thus, for example, the matter of geography: the term "land" is used in this book countless times. It was, therefore, necessary to define clearly the specific geographical entity we call "the land." This definition is based on the biblical data itself along with extant data about this particular piece of geography in documents of the ancient Near East. Further, analyses of the covenants and the notion of "holiness" are included. In addition, some of the theological notions depicted in the text are tested for their pertinence for our time.

SYNOPSIS OF FINDINGS: Upon completion of the doctoral dissertation upon which this book is based, the editor of the University of Judaism's publication probed via an interview of me the essence of the work. It is included here as a succinct summary of the findings of this book.

QUESTIONS FOR THE CONTEMPORARY SITUATION: It is apparent that the contents of this work suggest implications of all kinds for the issues that roil so many in and out of the Middle East in our time. We have, therefore, included a set of questions that appear to emerge from the biblical materials explicated. We leave it to the reader to grapple with the pointed issues raised from his or her own perspective.

The book concludes with notes for each chapter along with a bibliography and an index of the authors cited.

A Note About the Use Of God's Name

Jewish tradition has always distanced itself from uttering the Tetragrammaton (i.e., Greek "four letters"), the four Hebrew consonants (*yud, hay, vav, hay*) that spell the name of God. For example, Gen. 2:15, Ex. 3:2, Lev. 1:1, Num. 1:10, Deut. 1:6. Hence, the Hebrew word *Adonai* (Lord) was substituted whenever a biblical or liturgical text was pronounced in study or read aloud in a prayer setting. Thus, in place of the Tetragrammaton, the word "Lord" is used throughout this work.

About the Notes Section of the Book

In order to document in some detail or to amplify a number of elements in the body of the text, I have included a set of comparatively lengthy items in the notes. I have done this in order to avoid "cluttering" the main text with materials the reader may well feel he/she could do without. Some of these notes may be of benefit standing alone as brief thought units.

PART ONE

THE NATURE OF THE PROMISE

From its earliest beginnings and continuing down through the corridors of history, the promise of the Land of Israel, then known as Canaan, to the People of Israel has been at the heart of the Jewish experience. Indeed, it has been integral to this people's hopes and realities—and destiny.

In His first appearance to Abraham, God bids the patriarch to go forth "to the land that I will show you." The growth of his seed promised then and later to Isaac and Jacob was linked to that particular place on earth, and confirmed by two formal covenants—one unconditional and another conditional. Thus Canaan became "The Promised Land."

CHAPTER ONE

THE LAND AS GIFT

When the sun had gone down and it was dark, behold, a smoking fire pot and a flaming torch passed between the pieces. בַּיּוֹם הַהוּא כָּרַת ה' אֶת אַבְרָם בְּרִית לֵאמֹר לְזַרְעֲךָ נָתַתִּי אֶת הָאָרֶץ הַזֹּאת On that day *the Lord made a covenant with Abram saying: to your descendants I give this land* (Genesis 15:17-18).

––––––––––

In the book of Deuteronomy the word "land" appears consistently within the context of certain linguistic forms that amplify its meaning. One of these oft-recurring forms concerns the idea of land as having been given (נתן) to Israel's early patriarchs, namely, Abraham, Isaac and Jacob. Within the literary context of Deuteronomy, the land that is soon to be possessed by Israel is a territory destined to be Israel's because of a divine word in history about to be fulfilled.[1]

This literary saga begins long before Deuteronomy's time. According to Albrecht Alt,[2] the promise of the land was an original element of the pre-Mosaic cult of the God of the patriarchs. Here we are in the presence of a very old tradition. The God of the patriarchs had already promised possession of the land to the ancestors of Israel when they lived in tents on the edge of the settled territory.

The Covenant Stories

• This is evident in the first story about the covenant with Abram. The patriarch is commanded by God to leave his home in Haran and go to "the land I will show you." Though Canaan is not specifically mentioned in God's command, Abram apparently assumes it is and sets out for Canaan with his wife, Sarai, his nephew Lot, his household and possessions. He passes through the land and arrives at the terebinths of Moreh, which is in Shechem. It was there that "the Lord appeared to Abram and said:

לְזַרְעֲךָ אֶתֵּן אֶת הָאָרֶץ הַזֹּאת

'To your descendants I will give this land.' And he built an altar there to the Lord who had appeared to him (Genesis 12:1-7)."

• This promise is reiterated later when, after parting from his nephew Lot who had gone to settle in Sodom, Abram had another encounter with God. He had "settled in the land of Canaan" (Gen. 13:12). And it was there that:

> The Lord said to Abram, after Lot had parted from him: raise your eyes and look out from where you are, to the north and south, to the east and west, *for I give all the land that you see to you and your offspring forever...Up, walk about the land, through its length and its breadth, for I give it to you.* And Abram moved his tent, and came to dwell at the terebinths of Mamre which are in Hebron; and he built an altar there to the Lord (Genesis 13:14-18).

• The promise is especially evident in a third story—the striking description of Abram's encounter with God in a vision which, according to Albrecht Alt, has come down to us from this period (ca. 1800 BCE) almost intact. While at the terebinths of Mamre in Hebron (Gen. 14:13), Abram got word that his nephew Lot had been taken captive from Sodom. Abram then proceeded with three hundred and eighteen of his people, pursued the enemy as far as Dan and Damascus and succeeded in recovering Lot's stolen possessions as well as rescuing Lot and his family and bringing them back home to Sodom (Gen. 14). And then God appears to Abram in a vision and says:

> I am the Lord who brought you out from Ur of the Chaldeans *to give this land to you as a possession.*

To confirm this promise we read in the "Covenant Between the Pieces":

> When the sun had gone down and it was dark, behold, a smoking fire pot and a flaming torch passed between the pieces. בַּיּוֹם הַהוּא כָּרַת ה' אֶת אַבְרָם בְּרִית לֵאמֹר לְזַרְעֲךָ נָתַתִּי אֶת הָאָרֶץ הַזֹּאת *On that day the Lord made a covenant with Abram saying: to your descendants I give this land,* from the river of Egypt to the great river, the river Euphrates, the land of the Kenites, the Kenizzites, the Kadmonites, the Hittites, the Perizzites, the Rephaim, the Amorites, the Canaanites, the Girgashites and the Jebusites (Gen. 15:17-21).[3]

• The covenantal promise is spelled out yet again in a fourth story. Abram is now ninety-nine years old and has yet another vision in which God says to him:

> וַהֲקִמֹתִי אֶת בְּרִיתִי בֵּינִי וּבֵינֶךָ וּבֵין זַרְעֲךָ אַחֲרֶיךָ לְדֹרֹתָם לִבְרִית עוֹלָם
> And I will maintain my covenant between me and you, and your offspring to come, as an everlasting covenant throughout the ages.

> וְנָתַתִּי לְךָ וּלְזַרְעֲךָ אַחֲרֶיךָ אֵת אֶרֶץ מְגֻרֶיךָ אֵת כָּל אֶרֶץ כְּנַעַן לַאֲחֻזַּת עוֹלָם
> And I give you and your descendants the land of your sojournings, *all the land of Canaan as an everlasting holding* (Genesis 17:7-8).[4]

This promise of the land is a concept that is at the heart of the Hexateuch (the Pentateuch plus the book of Joshua). It was, moreover, a developing and dynamic tradition, interpreted from age to age so that it became a living force in the life of the people of Israel. So, for example, the assumed compiler of the literary strata known as "J" in the tenth century coinciding with the United Monarchy under David and Solomon, understood the promise more broadly than previously. Here the promise is understood to have been given to the patriarchs Isaac and Jacob as well as to Abraham.

> To Isaac: *I will give all these lands to you and to your heirs*, fulfilling the oath that I swore to your father Abraham (Gen. 26:3). To Jacob: I am the Lord, the God of your father Abraham and the God of Isaac: *the ground on which you are lying I will give to you and to your offspring* (Gen. 28:13). And again to Jacob: *The land that I gave to Abraham and Isaac I give to you; and to your offspring to come I will give the land* (Gen. 35:12).

Further, the promise is brought into relationship with the settlement under Joshua. The original promise was direct in its application; it did not envision emigration of the patriarchal group from the land followed by a second entry on their part. The compiler understood the promise of the land made by God to the patriarchs as pointing directly toward its fulfillment in the age of Joshua. According to Gerhard von Rad, "It must be stressed that it is the linking together of the promise of the land and its ultimate fulfillment (in the time of Joshua), with all the tensions this involves, which gives the Hexateuch as a whole its distinctive theological character."[5]

The promise is subsequently taken up as gift and articulated as such throughout the book of Deuteronomy. A set of representative examples:

> • And you shall eat and be full, and you shall bless the Lord your God for the good land *He has given you.* (אֲשֶׁר נָתַן לָךְ) – 8:10.

> • Do not say in your heart...it is because of my righteousness that the Lord has brought me in to possess this land...know that it is not because of your righteousness that the Lord *your God is giving you this good land to possess* (נָתַן לְךָ אֶת הָאָרֶץ הַטּוֹבָה הַזֹּאת לְרִשְׁתָּהּ), for you are a stubborn people. – 9:4-6.

- For you have not as yet come to the rest and to the inheritance which the Lord your God *gives you* (נֹתֵן לָךְ) – 12:9.

- There will be no poor among you for the Lord will bless you in the land which the Lord *your God gives you for an inheritance to possess* (אֲשֶׁר ה' אֱלֹהֶיךָ נֹתֵן לְךָ נַחֲלָה לְרִשְׁתָּהּ) – 15:4.

- He brought us to this place and *gave us this land* (וַיִּתֶּן לָנוּ אֶת הָאָרֶץ הַזֹּאת), a land flowing with milk and honey –26:9.[6]

Our discussion of the promise now proceeds to an analysis of it in the context of the book of Deuteronomy. What is its nature, and what are the implications of Deuteronomy's emphasis on the land as a gift of God to Israel?

1. The Promised Land as a Gift is Unconditional.

No Labor

Deuteronomy stresses that the land is acquired by Israel through no planning or strategies on her part, via no power or labor of hers, nor because of her superior strength in numbers (7:7, 17; 9:1). It is not gift arranged, but gift given. The refrain in 6:10-11, "cities you did not build...houses you did not fill...vineyards you did not plant...," emphasizes Israel's effortless acquisitions. The same view is found in 19:1, "...(when) you dispossess them and dwell in *their* cities and in *their* houses...." Again Israel is told that the land carries with it the gifts of civilization produced by others: these are *their* cities, *their* houses. Indeed, there are numerous other things of which Israel is the beneficiary, which clearly she did not earn via her own labors. The Lord is seen as giving: the rain (11:14), the grass (11:15), the fruits of the earth (26:10), cattle and sheep (12:21), blessings (16:17), all the good things (26:11), even, as in 8:18, "strength to accumulate wealth." In sum, Israel is the beneficiary of a good land fashioned and nurtured by people and forces other than her or hers. Canaan is unearned. It is a gracious gift. The "Promised Land" points to a power that promises and gives.

No Special Merit

Deuteronomy asserts, as well, that Israel receives her territory as a result of no special merit on her part. It goes to great lengths to describe Israel's rebellious history against God (9:7-25). No, it is not Israel's good character that motivates God to give her the territory. In 9:4-6 it is emphasized in four staccato-like phrases that it is not because of Israel's "righteousness" that she is going in to possess the land. Indeed, she is a "stubborn people." The fact that Israel will have overcome much more powerful nations than herself (9:1) might lead to a gross misunderstanding. She might conclude that God intervened on her behalf because of her own uprightness of character. Indeed, God had been moved to act by a set of different motives altogether. The conclusion to be drawn from the story of Israel's persistent rebellious temper (9:24) is that she received the land despite her character and not because of it.

No Stipulations

Moreover, the land is not only unearned and undeserved by Israel, but also what is clearly related to those factors: it is an unconditional gift. John Walvoord succinctly states the case that has been made for the idea of the unconditional nature of the Abrahamic covenant. We summarize his thinking on the matter:

In the statement of the covenant itself no conditions are itemized. When confirmations are given, while these sometimes arise from some act of obedience or devotion, it is not implied thereby that the covenant itself is conditioned. Further, the covenant with Abraham was confirmed by the unqualified oath of God symbolized by the shedding of blood and passing between parts of the sacrifice as described in Gen. 15:7-21.

While circumcision was required to recognize an individual as being within the covenant, it is not made the *sine qua non* of its fulfillment. In fact, the Abrahamic covenant was given before the rite of circumcision was introduced. Not only was the covenant confirmed without conditions to Isaac and Jacob, but later it was reiterated to the people of Israel in times of disobedience and apostasy, the most notable episode being that of the golden calf (Ex. 32:13-14) in addition to the assertions of the prophet Jeremiah (Jer. 33:25-26).[7]

Moshe Weinfeld has provided illuminating insight into the unconditional nature of biblical covenants. In studying ancient Near Eastern treaties (Hittite, Assyrian), Weinfeld distinguishes between "grant" types and "vassal" types and relates them to biblical covenants. The grant type constituted an obligation of the master to his servant, and the curse is directed toward the one who violates the rights of the servant; the grant serves mainly to protect the rights of the servant; it represents a gift to a servant; it is meant as an act of graciousness on the part of the master. On the other hand, the vassal type constitutes an obligation of the servant to the suzerain; the curse is directed toward the servant who violates the rights of the master; the treaty serves mainly to protect the master. Weinfeld sees the covenant with Abraham formulated in the style of the "grant" treaties. The gift of land to Abraham is unconditional; it is God who gives assurance; it is God who takes the solemn oath by passing between the pieces (thus taking the curse upon Himself, as it were). While it appears connected with faithfulness and presupposes loyalty, in its original setting the promise itself is unconditional.[8]

For a contrary view (in our opinion a mistaken one) that claims the Abrahamic covenant as conditional, see Supplement II.

An Historical/Literary Phenomenon

Here we come to an illuminating phenomenon. The significance of the idea of this geographical entity as gift becomes further apparent, not so much when we see it addressed to Israel on the eastern side of the Jordan River in the time of Moses in the 13th century BCE, but rather when we realize that, in the context of the book of Deuteronomy, it is being spoken to the Israel of Josiah's time 600 years later.

The Israelites who had been living for some six centuries in Canaan can be assumed to have established a comfortable, natural connection with their land. They had planted and cultivated and harvested their soil for generations. They were a landed people, ensconced on their own turf. Their land was their property. How striking, how jolting, therefore, must have been Deuteronomy's assertion that even *they* are creatures of a gift. Six hundred years after their occupation, a landed people still and again hears that their territory is a gift that they did not earn via their own labor or merit. The present Israelite occupants cannot separate themselves from their past and from the way their territory came to them. Simply living in the land and even over an extended period of time cannot change the fact that land is not simply property; it is first and foremost a gift of God, and Israel is receiving its benefits by His grace and beneficence still.

2. God's Gift and Human Action: Reconciling a Seeming Contradiction.

Although Deuteronomy asserts that the land is an unearned gift, it also understands that Israel cannot possess her territory and settle in it without her own active effort. The story of the twelve spies sent by Moses to scout out the territory in preparation for Israel's active move to occupy it reflects this notion. The human effort involved is clearly envisioned. Thus in Deut. 9:23 Israel is told, "Go up and take possession of the land I am giving you; you flouted the command of the Lord your God; you did not put your trust in Him and did not obey Him." In numerous other ways she is told to take the initiative on the matter (cf. 7:2, 7:24, 9:3).[9]

Questions

We are confronted here with an apparent contradiction. How is it that an unconditional gift from God has to be taken by human force? How can a land bestowed upon a people by a gracious God be considered unearned when this people must take specific, concrete action to gain possession of it? Have we not been told that Israel came to her territory through no effort of her own? Indeed, are the notions of divine gift and human action mutually exclusive?

Answers

Deuteronomy appears to answer this line of inquiry in two ways.

First, the two expressions "the land God gives you" and "to possess" are brought together linguistically, which is Deuteronomy's way of showing that precisely because the land is a gift, Israel is able to go in and possess it. *It is because of God's predetermined decision that Israel has title to this land that she has the opportunity via her own effort to successfully take it over.* The formula here is that God gives and Israel takes. We read: "And when the Lord your God gives them to you, you will smite them..." (7:2); "And when you will devour all the nations that the Lord your God gives you..." (7:16); "And when He gives their kings into your hand, you shall destroy their name under the heavens..." (7:24). Thus, the idea of divine gift and human participation are not incompatible; instead, they form a whole concept. The gift of land is the theological understanding of how Israel was able to come into possession of it.[10]

The *second* way Deuteronomy responds to our question is this: because the land is a gift, Israel must take the initiative; however, she cannot take it alone: her role is affected by divine action. It is God who destroys the nations (7:1, 22, 12:23, 8:20). He throws them into confusion (7:23); He brings them to their knees (9:3). These statements about God's primary role during the struggle for Canaan belong to the genre of narrative concerning Holy War in which God fights for Israel and gives her victory.[11] Because the land is a gift, God intervenes; He assists to assure Israel's taking possession of it. This Israel cannot do alone. When she tries, she fails, as in the aftermath of the twelve spies episode. When the people who were overcome by guilt attempted to invade Canaan on their own, the endeavor was destined for disaster for they were told, "The Lord will not be with you" (Numbers 14:43).

History

There may well have been an historical motivation for uniting the notions of God's gift with that of human action. It might well have been Deuteronomy's way of encouraging and validating King Josiah's campaign for Israel's independence from Egyptian rule and her repossession of the northern territories. God's promise of the land was invoked to validate Josiah's concrete efforts.

G. von Rad sees a connection of the militant piety of the book with Josiah's political expansion and military reorganization. Prior to Josiah's time, politics and the conduct of war had been the exclusive province of the king, his officials and mercenaries. Due to fiscal reasons, Josiah apparently could not afford such mercenaries and had to resort to the levy of free peasants for his soldiery; he needed the loyalty of the ordinary faithful Israelite for his wars. Under such circumstances, it would have been beneficial to Josiah to link the land as the gift of God to that of its active possession, thus motivating the faithful to work for his cause, to wit: acquisition of the land is a partnership between Israel and God. In this way, Deuteronomy's understanding of the promise of the land as gift makes its repossession not only a political and military mandate, but an act of faith as well.

3. The Promise as Gift: An Ever-Present Reality.

In Deuteronomy 26:1-11 we have a unit that deals with the ceremony of bringing of the first fruits, which illumines in a special way the idea of the land as a gift of God. The farmer is instructed to bring an offering of the first fruits of the harvest to the sanctuary and to recite a special declaration—the credo of an historic people walking on its path with God.

After recounting Israel's history from the patriarchs through Egyptian bondage and liberation, the farmer continues, "And He brought us into this place *and gave us this land,* a land flowing with milk and honey, and behold, now I bring the first of the fruit of the ground *which You, O Lord, have given me.*" With this statement the worshipper is attesting to God's promise of the realm to Israel and to its fulfillment in his time. Each individual Israelite in this cultic setting thus becomes a witness to the gift given and delivered.[12]

A Personal Experience

The notion of the land as a gift was viewed by the ordinary Israelite as an immediate experience rather than some long ago benefaction.

It is striking that even in the latest generations the farmer does not merely recall the gift of territory. He does not say, "My *fathers* have come into the land," but he says, "*I* have come into the land" (v. 3b). Each year and for generations into the future, the farmer declares that it is he himself who has experienced first hand the gift of territory. He is in effect saying, "I as an individual feel and profess myself as one who has come into this land, and each time I offer the first fruits, I declare it anew." Thus within this annual ceremonial framework the gift of land is ever kept alive, not as some abstract event of past history to be remembered, but as an ever-present concrete reality to be personally experienced ever anew.[13]

4. Source of the Gift: The Lord and Not the Gods of Canaan.

The credo recited by the farmer as he brings the first fruits of his harvest portrays God as the central force in Israel's history. The worshipper recites the main events of the saving history, beginning with the wandering Aramean, and ending with the gift of land. God's role in this credo is very active and very central; witness the following verbs: and the Lord "heard" (וַיִּשְׁמַע); "and saw" (וַיַּרְא); "and took us

out" (וַיּוֹצִאֵנוּ); "and brought us" (וַיְבִאֵנוּ); "and gave us" (וַיִּתֶּן לָנוּ). God is
here projected as the Lord of history who wills to save Israel and
fulfill His plan for her. The land stands at the end of a long chain of
historical events controlled and directed by God. It is, therefore, the
gift of that history.

There is another characteristic of the Giver that is adumbrated in
the credo. He is not only the God of history, but a God who is
ultimately responsible for that which transpires in nature. He gives
the fruit of the ground (רֵאשִׁית פְּרִי הָאֲדָמָה אֲשֶׁר נָתַתָּה לִי), which is to say
that He has fashioned the world in such a way that we can assert that
the growth and maturity of the crops are in His hands. He fashioned
the power that brings the rains and holds at bay locusts and blight,
mildew and scourges so that the yield of the fields could come to
harvest unscathed. Indeed, the Lord of history is, in this sense, also
the Lord of nature.

The Contrast

This idea that the Lord is the unseen yet ultimate power behind
the processes of nature stands out more sharply when viewed against
the prevalent Canaanite concept, which is that it is Baal who
guarantees the fertility of the soil and the abundance of rain. Baal
was the Canaanite "husband" or lord of the land, the object of the
farmer's adoration and supplication. When the Israelites settled in
the land, they too had to reckon with Baal and the result was a
syncretistic religion whose adherents wished to worship the Lord and
Baal at one and the same time. In I Kings 18:21 the prophet Elijah
stands on Mount Carmel; present are the prophets of Baal and the
prophet of Israel. A choice needs to be made. Elijah proceeds to
challenge his people, "How long will you go on limping with two
different opinions? If the Lord is God, follow Him; but if Baal, then
follow him."

A Life-and-Death Struggle

Indeed, Baalism and Lordism was a life-and-death struggle for
Israel as attested to in the prophetic literature. Hosea, who lived

approximately 500 years after the settlement in Canaan, felt impelled to remind Israel of God's role: "For she did not know that it was I who gave her the corn and wine and oil and multiplied for her silver and gold which they used for Baal" (Hos. 2:10).[14] A century later Jeremiah returned to the same theme: "And they did not say in their hearts, 'let us now fear the Lord our God who gives the former rain and the latter rain in due season, who keeps for us the appointed weeks of the harvest'" (Jer. 5:24).

In Deuteronomy, within the context of the credo, it is "the Lord your God" and not Baal who is affirmed as the Lord of nature, who controls the blessings of the earth. As Marvin Sweeney has suggested, Israel's God takes on Baal's identity, as it were, and functions as such in Deuteronomy. Moreover, the Giver of the yields of the fields is not limited to this natural sphere. Indeed, the God of fertility is the same God who acts in history. The Lord of nature and the Lord of history are one and the same.[15] Because this is so, the first fruits are to be viewed under the twin perspectives of history and nature. A credo that begins with the recollection of a wandering, rootless ancestor ends with a present of the soil. Thus, rootlessness and landedness are here brought together into a kind of integrated, organic thought unit, saying: God controls the processes of both history and nature.

5. Response to the Gift.

At the very end of the credo, the worshipper responds to God's blessings of history and of nature with a gratefulness appropriate to the gifts vouchsafed him. Insofar as the land is the gift of history, the worshipper places himself within that history and attaches himself to it. By declaring that he has come into the place promised to the patriarchs, he acknowledges a past that leads up to the present moment in which he stands as beneficiary. He responds to God's "bringing" (v. 9: "and *He brought* us to this place...") with a reciprocal "bringing" (v. 10: "And behold, now I bring the first fruit of the ground"). He (man) brings a gift of nature for a gift of history.

Insofar as the fruits are a gift of nature, coming from God's blessing, the Israelite responds by bringing the first of his fruits garnered from the soil as a symbol of recognition and thankfulness. In reverent demeanor, he worships before the Lord, rejoices in all the good things that he has, and shares his bounty with the landless Levite and stranger. Thus, God's gifts not only elicit fulsome thankfulness on a personal level to the Giver, but also motivate in man the desire for further giving and sharing with others. The gift of the first fruits becomes expanded to include not only "From Thee unto Thee," but also "From Thee unto Thine."[16]

CHAPTER TWO

THE LAND AS OATH

That your days and the days of your children may be
multiplied in the land *which the Lord swore to your
fathers* (אֲשֶׁר נִשְׁבַּע ה' לַאֲבֹתֵיכֶם) to give to them, as long
as the heavens are above the earth (Deut. 11:21).

In tracing the history of the promise, Ronald Clements asserts
that the most distinctive development which took place in the
tradition of the promise to the patriarchs is revealed in the book of
Deuteronomy: of the triad of promises to the patriarchs recorded in
Genesis, namely, progeny, land and blessing, only one is emphasized
in Deuteronomy and that is the promise of land.[1]

The most relevant development for our purposes in this chapter
is how the linguistic form of the promise is expanded. The Hebrew
verb נָתַן, "He gave," which characterizes the Deuteronomic account of
the land promise depicted in Chapter One, becomes also in
Deuteronomy נִשְׁבַּע, "He swore." Hence, the covenant which originally speaks of a promise of giving of the land takes on, in
Deuteronomy, the form of an oath. The expression "The land *sworn*
to your fathers" occurs quite frequently alongside the expression
given throughout the book. This indicates that the territory soon to
be possessed by Israel is not only "the promised land as gift," but also
"the promised land as oath," which has a more emphatic connotation
and which leads us to a set of additional characteristics of the
promise.[2] Note the following representative texts:

   • And when the Lord your God brings you into the land
   which *He swore* (אֲשֶׁר נִשְׁבַּע) to your fathers, to Abraham, to
   Isaac, and to Jacob, to give you... (6:10).

• And He brought us out from there, that He might bring us in and give us the land which He *swore* (אֲשֶׁר נִשְׁבַּע) to give to our fathers (6:23).

• And that you may live long in the land which the Lord *swore* (אֲשֶׁר נִשְׁבַּע) to your fathers to give to them and to their descendants... (11:9).

• And if the Lord your God enlarges your border as *He has sworn to your fathers* (כַּאֲשֶׁר נִשְׁבַּע לַאֲבֹתֶיךָ), and gives you all the land which He promised to give to your fathers (19:8)...

This emphasis on the promised land as God's oath to Israel suggests that the notion is clearly of prime significance in Deuteronomy's conception of Israel's territory. It implies a range of notions about the land, including the nature of the promise, Israelite history of the time, and other perspectives. And so we need now to arrive at an understanding of the nature of this notion and the reasons for its prominence in this biblical book.

1. The Power of the Word[3]

In the biblical world when a man swears, his oath is primarily self-cursing should he not be speaking the truth. This strengthens the human word and is meant to give assurance that what is said is true. This may be done by swearing by what is held to be valuable and sacred. Usually, to strengthen a statement, the witness of a deity is invoked. Thus the oath is a solemn statement whose force is enhanced by being linked to an authoritative source of power—to a witness whose testimony cannot be impugned. And so, the oath is a declaration that backs up a human statement; it guarantees the statement's veracity and is affirmed by divine cooperation.

Now, in the world of the Bible, God swears as well as man.[4] He can swear only by Himself. With an oath God guarantees the enduring truth of His word. He backs the declaration of His will by His majesty and holiness. He can even stake His life, as it were, as a pledge (Num. 14:21-23). Furthermore, the prophets viewed Israel's whole life as in some way dependent on the *word* of God. His word speaks, as it were, into history and speaks creatively in human events. This notion is expressed in Isaiah 40:7-8: "Grass withers, flowers fade when the breath of the Lord blows on them. Indeed, man is but grass: grass withers, flower fades, but the word of our God will stand firm forever." Indeed, the prophet saw the word of God as the real force and creator of Israel's history.

A Marked Emphasis

Although the concept of the word of God is current among all the prophets, there appears to be a marked emphasis on this idea in the seventh century BCE—the period of Deuteronomy. There is an increased use of the various forms of the prophetic word formula "The word of the Lord came to me," which appears, for example, thirty times in Jeremiah. This preoccupation with the word of God is reflected in Deuteronomy 13:3: "not by bread alone shall a man live, but on all that issues forth from the mouth of the Lord." Further, in Deuteronomy 9:5 the emphasis is on fulfilling the divine word: "not because of your righteousness or the uprightness of your heart are you going in to possess their land; but because of the wickedness of these nations the Lord your God is driving them out from before you, and that He may confirm the word, which the Lord swore (אֲשֶׁר נִשְׁבַּע) to your fathers, Abraham, Isaac and Jacob."

So, in Deuteronomy we have a "theology of the word" that sees divine utterance as the great bearer of power and moulder of events. God's swearing to grant the land to Israel was a way of affirming faithfulness to His word. He will do what He says He will do.

2. Reassurance in the Midst of Uncertainty: The Historical Context.

During King Josiah's reign (640-609), Judah had gained

independence from Assyria. For more than a century, the northern kingdom and then Judah had been subjugated, resulting in the dispersion of the populace of the former and vassal status of the latter. In Josiah's time the more laissez-faire Egyptian rule which had displaced the Assyrian was more easily resisted by Judah, which allowed Josiah to exercise a degree of sovereignty. Thus a restoration of the throne of David was on the horizon, with Josiah initially successful in his attempt to revive the old kingdom of Israel alongside the kingdom of Judah through taking some control of the northern provinces. Hence the land of Canaan was, in the mind of the Deuteronomist, being acquired anew, not only in the sense of being repossessed from foreign domination, but acquired anew in its territorial entirety. The opportunities for a new life on the land were opening up in a fresh new way.[5]

The people of Josiah's time, therefore, were in a situation comparable to that of the generation of the conquest: they were on the threshold once again of claiming their land. This historical *Sitz-im-Leben* of the Book of Deuteronomy explains why the idea of land is so prominent here. It was a major literary preoccupation because it was a major living reality. And if Moses is seen addressing, via his imaginary audience, the people of the seventh century, it signifies that this recent Israel is standing theologically between the promise of the land and the fulfillment of that promise, indeed quite close to the time of fulfillment. There is left for Israel an interim period that is full of optimistic anticipation, yet fraught with danger. Much can still happen to keep Israel from seeing the fulfillment of the promise of the land.[6]

The Need for Reassurance

There is thus a need to reassure Israel in her anxiety about her future and to bolster her confidence in her destiny. This is accomplished in Deuteronomy by constant reference to the divine oath to the patriarchs concerning Israel's possession of the land. The linguistic emphasis describing the place that is sworn spoke to the anxieties of both generations: would this land really be Israel's? The response is that God's oath stands with Israel in her claim to her land. The divine oath is an immutable guarantee that Israel is destined to inherit the land. In Deuteronomy the promise is expanded to oath in order to give reassurance that behind Israel's hold on Canaan lay the divine irrevocable word.

3. The Inclusive Embrace of the Oath.

Analysis of the Deuteronomic texts shows that in nine instances the sworn land is described as given to a varied set of recipients: the patriarchs (10:11), the patriarchs' children and their descendents (11:9), the patriarchs and their descendants forever (11:21), Moses' generation (6:10, 7:13, 19:8), and Josiah's generation (6:23, 26:3, 26:15).[7]

These texts reveal a striking phenomenon about the recipients of the land via the divine oath. The recipients are the patriarchs, but this is broadened to include their descendants as well. It becomes clear from this that Deuteronomy does not see one person or group of people as *the* recipients of the land. Rather, there appears here to be a continuum, stretching from "them" (i.e., the patriarchs of the past) to their descendants, ad infinitum. Arching across the generations are not only the recipients of the land, but the time span during which it is given.

But more: those being addressed by Moses are his generation about to enter the territory. And yet more: the recipients are those who had already settled in the land, i.e., those Israelites after the generation of Moses, including presumably those in Josiah's time, for the first fruits the farmer is to present to the priest as prescribed in Deut. 26 clearly alludes to a settled agricultural situation. And finally: the latter farmer is to make the following statement: "I have declared today to the Lord our God that I have come to the land which the Lord swore to our fathers to give to us" (Deut. 26:3). Since this is part of a fixed credo, it appears that each person in every generation is asked to see himself and his own generation as those for whom the oath of land was fulfilled.

From all of the above it becomes clear that Deuteronomy makes no distinction between the recipients of the oath: the patriarchs, those about to enter the land in Moses' time, those who had already entered and settled down, and those Israelites not yet born. The recipients of the land in God's oath are those Israelites of the past, present and future. The promise is not fixed in time but spans the generations.

What principles underlie this perspective that past, present and future are included in God's oath of the land to Israel? And how is the land oath that includes all the generations of Israel conceptualized? We suggest two responses:

Israel's Collective Consciousness.

Johannes Pedersen[8] sheds light on this question by offering an understanding of the way in which biblical man viewed the unity of the generations. To ancient Israel a people was not a collection of human beings more or less like each other. A people forms a psychic whole. "The people" is not visible. All common experiences are merged into the common soul and lend to it shape and fullness. Thus a psychic stock is created that is taken over from generation to generation, and is constantly renewed and influenced by new experiences. It is lived wholly in every generation. Yet, it is raised above it. The relationship to the ancestors becomes part of the common life. They (the ancestors and descendants) share their experiences with each other. Thus the people share the blessings of the fathers, but also their guilt. All events are connected because they contribute toward forming a psychic whole, a collective consciousness that is both horizontal and vertical.

That the land has been given to the fathers and to all subsequent generations means, therefore, that its acquisition is indissolubly bound up with the soul of the Israelites and is fused with them as part of their ongoing collective consciousness. Thus, when Deuteronomy speaks of the land sworn to the fathers, to their descendants, and to present and future generations, it is expressing the notion of a basic psychic wholeness, which is the people's collective consciousness.

Jon Levenson articulates this notion in historical terms. The major function of the array of texts about Israel's past history cited above has a collective dimension; it is, he writes:

> ...to narrow the gap between generations, to mould all Israel, of whatever era, into one personality that can give an assent to the divine initiative. "Your own eyes have seen what I did to the Egyptians" (Joshua 24:7). History is telescoped into a collective biography. What your ancestors saw is what *you* saw. God's rescue of them implicates *you*, obliges *you*, for *you*, by hearing this story and responding affirmatively, become Israel, and it was Israel who was rescued.
>
> Telling the story brings it alive. The historical brings the past to bear pointedly on the present. In the words of the rabbinic Passover liturgy (Haggadah), "Each man is obliged to see himself as if *he* came out of Egypt."[9]

Entering the Past Via the Cult

Gerhard von Rad[10] offers us insight into the notion of the inclusive nature of the oath. As we have noted, in Deut. 26:1-4 the generations long settled in the land declare within a ritual setting that the land was given to them as God swore to the fathers to "give to *us*" (לָתֶת לָנוּ). Now, if Moses in the 13th century BCE is addressing the people who are to possess the land, by virtue of what kind of understanding can this very declaration be made by future generations centuries later?

In cultic festivals, Israel did more than remember the past events with which the festival was associated. On these occasions Israel experienced the contemporaneousness of God's saving acts. She entered into the saving event in a quite actual way. By recitation and ritual, she re-entered the historic event to which the festival was related. Through this cultic experience, Israel, in each generation, was able to relive and enter again into the saving act and thus view itself as the generation to which the promise to the patriarchs applied. Psalm 114 gives us an idea of the cultic actualization of saving events, whereby events separated by many years are brought together in point of time. Here the events of the Exodus are recalled as well as the remarkable phenomena that accompanied Israel's crossing of the Reed Sea and later the Jordan river. These past events are made contemporary in verses 3-5 of the Psalm: "The sea looked and fled, Jordan turned back...what ails you, O sea, that you flee, O Jordan that you turn back?"

In leading Israel into her land there does not stand merely a momentary impulse of God that can be reversed capriciously tomorrow on a new impulse. What happens to Israel today is that which He swore as of old via His word. The projection of such an oath proclaims the faithfulness of God and His word. God's word, His oath within history, is the eternal bond that unites all the generations. It is His word that Israel hears as remaining steadfast throughout all time. And inasmuch as Israel saw her own peculiar history as a history with God, a road on which she traveled under God's guidance, every generation inevitably came under the aspect of the fulfillment of the oath to the patriarchs.

4. The Oath: The Historic Versus the Mythic Conception of the Land.

The land sworn to the patriarchs is a concept that expresses Israel's belief that God acts in history to realize His plans for the people. God had initiated in history a special relationship with Israel's ancestors in which He promised them and their seed the land of Canaan. Further, God is seen as dispossessing other nations at a given point in time in order to settle this people on the territory sworn to the patriarchs.

Now, Gerhard von Rad[11] has pointed out that there are two theological strands in the Hexateuch concerning the land: the historical and the cultic. The historical viewpoint sees the promise of land made to the early patriarchs pointing forward to the age of Joshua. This outlook dominates the narrative of the Hexateuch. On the other hand, there is the cultic concept, which sees Israel's relationship to the land in a-historical, mythical terms. In this view the place is seen as the Lord's land: "the land is mine, you are only strangers and sojourners with me" (Lev. 25:23). God controls this place; He functions within it, as it were, in response to the people's behavior.

This notion of a Divine force being somehow immanent in the earth informs much of the Pentateuchal legislation. For example, after listing a series of carnal transgressions, Lev. 18:25 states: "Let not the land spew you out for defiling it, as it spewed out the nation before you." In Numbers 35:34 we read, "You shall not defile the land in which you live, in the midst of which I dwell." Indeed, immoral behavior defiles the land (cf. Lev. 19:29, Deut. 21:23, 24:4) and its Owner will take action in response.

However, von Rad emphasizes that the mythic/cultic notion nowhere appears in Deuteronomy on anything like an equal footing with the historical conception.

The Contrast

In order to judge the uniqueness of the historical perspective, we may compare it to how peoples surrounding Israel explained the sanctity of their special places. Why is Babylon the holy city? Because following the battle in which Marduk conquered the chaos-dragon and built heaven and earth, the Annunaki, in gratitude, built the Temple Esagila and the Temple tower as a dwelling for Marduk, and so brought Babylon into being.[12] In the Assyrian period, in the city of Asshur, the same narrative was taken over as the basis for the holiness of the city and its Temple Esharra. Why is Thebes, the city of Amon, the holy center of Egypt? Because it is the "honorable hill of the primeval beginning, the beneficent eye of the lord of all, his beloved place, which bears his beauty and surrounds his entourage." Hermepolis and other Egyptian cities made similar claims, as have other locales in the ancient Near East.[13]

By contrast, Israel understands the sanctity of its territory not in mythic/cultic but in historical terms: it is the *sworn land*, that is, it is pledged to Israel via God's promise to her. In Israel, the category promise/fulfillment takes the place of the mythical orientation that permeated her environment. In this perspective, the land is not inherently holy because God Himself dwells in it, as it were, but is sanctified by virtue of it being at the center of God's oath to a people in history.[14]

CHAPTER THREE

THE LAND AND THE LAW

In Chapters One and Two, "The Land as Gift" and "The Land as Oath," the promise by God to Israel is an unconditional one, that is, there are no requirements about behavior attached to it. Side by side with that notion is a corpus of law that the Israelites were obligated to follow if they were to occupy the land: the place was promised by God *with* conditions. It is this latter notion we now examine.

The role of Law in Deuteronomy is of dominating significance. It is a major part of the core of the book, making up its central legal section, i.e., chapters 12-26, in which detailed excerpts from ancient law together with contemporary commentary and expansion are presented. In fact, there are some fifty instances where Deuteronomy links the law with the land in one form or another.

In this chapter we describe these laws, their basic ideas and purposes, and, when taken as a whole, are viewed as legislation emphasizing conditionality. We then show how this law corpus is identified with the conditional Sinai covenant and hence are, in fact, a set of requirements for Israel if she is to gain access to and endure on the land. In Chapter Four following, we will explore the relationship between the apparently contradictory promises—one unconditional and the other conditional—and how Deuteronomy integrates the two.

1. What is the Nature of the Laws?

Norm For Life In the Land.[1]

These texts convey the idea of ongoing, settled, established life. Two representative examples:

- These are the statutes and ordinances which you shall be careful to do in the land which the Lord, the God of your fathers, has given you to possess, all the days that you live upon the land (12:1). (That is to say: the laws are to be observed all the time, regularly, normatively.)

- When you come into the land which the Lord your God gives you for an inheritance, and have taken possession of it, and live in it, you shall take some of the first of all the fruit of the ground... (26:1-2). (That is to say: the produce of the land is the result of patient, ongoing effort.)

Indeed, the laws regulate normal life; they are the *modus operandi* for the people's functioning in the place. Here Israel learns what the guidelines for everyday life are, that is, how life under God and in community is maintained and happily enjoyed. The commandments are necessary for harmonious and satisfactory life in the land and are quite possible to fulfill and live by. They represent a consistently stable manner of living that human beings find necessary.

Laws Associated With the Land[2]

In these texts a connection has been forged between a specific law and Israel's existence on its territory. In some cases, blessings are motivations for obedience; in others, disobedience brings about negative consequences. Examples:

- Honor your father and mother, as the Lord your God has commanded you, that you may long endure, and that you may fare well in the land that the Lord your God is giving you (5:16).

- If a man committed a crime and was hanged on a tree, his body should not remain on the tree all night, but should be buried on the same day, for a hanged man is an affront to God. "You shall not defile your land that the Lord your God is giving you to possess" (21:22-23).

Land Laws.[3]

These are an integral part of the territory itself. Examples:

• The text in 21:1-9 tells us that if in the land a slain person whose slayer is unknown is found...the elders of the nearest city shall take a heifer and testify over it that they did not shed this blood nor did their eyes see it shed.

• In 23:25-26 we are told that when one enters a neighbor's field, one may eat one's fill of grapes, as many as one wishes, but that person must not put any of the grapes into his own vessel. Also, when one enters the field of his neighbor's standing grain, he may pluck the ears with his hands, but must not put a sickle to the neighbor's standing grain.

These regulations reflect both agricultural and "urban" life; they arise naturally from life in the place. Here the association between the laws and the land is an organic one.

Law as Condition.[4]

Here the notion of territory as given with conditions is heavily emphasized as indicated by a plethora of regulations. Some representative examples:

• When you have begotten children and children's children and are long established in the land, should you act wickedly and make for yourselves a sculptured image in any likeness, causing the Lord your God displeasure and vexation, I call heaven and earth this day to witness against you that you shall soon perish from the land (4:25, 26).

• Observe His laws and commandments which I enjoin upon you this day, that it may go well with you and your children after you, and that you may long remain in the land that the Lord your God is giving to you for all time (4:40).

• You shall walk in all the way which the Lord your God has commanded you...that you may live long in the land you are to possess (5:28-30).

• And if you will obey my commandments...I will give the rain for your land in its season...that you may gather in your grain and your wine and your oil...grass in your fields for your cattle and you shall eat and be full.... Take heed lest...you serve other gods...He will shut up the heavens so that there will be no rain and the land yield no fruit, and you will perish quickly off the good land... (11:13-17).

• See I set before you this day life and prosperity, death and adversity. For I command you this day to love the Lord your God, to walk in His ways, and to keep His commandments, His laws and His rules, that you may thrive and increase and that the Lord your God may bless you in the land you are about to enter and possess. But if your heart turns away and you give no heed...I declare to you this day that you shall certainly perish; you shall not long endure on the soil that you are crossing the Jordan to enter and possess (30:15-18).

Here, the cause-and-effect relationship between the Law and the land is clearly spelled out.

2. What Are the Purposes of These Laws?

Relationship to God

Insofar as man's relationship to God is concerned, Deuteronomy makes it unmistakably clear that the land can be entered into, lived on in peace, possessed in the long term only if the people adhere to the commandments as set forth. Israel must ever recognize the Source of her gift and live in accordance with His requirements.[5]

Relationship to Fellow Man

Insofar as man's relationship to his fellow man is concerned,

Deuteronomy, via presentation of its legal material, seeks to bring about a just and humane society.

• Concern for the poor and unfortunate is expressed in 15:1-6; every seven years a creditor should release his neighbor from the debt owed him so that there be no ongoing poor in the land. This text emphasizes that if there be among the people a poor brother *in any of* the towns within the land, one should not harden one's heart but should open one's hand to one's brother and lend him sufficient for his need, whatever it may be. And in 23:20 the Israelite is told not to make a loan to a fellow on interest because loans were usually occasioned by financial desperation and taking interest thus became a means of oppression.

• In 15:22-20 the law of the tithe on the yield of the fields gave special consideration to the disadvantaged. The fruit of this tax—grain, wine and oil—was to be given not only to the Levite, as heretofore, but to the alien, the orphan and widow as well.

• Deuteronomy 15:12-18 modifies the law in the Covenant Code (Exodus 21:1-11) that grants no compensation to a slave to be freed in the seventh year. Indeed, the slave *is* to be compensated liberally because the master has prospered from the slave's work. Further, the female slave is now entitled to the same rights of release as her male counterpart.

• There is a set of laws dealing with the fair treatment of one's neighbor. In 16:18-20 we're told that judges must rule impartially and according to the principle of justice if the people is to live and inherit the land... "You shall not judge unfairly: you shall show no partiality; you shall not take bribes, for bribes blind the eyes of the discerning and upset the plea of the just."

• And in 25:13-16 the dictum is clear that a merchant is to use full and just weights when doing business if he expects to have prolonged days on the territory.

• The land is a geographical entity upon which there is to be a general respect for life . In 18:10 it is emphasized that the pagan practice of child-burning through which the gods were thought to be appeased was banned; the "nations" were eliminated from the place for that reason—among others. In 21:1-9 the people are told that the elders of a city "in your land" must make expiation for a murder victim whose slayer is unknown.

There are numerous other laws in Deuteronomy of a disparate nature that have in common the notion that there is an organic relationship between possession of the land and the general upgrading of human life and concern for animal life on it, as well (e.g., 17:14-20, 22:10, 25:4). [6]

Criteria for Obedience

The overarching purpose of all these laws is Deuteronomy's emphasis that they are the criteria by which Israel's obedience to God is measured, and the land is the arena in which Israel does what God requires. Indeed, obedience is the *sine qua non* for continuing existence in the realm, for Israel's very life. Disobedience leads to loss of the realm. The people has no life apart from this realm for its national existence depends upon it.

Indeed, only a people that accepts the laws as the norm for its daily life, laws that enable her to live a happy, harmonious life...only a people that is aware that the gift of land comes with conditions... only a people that is aware of the Source of her gifts...only a people that fosters a just and humane society...only such a people is entitled to the blessings of a territory of her own and can retain it.

3. The Deuteronomic Law Corpus and the Sinai Covenant

We have spoken of the law corpus in Deuteronomy as an independent entity, which, of course, it is from historical and literary points of view. However, much of its basic content—including the condition-for-land belief detailed above—derives from an earlier era associated with the Sinai covenant. Sinai is the locus of Israel's conditional covenant. What is the basis for such an identification?

It is the scholarly consensus that the book of Deuteronomy derives from a cultic setting in which the original Sinai covenant was renewed. It was part of a liturgy through which the people of later generations identified itself with the original group at Horeb (Sinai). Thus Deut. 5:2-3, in introducing a restatement of the Ten Commandments, has Moses saying to the people: "...The Lord our God made a covenant with us at Horeb. Not with our fathers did the Lord make this covenant, but with us, who are all of us here alive this day...." Similarly, Deut. 28:69 reflects a covenant renewal ceremony whose words bear the stamp of liturgical expression, the origin of which was traced to Moses: "These are the words of the covenant which the Lord commanded Moses to make with the people of Israel in the land of Moab, besides the covenant which He had made with them at Horeb."

The Book of the Covenant

According to Deut. 31:9-13, the rites were to be solemnized every seventh year at the Fall pilgrimage to the central sanctuary, i.e., this was to become a regular service for all Israel. Josiah's reading in a public assembly at the Temple "the book of the covenant" that had been found "in the house of the Lord," and his making a covenant "before the Lord" to follow the laws of the book, and all the people joining in the covenant (II Kings 23:1-3), also indicate a covenant renewal ceremony through which Josiah made Deuteronomy operative in the life of the people. *Thus, Deuteronomy was a renewal or reconfirmation of the Sinai covenant.* Its law code is presented as the work and speech of Moses in its basic content features, and in its very wording claims to belong to the group of laws directly issuing from the Sinai covenant.[7]

Bernard Levinson has shown that the book of Deuteronomy is essentially a reiteration of the Book of the Covenant (Exodus 21:1 - 23:19) though with a set of major revisions prompted by new times and conditions. The catalog of laws contained in this covenant code are those that are integral to the covenant ascribed to Moses at Mount Sinai.[8]

And so, we see that Deuteronomy re-presents and represents the tradition of the Law given at Sinai as condition for Israel's possession of the land. This is the basis for the discussion in Chapter Four following regarding Deuteronomy's integration of the unconditional Abrahamic covenant with that of Sinai.

CHAPTER FOUR

THE INTEGRATION OF THE UNCONDITIONAL
AND CONDITIONAL COVENANTS

Either the promise of the land was given without
conditions or with conditions. Which is it?

———

As we have seen in Chapter Three, Deuteronomy emphasizes the
fundamental principle that Law is a condition for the land, the
promise of it to Israel embedded in the Sinai covenant. This concept
is one of Deuteronomy's most characteristic ones and is a central,
controlling element of the book's overall theological perspective.

In Chapters One and Two, on the other hand, we have seen that
the concept of the land as having been promised by God to Israel's
patriarchs—Abraham, Isaac and Jacob—is also clearly of significance
in Deuteronomy, its prominence manifest. Here the land is granted
to Israel without conditions; it is hers because of a divine word in
history; it is to be possessed not because of any inherent merit on her
part nor because of any particular effort of hers, but because God had
bound Himself by His word to Israel's founding fathers, "To your
seed will I give this land" (Gen. 15:18). Thus this concept—the
promise as unconditional—is also a central element in the Deuteronomic theology of the land.

We must now inquire: do not these two concepts contradict each
other? Either the promise of the land is unconditional, not subject to
Israel's behavior, or it is conditional subject to Israel's behavior.
Which is it? Our answer is that there is no contradiction between the
two promises and that they, in fact, exist in Deuteronomy side by
side and each is valid and operative in Israel's life. How this can be so
is the subject of this chapter.[1]

Three Covenants

As we have noted, the unconditional promise of the land to Israel is embedded in the Abrahamic covenant, and the conditional promise in the Sinaitic covenant. The Davidic covenant, as we shall soon show, was an adumbration of the Abrahamic in that it is unconditional. And so we begin by tracing the historical forces that forged the relationship between the three pacts; this will serve to clarify why it is the Abrahamic and Sinaitic covenants alone with which we need to deal here; it also serves as the backdrop for our demonstration of the organic relationship between these two promises. We follow with examination of a number of views on the subject by a set of leading scholars and evaluate what, in our opinion, is the cogency of these views insofar as they respond to the basic question at hand. We then present our own view along with the Deuteronomic texts that buttress it.

What were the historical factors that led Deuteronomy to relate the covenants to each other?[2]

In the beginning, there was the Abrahamic covenant. This unconditional promise of the land to Abraham had its origin during the early patriarchal period itself and was a formative, dominating force in the life of the Israelites down through the period of the Judges (Genesis 12:1-7; 15:17-21; 17:7-8). During the era of the Israelite amphictyony (confederation) between ca. 1200-1000 BCE, when Israel settled in the land and the tribal league functioned at its fullest, a body of laws governing the life of the people developed, and was linked to the covenant between God and Israel at Mount Sinai during the time of Moses (Exodus 19:1-12).

Then there arose the Israelite monarchy with all the brilliant achievements of David and Solomon. Israel was at last in full possession of the land promised to the fathers and had become a nation strong and great. During this period a theology developed that God had chosen Zion as His eternal dwelling place and had made a covenant with David that the latter's line would rule forever. The substance of this theology (as best evidenced in the royal Psalms) is that God's promise was indeed eternal. The Davidic covenant developed the pattern of the patriarchal covenant in that it was based upon God's promises for the future and was unconditional in character (II Samuel 7:8-16).

The development of the Davidic covenant could not help but affect the fortunes of the Abrahamic and Sinaitic ones. The Abrahamic covenant was perceived in this period as having its fulfillment in the extension of the Davidic kingdom, for was not the promise to Abraham of the rise and triumph of that kingdom? The local, limited physical dimension of the land was expanded to a much larger area by virtue of David's expansive activity. Thus, the unconditional character of the Davidic covenant reigned.

However, during this heyday of the monarchy, the tradition of the Abrahamic covenant held and was preserved in the David court circle, underground, as it were. Furthermore, the conditional Sinai covenant remained in force due to the continued influence of the prophets at the time and of the ongoing observance of the cultus. Both, however, were overlaid in the popular mind by the Davidic covenant: the Abrahamic was subsumed in the Davidic, and the Sinaitic, with its demands and conditions, was subordinated to the confidence of the people in the unconditional promises to David and his royal successors.

The Shaken Davidic Covenant

Then came the events of the eighth century with the shattering of the northern kingdom, and the experience of the seventh century with the vassalage of the kingdom of Judah and the constant threats of disaster at the hands of their now Egyptian and subsequent Babylonian overlords. These developments could not help but affect the fortunes of the now shaken and problematic Davidic covenant and bring about a realignment of the relative status of the Sinaitic and Abrahamic covenants. It is at this point in time that the work of Deuteronomy enters onto the stage of history.

Deuteronomy declared with desperate urgency that the nation's very life depended upon a return to the covenantal relationship on which the national existence had previously been based, i.e., the covenant at Sinai. It restates and reemphasizes the stipulations of that covenant and urges upon Israel obedience to them if the nation hoped to continue existence on its land. By implication, Deuteronomy was saying that the nation was living in a "fool's paradise" in assuming that God, through His promises to David, was irrevocably and unconditionally committed to its defense: witness the crumbled kingdom of Israel and the endangered kingdom of Judah! Indeed, it is the conditional Sinaitic covenant by which Israel lives and not that of the shaken unconditional Davidic covenant.

But, what about the unconditional Abrahamic covenant? It had long since been in existence, and a humiliated and endangered people could not function without hope for its future. Thus, in Deuteronomy, the Abrahamic covenant also gained new recognition and importance. Though the Sinai covenant in Deuteronomy is given preeminence, appeal is also made to the promise to Abraham in order to gain reassurance that behind Israel's existence and its tenure on the land of Canaan lay the divine promise.

The Abrahamic Covenant Persisted

Thus the unconditional promissory form of the Abrahamic covenant is retained; it is now referred to as made with all three patriarchs, is understood as exclusively concerned with the land of Canaan, and the land is given and oathed to Israel as a whole. In Deuteronomy's speeches about the significance of the land, the Abrahamic covenant is appealed to in order to emphasize that Israel's entitlement to it is the result of an act of divine grace. In this way, Deuteronomy appealed behind the Davidic covenant to that with Abraham; both were unconditional, but only the latter could fulfill the need of the historical hour.

This, then, is the historical background of the three biblical covenants. The two that remain before us in the context of Deuteronomy are both authoritative and operative. Yet they appear to contradict each other: the Abrahamic is a promise *without* conditions, the Sinaitic is a promise *with* conditions. Do they actually stand together without contradiction? It is to this question we now turn our attention.[3]

Efforts That Deal With the Two Seemingly Contradictory Covenants

In examining a set of representative scholars who have analyzed the subject at hand, we find this essential position: the claim that the Abrahamic covenant was cancelled by the events of history, leaving the Sinaitic covenant and its requirement of adherence to the laws the sole pact intact. Since, in their view, the Abrahamic covenant lapsed, was no longer valid and operative in the life of Israel in the Deuteronomic period, no two contradictory covenants were in existence any longer.

We dissent from this position. As we have demonstrated, the Abrahamic covenant was unconditional and never lapsed (Chapters One and Two) and existed side by side in the mind of the Deuteronomist with the conditional Sinaitic covenant (Chapter Three), and were retained intact in integrated form by the Deuteronomist, as we will seek to demonstrate in what follows. But first let us hear what the scholars say about our subject. (The italics are mine.)

David Noel Freedman.[4]

Freedman asks: how can we reconcile two apparently incompatible covenants—a covenant of divine commitment involving an irrevocable promise to His people on the part of God, and a covenant of human obligation in which the continuity of the relationship depends upon the behavior of the human party? Can a covenant bond be broken – and at the same time persist? Can one sever a relationship as a result of covenant violations – and nevertheless maintain it in perpetuity?

Freedman responds to his own line of inquiry this way: logically one might argue that the divine commitment to Abraham was discharged when its terms were fulfilled in the conquest and settlement in the land, or certainly by the time of David and Solomon. From that point on, the fate of Israel was contingent upon her obedience to the terms of the pact at Sinai. After God fulfilled His commitment, it became the responsibility of Israel to maintain the Sinai pact by performing its obligations to God or face the consequences. For the Deuteronomic historian this appears to be the situation of Israel in his time.

The difficulty with this view is that the unmistakable implication of saying that "the divine commitment to Abraham was discharged" through the conquest and settlement is that this covenant thereby lapsed, was over with, already fulfilled, and that at least from the time of David and Solomon on, the Sinai covenant took over, as it were. If this is so, what then could be the basis of Deuteronomy's hope for the future in the face of Israel's past disasters and impending dangers? Freedman claims that "at the same time, and in the face of this all but total destruction, hope persisted...." In light of Freedman's own statement that the promise to Abraham was "discharged," there is no basis for this last statement of his. The two covenants remain contradictory since, in our view, they both are operative.

George Ernest Wright.[5]

Referring to Deut. 11:8-9, Wright notes the book's claim of obedience to the commandments as condition for the land. "God's promise of the land," Wright says, "was contingent upon the nation's acceptance and maintenance of the covenant. Election with its accompanying blessings was dependent upon the nation's acceptance of its responsibility made clear in the revelation of the law at Sinai.

Law and obedience are thus the condition for the land's possession. In this way, Deuteronomy interpreted the disasters that befell the nation, especially the threatened loss of the land and of independent national existence." Wright goes on to say that *Deuteronomy reinterpreted the Abrahamic covenant in the light of the new historical conditions, whereby the heretofore unconditional Abrahamic covenant was transmuted by means of the Sinaitic covenant into a conditional one.*

The difficulty with this interpretation is that the unconditionality of the Abrahamic pact does not yield so easily to such a change both in terms of the history of this tradition as well as Deuteronomy's own understanding of it as independent of Israel's deeds, such as Moses' fervent plea in Deut. 9:26-27: "...O Lord God, destroy not Thy people and Thy heritage... Remember Thy servants, Abraham, Isaac, and Jacob; do not regard the stubbornness of this people, or their wickedness, or their sin." Thus, Wright's view is not adequately rooted in our texts. Our two covenants thus remain in seeming contradiction.

Gerhard von Rad.[6]

In analyzing the relationship between the Abrahamic and Sinaitic pacts in the book of Deuteronomy, von Rad with reference to Sinai poses this highly suggestive rhetorical question: "Does not the promise of the land in this conditional form pave the way for a declension from grace into law?"

The clear implication of von Rad's question is that the Abrahamic covenant was subjected to a major shift of stress (as the dictionary defines the word "declension")—to a reinterpretation by the Deuteronomist from unconditionality to conditionality in terms of entitlement to and possession of the land, from, as von Rad puts it, "grace into law." This indicates that Deuteronomy reflects a substantially more advanced situation, a development of the promise idea from that of the earlier biblical writers for whom the land was a pure gift from God to a revised notion prompted by historical conditions. Further ground for understanding von Rad in this way is the fact that the overall context and thrust of his work on Deuteronomy is the attempt to show the developmental, innovative, more advanced character of the Deuteronomist as against the older traditions.

Here, too, assuming that von Rad is contending that the Abrahamic covenant was no longer operative, dissent with such a contention is required by the nature of biblical texts about that pact.

John Bright.[7]

Bright discerns that the patriarchal covenant containing God's promise of the land for the future was in a certain tension with the Sinaitic covenant. There was a similar tension during the period of the monarchy when the (unconditional) Davidic covenant was dominant in the national mind. In this situation—in light of the disastrous events of the eighth century—the prophets put strong stress on the demands of the old Sinai covenant. This work of the prophets was probably a primal impulse in the formation of the Deuteronomic law. Indeed, *Deuteronomy committed the nation to obedience to the stipulations of the old Sinaitic covenant; its reform called the nation back behind the official theology of the (unconditional) Davidic covenant to an older notion of covenant— the conditional Sinaitic one.*

As we have pointed out, the Davidic pact is in essence a thematic adumbration of the Abrahamic. Hence, it appears that Bright sees Deuteronomy as having jettisoned the unconditional Davidic/ Abrahamic pact in favor of a now exclusive Sinaitic covenant with that pact's array of required laws and regulations. For the same reasons indicated in connection with the positions of Freedman, Wright and von Rad, we dissent from Bright's view.

Jon Levenson.[8]

In challenging the concept that Christians inherit the status of

Israel without the obligation to fulfill the Mosaic law, Levenson writes this:

> The covenant without stipulations, the Abrahamic covenant of Genesis 15 and 17, *is only a preparation for the Sinaitic covenant, into which it is absorbed.* Thus, observance of the Mosaic Torah is the opposite of an obstacle to a loving and intimate relationship with God. It is the vehicle and the sign of just that relationship.

Levenson, who, to our puzzlement, mentions the Abrahamic pact but once (here) in his entire book about Israel's covenants, proceeds to discuss another of the covenants—the Davidic, this one unconditional, as is the Abrahamic. He confirms that the dynastic promises of Nathan to David in II Samuel 7:8-16 clearly are without stipulation, without terms that David and his descendants must fulfill in order to inherit a permanent dynasty. Psalm 89:4-5, like Nathan's oracle, states distinctly that God will uphold David's posterity at all cost even—and here the contrast with Sinai could not be sharper—if they break the commandments and desecrate divine law.

However, Levenson then points to I Kings 8:24-25, which departs from Nathan's oracle in that it *does* make continuation of David's dynasty conditional upon observance of stipulations. Based on this, Levenson concludes:

> The subordination of the Davidic covenant to the Sinaitic in I Kings 8:25, therefore, must be seen as a reinterpretation of the pristine Davidic covenant material, a reinterpretation that reflects the growing canonical status of the Sinaitic traditions that will become the Pentateuch.

In this construct the heretofore unconditional Davidic/ Abrahamic covenant is no longer valid and operative in Israel's life. Again for the reasons proffered in connection with the views of

Freedman, Wright, von Rad and Bright, we cannot concur with Levenson's conclusion.[9]

The Seemingly Contradictory Covenants Seen as Integrated: Our View

Based on our analysis of the promise of the land to Abraham as depicted in Chapter One, "The Promised Land as Gift," and on our critique of the above scholarly positions, we differ from those positions. *In our view, the notion that the Abrahamic covenant was superseded by the Sinaitic, that it was no longer valid and operative in the biblical mind during Deuteronomy's historical point in time (i.e., the 7th century BCE), is inaccurate. And so, we proceed here to set forth our view on the subject.*

The Ground of Our View

We believe that the groundwork for the solution to our problem we have found in two trenchant articles, one by Uriel Simon, and the second by Lawrence Kaplan.[10] The latter article is an amplification of the former and, taken together, *they establish the following principle with regard to the Abrahamic covenant: the divine promise was unconditional; its realization, its actualization was conditional.* (The Sinai covenant is not discussed in these articles.)

Abraham was not born in the promised land; his attachment to it was based on a command interwoven with a promise: "Go from your country and your kindred and your father's house to the land that I will show you. And I will make of you a great nation, and I will bless you, and make your name great, so that you will be a blessing" (Gen. 12:1-2). However, Abraham's adherence to this command was only the beginning of a long path. At the "Covenant Between the Pieces" (Gen. 15) he was informed that his children would inherit the land only after 400 years; Abraham's son Isaac was born only after long years of barrenness. His dwelling in the land promised him was as a "stranger and sojourner." His wells were stopped up by the Philistines. Only when he had to bury his wife did he acquire an actual foothold in the land in the form of a small grave site. *Clearly, there is a wide time gap here between the promise to Abraham and its actualization.*

Attachment to Land: Natural vs. Promised

To understand the meaning of the above facts, we must distinguish between natural attachment to any land and Israel's attachment to its particular place. The nations of the world understand their possession of their lands as a natural right that is a product of weighty historical facts, such as primal possession, conquest, extended possession, development of culture, etc. A natural attachment is grasped in the national consciousness as a basic given: a nation may occasionally be forced to defend its freedom or sovereignty, but not its very existence on its land; the danger of exile is not an actual threat and is thus far from consciousness.

Israel, on the other hand, understands her possession of her land as a result of a divine promise that preceded (in time and in principle) actual possession. *Therefore, this right is not dependent upon actual possession.*

The natural attachment of the nations to their lands is continuous, but the claim to it could eventually end, *whereas the attachment of Israel to its land, while sporadic, is eternal.* The text of Amos affirms this distinction between Israel's temporary rule over the land and her permanent survival as a nation: "Behold, the eyes of the Lord God are upon the sinful kingdom, and I will destroy it from the surface of the ground; except that I will not utterly destroy the house of Jacob, says the Lord" (Amos 9:8). The kingdom of Israel will be destroyed because of its sin, but it is promised that the House of Jacob will never be destroyed; it will survive in exile and finally return to its land:

> "I will set up the fallen booth of David. I will mend its
> breaches and set up its ruins anew. I will build it firm as in
> days of old. I will restore my people Israel...I will plant

them on their soil nevermore to be uprooted from the soil I
have given them (Amos 9:11, 14-15).

*Thus, the promised attachment of Israel to its land is not
dependent upon changing historical conditions.* This idea is
expressed in the Torah through the divine promise to the fathers—
with the realization of that promise anticipated, the actual possession
in the future. A further indication of this idea is the fragile hold of the
patriarchs on the land that stood in contrast to their promised right
to it. For example: the "territorial compromise" Abraham made with
Lot; for the sake of peace Abraham made this compromise though he
surely would not have done so if it implied a limitation of the
promised permanent entitlement to the place. Indeed, Abraham's
action was taken in light of the trust that "all the land which you see,
to you I will give it, and to your seed forever" (Gen. 13:15).

Now, how does the realization of the promise to Abraham come
about? Simon quotes Gen. 18:19 in response: "For I have chosen
him, that he may charge his children and his household after him to
keep the way of the Lord by doing righteousness and justice; so that
the Lord may bring to Abraham what He has promised Him." In
other words, *the realization of the promise is conditional upon
Israel's observance of God's prescriptions.*

Distinction Between Promise and Realization

In amplifying Simon's argument as outlined above, Kaplan
stresses the distinction between the divine promise itself and its
actualization. It is the realization of the promise, i.e., Israel's actual
possession of the land, which is dependent upon her righteousness.
Since the realization of the promise is conditional, if Israel does not
live up to the conditions specified, she may be exiled. This was the
burden of the message of the prophets against those who felt that
God would never allow His Temple to be destroyed and His nation
exiled. This was also the message of Deuteronomy—which we will
discuss shortly. (And we may add, this was also the message of Rabbi

Yohanan ben Zakkai in the first century C.E. against the zealots who felt that God would not allow Jerusalem to be captured by the Romans.)

From this Simon-Kaplan analysis, the following basic notion emerges: It is only the realization, the actualization of the promise to the patriarchs that is conditional, which is dependent upon the performance of certain stipulations. *The promise itself, however, has an absolute, unconditional quality insofar as this promise stands no matter if its realization is delayed or cancelled.* The promise itself is never withdrawn. If Israel sins the land will vomit her out; sin leads inexorably to exile. However, though it negates the realization of the promise, the exile does not negate the promise itself.

Those texts (e.g., Gen. 13:15, Gen. 17:8) that suggest the unconditionality of the promise only refer to the enduring validity and the permanent character of the promise itself. They do not in any way suggest, nor indeed could they suggest, that the realization of the promise is not dependent upon Israel's observing the stipulations set forth in the Torah.

Summary

In a summary restatement of Simon's views, Kaplan asks: what then is the nature of Israel's attachment to the land insofar as it derives from the promise to the early patriarchs? And he responds: it is an eternal attachment, that is to say, the right to the land rests on a divine promise that preceded (in time and in principle) actual possession. As such, this right is not dependent upon actual possession and changing historical conditions. To put it another way, while the *actual possession* of the land is dependent upon Israel's merits and deeds, the *eternal entitlement* to it is based upon the immutable and everlasting divine promise.

What Deuteronomy Did

Here we have the conceptual key to understanding Deuteronomy's integrating two seemingly contradictory promises, to grasping the way in which the book fuses the unconditional Abrahamic with the conditional Sinaitic covenants. Indeed, the basic principle expounded by Simon-Kaplan, as we apply it to Deuteronomy, provides us, we believe, with what we need to understand how it handles our problem.

What Deuteronomy in essence understood was the following: *The divine promise of the land to the early patriarchs was indeed without conditions, and this promise stands permanent and eternal; however, the realization of that promise, Israel's actual possessing and living on the land, does depend upon her observance of the laws stipulated in the Sinai covenant.*

The texts clearly support this construction. Note how each of the following statements about possessing the land is linked to observance of the commandments and is then immediately followed by iteration of the oath made to the patriarchs. Thus the consensus point of these passages is that Israel can actually possess the land if she conforms to the Law; this is so because of an irrevocable oath God made to her ancestors:

- You shall diligently *keep the commandments*...that you may go in and take possession of the good land which the Lord *swore to give to your fathers* (6:17-19).

- And because you *hearken to these ordinances*...He will bless the fruit of your body and the fruit of your ground, your grain, wine and oil...in the land which He *swore to your fathers* (7:12-13).

- *All the commandments* which I command you this day you shall be careful to do, that you may live and multiply, and go in and possess the land which the Lord *swore to give to your fathers* (8:1).

- You shall *keep all the commandments*...that you may

be strong and go in and take possession of the land...and that you may live long in the land which the Lord *swore to your fathers to give to them as long as there is heaven over the earth* (11:8-9).

- You shall *lay up these words* of mine in your heart and soul; and you shall bind them as a sign upon your hand, and they shall be as frontlets between your eyes...and you shall write them upon the doorposts of your house...that your days and the days of your children may be multiplied in the land the Lord *swore to your fathers* (11:18-21).

- For if you will be careful to *do all this instruction*...then the Lord will drive out all these nations before you...the Lord will lay the fear and the dread of you upon all the land that you shall tread, *as He promised you* (11:22-25).

- And if the Lord your God enlarges your border, as *He has sworn to your fathers*, and gives you all the land which He promised to give to your fathers—provided you are *careful to keep all this commandment*... (19:8-9).

- When you have finished paying all the tithe of your produce...then you shall say before the Lord...I have *not transgressed any of Your commandments*... Look down, therefore, from Your holy habitation and bless Your people Israel and the ground which You have given us, *as You swore to our fathers* (26:12-15).

Taken together, these passages speak clearly: God has promised you the land, people of Israel; His word in history guarantees your eternal claim; however, you must observe His commandments if you expect to actually possess it and enjoy its benefits. In other words, the realization of God's promise in specific, concrete terms, that is, to experience in physical reality the "word" of that promise in the ongoing life of the people, depends upon the behavior of that people.

Thus we see the way in which Deuteronomy wove the unconditional Abrahamic and the conditional Sinaitic covenants together into a seamless, consistent thought line. The two pacts were fused in a way that removed their apparent contradiction, successfully integrating them into a perfect unity. This was a theological achievement of monumental proportions.

Conclusion

We conclude this analysis with an additional comment that validates, we believe, the principle that helps us grasp how Deuteronomy successfully integrates the two covenants.

We ask the basic question again: if Israel believes with a perfect faith in the divine promise to Abraham that the land is hers no matter what her deeds, what then is the purpose of the laws of Sinai and why perform them?

The answer: *the realization of the promise is made possible by the unconditional promise itself*; the latter provides the "official entitlement" to the land, as it were, the ground for it, and thus the motivation to work and strive, via deeds, via adherence to the laws, in order to translate promise into reality. For without the basic right, a right granted in the Abrahamic pact, which was rooted in transcendent authority, the effort of man himself—an effort demanded by the Sinaitic pact—would be pointless and futile. The unconditional promise does not free Israel from observing the laws of the Torah—to repent and return; on the contrary, belief in that promise spurs her on to a life of covenantal loyalty in order to make promise reality.

And we might add, the covenant of Abraham was retained in Deuteronomy as unconditional in principle because if its promises were dependent upon the worthiness of Abraham's seed, the probability of human failure would have robbed the promise of any real hope of actualization. The Sinaitic covenant, as it is brought into context with the Abrahamic in the book of Deuteronomy, says that it is, indeed, possible for even weak, finite, erring man, through his deeds, to realize the destiny of the people Israel.

CHAPTER FIVE

THE LAND IN THE PROPHETS
AND THE WRITINGS (*KETUVIM*)

Is the connection between Israel's religio-moral behavior and loss of land as formulated in Deuteronomy to be found in the prophetic and *Ketuvim* teachings as well? And, simultaneously, is the idea of the unconditional claim to the land as a source of hope similarly to be found in the prophetic and *Ketuvim* literature? If so, on what is this optimism grounded?

The Term "Brit"

It is significant that the actual term *brit* (covenant) rarely appears in the prophetic literature. The term is found in a few isolated cases, such as when Hosea refers to Israel's sinfulness because "they have broken my covenant (*briti*) and Torah (8:1)." Similarly, Jeremiah laments that his compatriots "forsook the covenant *(brit)* of the Lord and worshipped other gods and served them" (22:9).

However, given the extensive prophetic literature, the term *brit* itself is, in fact, largely avoided. This is, indeed, ironic since at the very core of the prophetic message are the concepts of election and binding agreement between God and Israel. It may be that the word *brit* was eschewed because of the widespread misunderstanding of it—the interpretation of the concept of covenant being food for a narrow, exclusive nationalism. Nonetheless, the notion was implacably present in the prophetic mindset, as David Napier, in his analysis of the work of the great prophets, has emphasized:

> The notion of covenant is unmistakably and persistently present. Covenant is the working extension and imple-
> mentation of election, the formal and continuing

application of what is implicit in election—namely, the concrete responsibilities assumed by the elector and the obligations of the electee freely undertaken in response. Election with reference to Israel is perpetuated and realized in covenant. Covenant in the Hebrew Bible is the working contract between unequal partners, instigated, initiated by the senior partner in the act of election.[1]

When, then, we depict below the prophetic linking of Israel's backsliding with the cause for exile—that her non-adherence to the moral and ritual requirements is the reason for diaspora—we are justified in assuming that the ground for such thinking is rooted in the conditional Sinai covenant.

We need to point out, as well, that the unconditional Abrahamic covenant is similarly rarely directly referred to in the prophetic literature. However, here too, as we shall see, that covenant was embedded in the prophetic message, serving as the basis for the prophetic declarations of hope for renewal and assurance of Israel's return from exile to the promised land.

The Prophetic Perspective

Beginning with the prophet Amos in the mid-8th century BCE, and expressed with different emphases and nuances, the prophets of ancient Israel evaluated the national condition and, speaking in God's name, declared that the people had fallen away from the paths of righteous living and away from exclusive loyalty to the one God. Israel had flaunted the provisions of the Sinai covenant both in the areas of morality and cult.

Punishment: This basic prophetic view mirrored that of Deuteronomy: for such behavior there were consequences. With dire threats and warnings, articulated in stinging rhetoric, the prophets alerted their countrymen to the serious consequences that would follow as a result of their rebelliousness and alienation from God and

His requirements of them. They would be held accountable for following the Canaanite gods and for their disregard of justice vis-à-vis their compatriots. These prophetic teachers rebuked their fellows in the hope of shattering the national complacency and affecting repentance and change.

The prophetic idea enunciated for close to two hundred years prior to the exile was essentially the same throughout: God, the presumed champion of Israel, would in fact abandon His people and allow their enemies to overtake them; they would lose everything they held dear: Temple, land, national existence; and worst of all, they would be forced to go into exile. The only way to avoid the oncoming catastrophe would be to return to the Sinai covenant and embrace its teachings.

Hope: However, in reacting to the national disaster, the prophetic view mirrored Deuteronomy's as well: hope remained eternal; exile would never be permanent; God promised Israel's patriarchs that the land was to be Israel's. Thus, accompanying the prophetic word of doom is its word of hope and restoration. These inspired leaders are filled with conviction that God not only rebukes and chastises, but also loves and restores His people to their land.

To illustrate this dual idea of sin/exile and hope/restoration, we note in what follows the works of a set of representative prophets.

The Prophecy of Amos

Amos of Tekoa, cattle breeder and tender of sycamore trees, went north to the kingdom of Israel whose assimilation was more pronounced at the time (8th century BCE) than that of the kingdom of Judah. His preaching flows from the covenant relationship between God and Israel initiated at Sinai: "You alone have I singled out of all the families of the earth. That is why I will call you to account for all your iniquities" (3.2).

The prophet decried the injustice to the poor and the subversion of the cause of the needy. He mocked the greed rampant in the popular culture, the dishonesty in business dealings by manipulating the selling of "goods," substituting the bad for the good:

> Listen to this, you who devour the needy, annihilating the poor of the land, saying: if only the new moon were over so that we could sell grain, the Sabbath so that we could offer wheat for sale using an ephod that is too small and a shekel that is too big—tilting a dishonest scale and selling grain refuse as grain and buying the poor for silver, the needy for a pair of sandals (8:4-6).

Amos attacked his listeners for their empty rituals and holy day celebrations in the absence of righteous living. He declared their sacrifices to God meaningless in view of their outrageous moral behavior.

> I loath, I spurn your festivals, I am not appeased by your solemn assemblies. If you offer me burnt offerings or meal offerings, I will not accept them; I will pay no heed to your gifts of fatlings. Spare me the sound of your hymns, and let me not hear the music of your lutes. But let justice well up like water, righteousness like an unfailing stream (5:21-24).

For the sins of faithlessness and injustice, Amos dares to prophesy the inconceivable: the people will lose their land and go into exile. The hedonistic leaders who were indifferent to the plight of the people "shall lead the column of exiles" (6:4-7). In his encounter with the priest Amaziah at the shrine of Bethel, Amos rebukes the priest and again foresees exile: "Your wife shall play the harlot in the town. Your sons and daughters shall fall by the sword, and your land shall be divided up with a measuring line. And you yourself shall die on unclean soil, for Israel shall be exiled from its soil" (7:17).

However, Amos sees some light through the doom and gloom.

Although he foresees enemy attack, plunder and exile, he does *not* foresee an absolute end; God will not utterly destroy Israel. There is reason for hope about the morrow, and this is expressed via the existence of survivors.

A Remnant

The prophet articulates this view of hopefulness by means of the idea of survivors, which is reiterated and expanded by the prophets who follow him. Despite the judgment that hovers over Israel, God's graciousness is ever present. Yes, Israel will be punished but not with finality: "Hate evil and love good and establish justice at the gate. Perhaps the Lord, the God of hosts, will be gracious to the remnant of Joseph" (5:15).

This idea of a remnant is expressed in symbolic language: "As the shepherd rescues from the lion's jaws two shank bones or the tip of an ear, so shall the Israelites escape who dwell in Samaria—with the leg of a bed or the head of a couch" (3:12).

Once again we see this dialectic of ruination and hope in the final chapter of Amos: "Behold the Lord God has His eyes upon the sinful kingdom: I will wipe it off the face of the earth! But I will not wholly wipe out the house of Jacob, declares the Lord" (9:8).

Thus we see from the "pioneer prophet" that Israel was indeed ripe for a national calamity of major proportions. For her betrayal of the stipulations of the Sinaitic covenant with God—for a life devoid of justice and mercy—Israel will forfeit her land and nationhood and will experience exile. This perspective of Amos reflects the nexus in Deuteronomy between sinfulness and landlessness.

But then, a qualifying notion emerges. In the last chapter of the book of Amos we find the idea of hope and restoration of the people to its land. Perhaps not from the mouth of the prophet Amos himself, but from the mouth of an exilic prophet, we find words of comfort and hope.[2] Here we have adumbrated Deuteronomy's notion of a land and a people being resurrected. The people Israel will live on, and her land will be returned to her. This optimism and faith in the future is rooted in God's promise:

> In that day, I will set up the fallen booth of David: I will mend its breaches and set up its ruins anew. I will build it firm as in days of old (9:11). I will restore my people Israel. They shall rebuild ruined cities and inhabit them; they shall plant vineyards and drink their wine. They shall till gardens and eat their fruits. And I will plant them on their soil, nevermore to be uprooted from the soil I have given them—said the Lord your God (9:14, 15).

Thus we see reflected here the notion of the nucleus of national regeneration and return from exile to the land.

The Prophecy of Isaiah

Isaiah mirrors Deuteronomy's perspective of permanent and impermanent settlement of the land, i.e., permanence for covenant fulfillment and impermanence for covenant abrogation. He, too, is ever mindful of the restoration of Israel to her land due to a non-conditional promise that hearkens back to the patriarchs.

With rich imagery, symbolism and parable, the prophet calls attention to the iniquity rampant in Judah. His message derives from a unique theology. For Isaiah, God is the exalted one whose glory and holiness fill the entire earth. This divine holiness is not neutral but rather bound up with righteousness and justice (5:16). The "Holy One of Israel" has a purpose for history and nations and makes demands of Israel, His people. In light of God's sovereign righteousness, Israel's sins are an affront, an insult to God and, as such, are insufferable. The prophet is angered and repelled:

> Ah, sinful people, people laden with iniquity.
> Brood of evil doers, depraved children!
> They have forsaken the Lord, spurned the Holy One of Israel,

Turned their backs on Him (1:4).

Like Amos, Isaiah takes his people to task for believing that rituals alone are actions pleasing to God, that by bringing sacrifices to God they have discharged their religious obligations. These are not the things faith demands:

> Hear the word of the Lord, you chieftains of Sodom.
> Give ear to God's instruction, you folk of Gomorrah!
> What need have I of all your sacrifices, says the Lord.
> I am sated with burnt offerings of rams and suet of fatlings, blood of bulls.
> I have no delight in lambs and he-goats that you come before me.
> Who asked that of you? Trample my courts no more (1:10-12).

Isaiah depicts Israel's leaders who thrive in a materialistic, hedonistic culture. He deplores their extravagant living and attachment to foreign gods:

> Their land is full of silver and gold
> There is no limit to their treasures;
> The land is full of horses; there is no limit to their chariots
> And their land is full of idols;
> They bow down to the work of their hands
> To what their own fingers have wrought (2:7-8).

Attacking the social ills of his countrymen, Isaiah declares:

> Alas she has become a harlot, the faithful city
> That was filled with justice where righteousness dwelt—
> But now murderers.
> Your silver has turned to dross, your wine is cut with water
> Your rulers are rogues and cronies of thieves
> Every one avid for presents and greedy for gifts;
> They do not judge the case of the orphan

And the widow's cause never reaches them (1:21-23).

Here, too, like Amos, Isaiah links such behavior to calamitous consequence. The people cannot expect immoral behavior and the corruption of its rulers to be exempt from punishment. The prophet declares:

> Your land is a waste, your cities burnt down; before your
> eyes, the yield of your soil is consumed by strangers—
> A wasteland—as overthrown by foreigners (1:7).

Isaiah dares to give voice to the unimaginable—a people who rejected its God has forfeited the privilege of living on its land:

> Assuredly my people will suffer exile for not giving heed,
> Its multitude (will be) victims of hunger
> And its masses (will be) parched with thirst (5:13).

Isaiah asserts, however, that from the devastation and carnage there will emerge survivors—remnants who will form the nucleus of a revived people. He offers words of hope:

> Fair Zion is left like a booth in a vineyard, like a hut in a
> cucumber field. Had not the Lord of Hosts left us some
> survivors, We would be like Sodom, another Gomorrah
> (1:8-9)

> For a remnant shall come forth from Jerusalem and
> survivors from Mount Zion. The zeal of the Lord of Hosts
> shall bring this to pass (37:32).

By means of a striking metaphor, Isaiah points to the vivifying role of this remnant. While the land and people are ravaged and resemble a felled terebinth and oak from which only a stump is left, something startling happens: from this very stump new growth will emerge, "its stump shall be a holy seed" (*zerah kodesh matzavta*, 6:13).

Isaiah proclaims: "But the Lord will pardon Jacob, and will again choose Israel, and will settle them on their own soil. And strangers shall join them and shall cleave to the House of Jacob. For peoples shall take them and bring them to their homeland..." (14:1, 2a).

It is significant that the exilic prophet of comfort and hope, who is referred to as Second Isaiah, associates the nascent people with its ancestor Abraham:

> But you, O Israel, my servant, Jacob who I have chosen,
> Seed of Abraham my friend—
> You who I drew from the ends of the earth
> And called from its far corners, to whom I said:
> 'You are my servant; I chose you, I have not rejected you.
> Fear not for I am with you, be not frightened, for I am your God.
> I strengthen you and I help you.
> I uphold you with my victorious right hand' (41:8-10).

Because of God's special relationship with Israel's patriarchs, their descendants merit God's loving care. The memory of Abraham and Jacob serve as reassurance and as a reminder that those being addressed are still God's chosen.

To those who were doubtful about the viability of the community of returned exiles because of its small size, the prophet again calls to mind their founding patriarch and matriarch:

> Listen to me you who seek justice, you who seek the Lord:
> Look to the rock you were hewn from, to the quarry you were dug from.
> Look back to Abraham, your father, and to Sarah who brought you forth.
> For he was only one when I called him, and I blessed him and made him many (51:1-2).

Here again those addressed are being asked to associate

themselves with the nation's founding couple and with God's blessings of them. The exiles are thus reminded that God's gracious love to Abraham filters down to and envelopes them.

The Prophecy of Micah

It is significant that Micah, who followed in the ideological footsteps of his contemporaries Amos and Isaiah, specifically alludes to the oath God made to the patriarchs Abraham and Jacob as the basis for hope in Israel's future. This was the same unconditional oath to Israel alluded to in Deuteronomy:

> Who is a God like You, forgiving iniquity and remitting transgression,
> Who has not maintained His wrath forever against the remnant of His own people
> Because He loves graciousness!
> He will take us back in love, He will cover up our iniquities.
> You will hurl all our sins into the depths of the sea.
> You will keep faith with Jacob, loyalty to Abraham, as you promised on oath to our fathers in days gone by" (Micah 7:18-20).

The Prophecy of Jeremiah

While the pre-exilic prophets felt mandated by God to warn Israel and Judah of impending doom should they fail to repent, it fell to Jeremiah to not only prophesy the imminence of the national catastrophe, but be witness to it.

Driven by the conviction that the people of Judah are standing on a precipice, oblivious to the immediate danger, his words are sent forth as sharp and pointed arrows meant to disturb, to shock and to warn.

Jeremiah's prophecy has as its starting point the partnership between God and the people Israel. This relationship is variously described: Israel is the loyal bride who follows God faithfully in the wilderness (2:2); she partakes of the sacred quality of the first fruits which belong to God (2:3); she is "a choice vine" planted by God 2:21); she is a loincloth which clings to the loins of a man (13:11). However, Israel has betrayed that intimate relationship. Led by irresponsible leaders, she left her God to follow Baal, the god of Canaan. This rebelliousness has a long history:

> Hear the word of the Lord, O House of Jacob,
> Every clan of the House of Israel,
> Thus said the Lord:
> What wrong did your fathers find in Me that they abandoned Me
> And went after delusions and were deluded?
> They never asked themselves, 'Where is the Lord who brought us up from the land of Egypt,
> Who led us in the wilderness, a land of deserts and pits
> A land of drought and darkness...'
> I brought you to this country of farm land to enjoy its fruit and its bounty
> But you came and defiled My land, you made My possession abhorrent.
> The priests never asked themselves, 'Where is the Lord?'
> The guardians of the Torah ignored Me, the prophets prophesied by Baal
> And followed what can do no good (2:4-8).

The people are thus chastised for ungratefulness to the Source of their blessings and for preferring Baal worship to the worship of the One who sustains them. This has led the people to the abhorrent practice of child immolation (7:31, 19:5, 32:35) against which the prophet rails. Baal worship has even entered the sacred precincts of the Temple itself (19:4).

Accompanying the illegitimate worship of a foreign god, there emerged a social climate of corruption and deceit:

From smallest to greatest they are all greedy for gain;
Priest and prophet alike, they all act falsely (6:13).
They bend their tongues like bows for treachery, not
honesty in the land.
They advance from evil to evil; they do not know Me,
declares the Lord.
Beware every man of his friend! Trust not even a brother!
Every brother deals crookedly, every friend carries gossip,
One man cheats another.
They will not speak truth, they have trained their tongues
to speak falsely,
They wear themselves out working iniquity.
You dwell in the midst of deceit,
In their deceit they refuse to heed Me—declares the Lord
(9:2-5).

Despite their Baal worship and personal immorality, the people
still wish to gain God's favor by bringing Him sacrifices at the
Jerusalem Temple. For this misplaced religiosity, the prophet
reiterates the rebuke of his predecessors, i.e., the substitution of the
sacrificial ritual for inner devotion and loyalty to His teachings is
abhorrent to God:

What need have I of frankincense that comes from Sheba
Or fragrances that come from a distant land?
Your burnt offerings are not acceptable and your sacrifices
are not pleasing to Me" (6:20).

For their transgressions and waywardness, the prophet declares
an end to the national life:

I will turn Jerusalem into rubble, into dens for jackals;
And I will make the towns of Judah a desolation without
inhabitants (9:10).
You will forfeit by your own act the inheritance I have
given you.

I will make you a slave to your enemies in a land you have
never known
For you have kindled the flame of My wrath, which shall
burn for all time (17:4).

But then Jeremiah proceeds to soften his rhetoric and alludes to a
future of hope. He offers a prescription for living that would enable
his people to remain in the land. Note the eternal claim to the land at
the conclusion of the following passage:

> Thus said the Lord of Hosts, the God of Israel: Mend your
> ways and your actions and I will let you dwell in this place.
> Don't put your trust in illusions and say, "The Temple of
> the Lord, the Temple of the Lord, the Temple of the Lord."
>
> No—if you really mend your ways and your actions, if
> you execute justice between one man and another, if you
> do not oppress the stranger, the orphan and the widow, if
> you do not shed the blood of the innocent in this place, if
> you do not follow other gods to your own hurt—then only
> will I let you dwell in this place, in the land that I gave to
> your fathers for all time (7:3-7).

Despite Jeremiah's personal struggles and despite his having
witnessed the siege and invasion of Jerusalem and the capture of
King Jehoiachin, his faith in God remained strong; he also firmly
believed in God's continuing love for His people. Jeremiah proclaims
that the people will eventually return to their land:

> Thus said the Lord:
> A cry is heard in Ramah, wailing, bitter weeping—
> Rachel weeping for her children.
> She refuses to be comforted for her children who are gone.
> Thus said the Lord:
> Restrain your voice from weeping, your eyes shedding tears;
> For there is a reward for your labor—declares the Lord

They shall return from the enemy's land.
There is hope for your future—declares the Lord
Your children shall return to their country (31:15-17).

The prophet foresees the ingathering of the remnant: "And I Myself will gather the remnants of my flock from all the lands to which I have banished them, and I will bring them back to their pasture where they shall be fertile and increase" (23:3).

And significantly, hope for the future restoration derives from God's covenant with the people's forebears:

> Thus said the Lord: As surely as I have established My covenant with day and night—the laws of heaven and earth—so I will never reject the offspring of Jacob and my servant David; I will never fail to take from his offspring rulers for the descendants of Abraham, Isaac and Jacob. Indeed I will restore them from captivity and will have mercy upon them (33:25).

Jeremiah personalized this fervent belief in return to the land during the siege of Jerusalem. While in the prison compound and with the enemy surrounding the city, he negotiated the purchase of a piece of ancestral land in the town of Anatot, in the territory of Benjamin. With the documents and deed of purchase being placed in an earthen jar for preservation, Jeremiah declared in God's name, "houses and fields and vineyards shall again be purchased in this land" (32:15).

The Prophecy of Ezekiel

This confidence in a better tomorrow is emphasized by Ezekiel as well. In his famous vision of the valley of dry bones, the prophet proclaims in God's name:

> Then he said to me, "Son of man, these bones are the whole house of Israel. Behold, they say, 'Our bones are dried up,

and our hope is lost; we are clean cut off.' Therefore prophesy, and say to them, thus says the Lord God: Behold, I will open your graves, and raise you from your graves, O my people; and I will bring you home into the land of Israel. And you shall know that I am the Lord, when I open your graves, and raise you from your graves, O my people. And I will put my Spirit within you, and you shall live, and I will place you in your own land; then you shall know that I, the Lord, have spoken, and I have done it, says the Lord" (37:11-14).

The *Ketuvim* – The Writings

In the third section of scripture we find a set of passages that brim with hope for Israel's future based on God's promise of the land to Abraham and his descendents.

The Psalmist praises God for all the blessings He has bestowed on His people Israel in the past and will bestow in the future:

> He is the Lord our God; His judgments are throughout the earth. He is ever mindful of His covenant, the promise He gave for a thousand generations, that He made with Abraham, swore to Isaac and confirmed in a decree to Jacob, saying: "to you I will give the land of Canaan as your allotted heritage" (Psalm 105:7-10, 42).

Nehemiah is addressing a disconsolate people who had returned to the land from exile, yet were few and bereft. He gives hope for a better tomorrow with these words addressed to God:

> You are the Lord God who chose Abram, who brought him out of Ur of the Chaldeans and changed his name to Abraham. *You made a covenant with him to give to them the land of the Canaanites*...to give it to their descendants. And you kept your word for you are righteous (Nehemiah 9:7-8).

The Chronicler describes the terrible backsliding of the Israelites during the reign of King Menassah. He roundly condemns them while also invoking the past which embraces assurance for the morrow. He quotes God as saying, "I will never again remove the feet of Israel *from the land I assigned to their fathers*, if only they observe faithfully all that I have commanded them—all the teaching and the laws and the rules given to Moses" (II Chronicles 33:8).

While noting the relative paucity of references to the Abrahamic covenant in the *ketuvim*, W. D. Davies avers, along with R. Clements, that "the covenant with Abraham was at the foundation—assumed and often unexpressed—of the people of Israel. Like the foundation of a building, it was often hidden from view and not actively discussed."[3]

Conclusion

In all these works we see the spiritual genius of the Hebrew people. Despite the threat of exile and its actual coming to pass, stress was emphatically put on the landed experience of Israel proclaiming that the notion of the eternal inheritance of her land still had power and effect. That notion speaks of the free gift of land to God's covenant partner, Israel. The language of hope and promise for the future remains alive. The land is seen as the gifted arena of God's encounter with His people. Standing over against the experiences of land loss, of dispossession, these works assert the reality of God's closeness and His promise to restore His people to their heritage.

And so we may say that the prophets of Israel mirrored the dual perspective of Deuteronomy: Israel's sins caused her abandonment and exile as per the Sinai covenant, combined with hope for and confidence in restoration as per the Abrahamic covenant.[4]

CHAPTER SIX

THE LAND IN TALMUDIC
AND MEDIEVAL PERIODS

We now inquire about the post-biblical period: Do we find Deuteronomy's dual perspective concerning the land still in place in Jewish life and thought after destruction of the second Temple and Jerusalem, the dismemberment of Israel's national life in 70 CE and subsequent exile? Yes—the rabbis led their people in accordance with the twin perspective of physical detachment from the land and spiritual closeness to it—of exile and dream of return in real time. They were both realistic and idealistic.

The reality was that the Babylonian exile had distanced the nation from its religious and national center. They no longer had an independent sovereign state. There were new kings and authorities to whom homage was due. They paid taxes to a foreign government and were powerless pawns. They had no choice but to obey the civil authorities and their laws.[1] They no longer could seed and harvest their own fields and bring the first fruits to Jerusalem and celebrate there. No longer could they bring atonement sacrifices and thanksgiving offerings to the altar in the Temple. No longer could the priests serve as the people's intermediaries before God. The city that was the national crown jewel, Jerusalem, was in ruins.

To the rabbis fell the responsibility of interpreting this national catastrophe at the hands of the Romans when Jerusalem was razed. They would have to find a way to provide alternative ways of remaining a viable people still attached to its faith, lest exile and despair lead to national disintegration and eventual disappearance.

And so in the disorientation that followed the destruction and subsequent exile, the sages sought to extract meaning from what had happened to this people through a process of introspection. They proceeded to describe God's judgment and punishment as consequences of the failure of the Israelite community to live up to its own highest ideals. The religious leaders followed in the biblical tradition as understood by Deuteronomy, which affirmed that what happened to Israel was a result of her own rebelliousness and unwillingness to conform to God's will.

The loss of Israel's land and its national humiliation needed to be explained to a perplexed people and was, therefore, viewed theologically as punishment, a reality that had to be faced and that provided meaning to the cataclysm. However, side by side with the notion of punishment, the conviction firmly held by the rabbis was that this punishment would not mean annihilation nor permanent detachment from the land. Indeed, they faced the reality of exile combined with the hope of return, with the dream of concrete restoration.

Creative theological thinking was exhibited by the rabbis: they negotiated the ambiguity of Israel's physical detachment from her ancestral home along with her tenacious sense of closeness, immediacy and concrete attachment to it. To the details of this thought line we now turn our attention.

In the Talmud and Liturgy: Sin the Reason for Exile

The rabbinic perspectives are contained in two basic literary creations that developed over the millennium following the exile—the Talmud and the Liturgy. It is in these works of the mind and spirit of a living people that we find mirrored Deuteronomy's twin concepts of punishment for sin and hope for the future. There are a number of allusions in the Talmud to the theme of self-blame. They speak to the idea of Israel's collective sin that led to loss of Temple and loss of land. They thus express a national angst that rests on theological assumptions. Some examples:

> Why was the first Temple destroyed? Because of three
> things of which Israel was guilty: idolatry, sexual immoral-
> ity and acts of murder...but during second Temple times
> when Jews were involved in Torah study and did observe
> the commandments, why was the Temple destroyed?
> Because baseless hatred was rampant (*Yoma* 9b).

Another sage explains the plight of his people this way:

> Invaders exiled the inhabitants of the land and others came
> to settle in their place because of the cessation of the
> observances of *shmitta* and *yovel* (the sabbatical and
> fiftieth year when cultivating the land is proscribed in
> scripture) (*Shabbat* 33a).

In yet another passage we find a new reason for the exile:

> We were driven from our land because we did not set aside
> the heave offerings and the tithes (the Torah required)
> (*The Fathers According to Rabbi Nathan* 20).

This notion of self-blame articulated in the rabbinic literature
continued to be expressed in the synagogue liturgy that developed in
the generations to follow. The synagogue was an institution in the
exile that took on a special role in the life of Jewry. It served as a
religious rallying point in the absence of the Jerusalem Temple. In
lieu of sacrifices of thanksgiving, atonement and purification et al.,
words of prayer, chants and hymns were fashioned. Gradually the
poets, mystics and scholars developed a "service of the heart"
whereby an awareness of God could be nurtured and religious and
national needs and yearnings expressed. Thus over many generations
the liturgy was created and subsequently codified in the mid-ninth
century by Amram Gaon, the head of the Babylonian Academy
located in the city of Sura.

Through this authoritative *Siddur* (prayer book) the basic Jewish practices, beliefs and dreams were expressed. Embedded in this liturgy like a silver thread in a variegated tapestry is the theme of Zion—Zion lost and Zion restored.

In this liturgy we find again the theme of Israel's collective sin leading to the loss of Temple and land. Inserted in the Amidah for the Festivals we read as follows:

וּמִפְּנֵי חֲטָאֵינוּ גָּלִינוּ מֵאַרְצֵנוּ וְנִתְרַחַקְנוּ מֵעַל אַדְמָתֵנוּ

And on account of our sins we were exiled from our land,
and removed far from our country, and we are unable to go
up in order to appear and prostrate ourselves before You,
and to fulfill our obligations in Your chosen house, that
great and holy temple which was called by Your Name,
because of the hand of violence that has been laid upon
Your sanctuary (*Hertz Siddur*, p. 821).

The same perspective is expressed in the penitential prayers known as תַּחֲנוּן (*supplication*), the somber elegy known as "the long v'hurachum" recited on Monday and Thursday mornings and at one time observed by some as fast days. These prayers are filled with woe over Israel's suffering. Consciousness of sin is the opening note here passing into lamentations and transitioning to trust in God's gracious love.

> O Lord, according to all your righteous acts, let Your anger
> and fury be turned away from Your city Jerusalem, Your
> holy mountain. Because of our sins and the iniquities of
> our fathers, Jerusalem and Your people have become a
> byword among all who are round about us. Listen, our
> Lord, to the prayer of your servant and to his supplications
> and cause your face to shine on the sanctuary that is
> desolate...Our Father and King be gracious to us and
> answer us for we have no good works of our own...
> remember for us the covenant of our fathers and save us
> for Your name's sake (*Hertz Siddur*, p. 171).

In the penitential prayers (*slichot*) we again find expressions of sinfulness and penance. In one of these prayers for the *17th day of Tammuz*, the day the walls of the Temple were first breached, the poet expresses guilt combined with a plea for forgiveness:

> We have come before You sighing with heavy hearts because of our iniquities and crying aloud because of the harsh decrees...Because we provoked You to anger we were given up to destruction...We rebelled against Him and were therefore scattered in all directions...For being a stiff-necked people we suffered great calamity...Behold, O Lord, deliver us from calamity and convert the *17th of Tammuz* into gladness and joy...Turn to us and gather our dispersed from the four corners of the earth. Say to Zion, arise! And we shall rise (*Selichot for the Whole Year, London*, p. 366).

In passing, note the comment by Moritz Lazarus in his *Ethics of Judaism* in this connection:

> The Jews have always been the people of self-criticism. Thus our propensity for self-accusation fosters prejudice against us. Often the spirit is rife (as with Goethe) that Jews must be so much worse than other people because their prophets and leaders have always rebuked them for their wickedness. It is not that our faults have been greater than other peoples, but that our condemnation of ourselves has been more severe.

In the Talmud: Hope for Restoration

As the concluding passages of the above penitential prayers and others of this genre express, more than national sorrow for the exile is indicated. In them we hear the yearning of a people who dare to hold on to a shred of hope—that the redeeming God of history will not abandon Israel utterly, will not forsake her forever. Indeed, the dream for Zion reborn was kept alive.

And so we turn our attention to the second perspective of Deuteronomy, to that of hope derived from the conviction that God's unconditional promise of the land still holds firm. It was the reality of this promise that remained operative in the rabbinic mind. This eternal oath to Israel's patriarchs is mirrored in the writings of the talmudic sages. And it was this promise that filled the hearts of the poets and hymnists in their religious outpourings, which in turn fill the pages of the Jewish liturgy.

The Sense of Exile

With the passage of time, Jews acclimated to their new surroundings. However, despite the fact that many Jews actually prospered in Babylonia and elsewhere in the diaspora, despite the study of Torah, performance of *mitzvot*, employment of prayer in place of sacrifice, substitution of synagogue in place of Temple, a striking phenomenon remained in place: a pervasive sense of exile. It was the recognition that Jewish existence was partial at present and that the diaspora was an interim condition. The memories of the homeland and the tenacious attachment of the people to it persisted.

The very study of Torah and the pervasive presence of the land in it, in prayer and the performance of *mitzvot*, enabled the memory and yearning to live on. Indeed, the continuity of the people Israel and the theological underpinnings of promise, covenant and land are writ large on the pages of Talmud and adumbrated everywhere in ritual and liturgy. Moreover, it is in the rabbinic writings that so much of Israel's laws pertaining to the land are formulated. As the rabbis in the academies interpreted scripture, the homeland was made to retain its actuality; it remained real, a sacred geography, a very concrete place charged with magnetic force. The theological perspective remained: the exile was a temporary condition despite its seeming permanence. The time would come when a physical return to Zion would be possible.

Hope: Keenly Felt

The hope of regaining the land was felt so keenly that one third of the Mishna (the pharisaic legal code) is devoted to laws dealing with the land. The bulk of the first order of the Mishna *Zeraim* (seeds), of the fifth order *Kodshim* (hallowed things), of the sixth order *Taharot* (clean things) deal with rules concerning the land. There is much the same in other parts of the Mishna. This all is no accident, because the connection between Israel and its land was seen as an integral part of the Divine purpose for this people.

The rabbis conjured with various aspects of the land—its sanctity, its borders, its divisions, its laws pertaining to the Temple, its utensils and sacrifices. When one reads the Talmud, one begins to comprehend the utter reality of this holy place in the Jewish psyche and the undaunted belief in possessing it again.

The sages refer to the land of Israel simply and affectionately as *ha-aretz* ("the land") in contradistinction to all other places, which are referred to as in Taanit 10a as חוּץ לָאָרֶץ ("outside the land"). The term used in describing migration to the place is לַעֲלוֹת ("to go up") because it is symbolically higher than any other place (*Tanhuma Kedoshim* 10). Indeed, there were no constraints on hyperbole: this locale is the center of the world, yet more—the foundation stone upon which the world is based (ibid.).

The Talmud expatiates at length on the "precepts dependent on the land" (*Kiddushin 37a*) and avers that it was only in that locale that the agricultural mitzvot could be performed and nowhere else, e.g., *Orla, Omer, Shmitta, Peyah, Shikcha, Ma-aser, Bikkurm.*[2] It was permitted to calculate and proclaim the onset of a new month and declare a leap year only in the land (*Mishna Kiddush Hachodesh* 1:8). Moreover, authorizing the position of a judge could be done only in the land (*Sanhedrin* 14a).

Yearning for the land and the desire to experience its sanctity form the basis for several rabbinic statements. For example, they asserted that to reside in the land is equal to all the precepts of the Torah (*Ketubot* 25a). Some maintain that not only he who lives in it permanently, but even he who walks four cubits in it is assured of life in the world to come (*Ketubot* 111a). The great sages would kiss its stones and roll in its dust (*Mishna Melachim* 5:10). Whoever is buried in the land of Israel is as if he's buried beneath the Temple altar (*Ketubot* 111a). For those living outside the land, it became a custom to place in the grave some earth from the land of Israel (*Mishna Kilayim* 9:4).

From this all we see that in the Talmud the land not only evokes deep emotional ties but in the rabbinic mind the place remains a concrete reality with hope that someday Israel would repossess it.

Rabbi Akiba

The Midrash records the attempts of the rabbis to offer hope of restoration. It is related that one day, Rabbi Akiba and his colleagues were walking near the site where the Temple once stood. There they noticed a fox running out from the area that had once been the Holy of Holies, the most sacred place of the Temple. The rabbis wept but Rabbi Akiba remained composed. He seemed almost happy. When asked by his colleagues how he could remain so serene at this scene of utter destruction, Akiba said that he had been thinking of two separate prophecies—the doom announced by Zechariah, Micah, Jeremiah, and the prophecy of comfort pronounced by Zechariah (8:4), "old men and old women will yet sit in the streets of Jerusalem, each with staff in hand because of old age." The sage then concluded by assuring his colleagues that if the prophecies of doom had been fulfilled, then we might also expect the prophecies of consolation to come true. When the others heard this they said to him, "You have comforted us, Akiba" (*Sifre on Deut.* 43).

In the Liturgy: Hope for Restoration

The memory of Zion and hope for its restoration was carried

forth in every prayer service in synagogue and home. The early rabbis at Yavneh substituted morning and afternoon prayer units for the sacrifices that had been offered daily in the Temple in Jerusalem as a way to link their present to their past, to keep the memory of that worship pattern alive in anticipation of its restoration. The *Amida* (the silent prayer recited standing) that was integral to these prayer units was required to be said daily (*Mishna Brachot* 4:1 ff), and reflects this aspiration in a number of ways.

Embedded in the midst of the *Shmoneh Esray* (the eighteen blessings—actually nineteen—which constitute the *Amida*) are prayers for understanding, pardon, redemption, healing, prosperity et al. Here we find, as well, fervent yearning for Jerusalem and Zion:

> And to Jerusalem, Your city, return in mercy, and dwell therein as You have spoken. Rebuild it soon in our days as an everlasting building and speedily set therein the throne of David. Blessed are You, O Lord, who rebuilds Jerusalem.

Referring to the Temple in the holy land, the prayer reads:

> Accept, O Lord our God, Your people Israel and their prayer; restore the service to the inner sanctuary of Your house; receive in love and favor both the offerings of Israel and their prayer; and may the worship of Your people be ever acceptable to You.

And again:

> And let our eyes behold Your return in mercy to Zion. Blessed are You, O Lord, who restores Your divine presence to Zion.

And then, as if the sentiment had not yet been adequately expressed, the liturgists added an addendum at the very conclusion of the Amida:

> May it be Your will, O Lord our God and God of our
> fathers, that the Temple be speedily rebuilt in our days,
> and grant our portion in Your Torah. And there we will
> serve You with awe as in days of old and as in ancient
> years. In the words of the prophet Malachi 3:4: Then shall
> the offering of Judah and Jerusalem be pleasant unto the
> Lord, as in days of old, and as in ancient years.

In the Shabbat and Festival *shacharit* service embedded in the
prayer preceding the Shema is the plea:

> O bring us in peace from the four corners of the earth and
> make us go up proudly to our land.

In the prayers chanted as the Ark is opened in preparation for the
Torah reading on Shabbat and Festival, the following yearning is
proclaimed:

> Father of mercies, do good in your favor to Zion; build the
> walls of Jerusalem...For out of Zion shall go forth the
> Torah, and the word of the Lord from Jerusalem.

And in the Shabbat *musaf* service the prayer is yet again recited:

> May it be Your will, O Lord our God and God of our
> fathers, to lead us in joy to our land, and to plant us within
> our borders.

The focused concern for Jerusalem in prayer motivated the
rabbis to promulgate particular rules for prayer. In the *Mishna
Brachot* 4:5, for example, we read as follows:

> If one is riding on a donkey when the time for prayer is
> upon him, he should dismount to say the *Tefilla* (the
> A*mida* prayer). If he cannot dismount, he should turn his
> face toward Jerusalem; and if he cannot turn his face, he
> should direct his heart to the Holy of Holies.

Certain liturgical practices were observed זֵכֶר לְמִקְדָּשׁ, "in memory of the Temple." For example, during Temple times the *lulav*, the palm branch used during the Sukkot festival, was carried for seven days in the Temple, but in the provinces one day only. After the destruction, Rabbi Yochanan ben Zakkai ordained that in the provinces the *lulav* should be carried for seven days in memory of the Temple.

In the Passover Haggadah this זֵכֶר לְמִקְדָּשׁ idea can also be found. Before one partakes of the Hillel sandwich of matzo and bitter herbs, one says as follows: "I do this in memory of the Temple as Hillel did during Temple times; Hillel would combine matzo and marror and eat them together."

Other elements in the liturgy came to be called זֵכֶר לְחָרְבָּן, "in memory of the destruction." For example, *Tisha B'av*, the ninth day of the Hebrew month Av, a commemorative occasion each year, is a fast day because it is on this day the Temple is said to have been destroyed and the subsequent exile occurred. The book of Lamentations is read in the synagogue on this day. This biblical dirge depicts the devastation of the land, the physical pain, the anguish of the people, the loss of life and limb, the dashing of spirit— this all caused by the destruction. Jews identified thereby with the land's fate throughout the ages.

Twice a year in liturgical settings the yearning to return to Zion is expressed in the outcry: "Next year in Jerusalem." At the conclusion of the Day of Atonement when the Jew feels spiritually cleansed, and at the conclusion of the Passover Seder when he feels a sense of liberation, he/she looks forward to the greatest liberation of all: exit from exile and return to homeland.

On Festivals in the synagogue, those in the congregation who are of priestly lineage offer the priestly blessing upon the assemblage. The blessing formula was given to Aaron the priest back in biblical times. Amplifying this blessing, these later priests pray as follows:

> May our prayer be acceptable to You...You, O God, who are
> merciful, we beseech You to restore Your divine presence
> to Zion and the ordained service in Jerusalem. Let our eyes
> see Your return in mercy to Zion, and there we will worship
> You in awe, as in days old and as in ancient years
> (*Numbers* 6:24).

It is noteworthy that the hope for return to Zion is not only
expressed in the communal, collective religious life, but in the
prayers of the personal life as well. When a bride and groom stand
under the *huppah*, the wedding canopy, a quintessentially joyous
moment, the groom breaks a glass at the conclusion of the ceremony.
This is viewed as fulfilling the oath of the ancient exiles as portrayed
in Psalm 137: "If I forget thee, O Jerusalem, may my right hand
wither, may my tongue cleave to the roof of my mouth if I remember
thee not, if I do not invoke Jerusalem above my chiefest joy."

At this wedding occasion, as well, when two lives are being
happily united, a sentiment of joy is expressed in the seven blessings
that are chanted, one of which reads:

> May the barren one bereft of children (i.e., the homeland)
> rejoice and be glad in the ingathering of her children to
> herself in joy. Blessed are You, Adonai, who causes Zion to
> rejoice with her children. Speedily, O Lord our God, may
> there be heard in the cities of Judah and the streets of
> Jerusalem the sound of mirth and the sound of gladness,
> the voice of the groom and the voice of the bride—the
> joyful sounds of grooms from their wedding canopies and
> the youths from their song-filled banquets...

And then in the Grace after Meals, recited after each meal when
bread is eaten, Zion and Jerusalem are repeatedly invoked.
Examples:

- Have compassion, O Lord our God, on Israel Your people,

on Jerusalem Your city, on Zion the abiding place of Your glory, on the kingdom of the house of David Your anointed, and the great and holy house that was called by Your name.

- Rebuild Jerusalem, the holy city, speedily in our days. Blessed are You, O Lord, who in Your compassion rebuilds Jerusalem. Amen... May the all-merciful break the yoke from off our neck and lead us proudly to our land.

During the *Brit Milah* (circumcision ceremony), when an eight-day-old male is initiated into the Jewish faith and community, there are a number of blessings invoked for the child's physical and spiritual well-being. One of them reads: "May this tender infant...live to appear before the divine presence three times a year (for the annual pilgrimage festivals in the land)." Thus even at such a joyous family occasion, there is a consciousness of the national condition of exile, and so the following is chanted: "May the All-merciful send us the righteous anointed one to bring good tidings and consolation to a people that is scattered and dispersed among the nations."

The Source of the Hope for Restoration

From the foregoing, it becomes clear that throughout the years of exile, there existed an invisible "umbilical cord," as it were, connecting a people to its land. We have seen how rabbinic thought and Jewish liturgy expressed a tenacious longing to return to the homeland. The question we must now respond to is this: what is the source of this unyielding hope? What theological understanding preserved the dream of return?

From the liturgy comes the answer. Although in exile, Jews believed that the Abrahamic covenant with God was still in force. Exile had not ended this fundamental relationship. Rather, the sages viewed exile as an instrument of atonement, a cleansing that would restore this people to its God. A morning prayer offers the prevailing religious sentiment: "For we are Your people, the children of Your covenant." And because they were still God's people, God was still their God. He is the *Shomer Yisrael*, "the Guardian of Israel"; He is the אוֹהֵב עַמּוֹ יִשְׂרָאֵל, "the Lover of His people Israel"; He is the גּוֹאֵל יִשְׂרָאֵל, "the Redeemer of Israel"; He was the Redeemer in the past, גָּאַל, and is still the Redeemer in the present, גּוֹאֵל. God's role in Israel's redemption is affirmed again and again.

This unshakable belief was rooted in God's promise of the land to Israel's patriarchs which was given to them unconditionally, and the promise applied to all subsequent generations. And so the supplication section in the prayer book recited during the end of every morning service continually harkens back to God's promises to the patriarchs; note the following passages in the Hertz Siddur:

> • We beseech You, O gracious and merciful King, remember and give heed to the Covenant between the pieces with Abraham... (saying: to your descendants I give this land...) (p. 174).

> • Hear our voice and be gracious, and abandon us not into the hands of our enemies to blot out our name. Remember what You swore to our fathers that we would be as the stars in the sky though now we are few in number (p. 184).

> • Lord our God, listen to the voice of our supplications and remember for us the Covenant of our fathers and save us for Your name's sake (p. 170).

Furthermore, appeal to the patriarchs does not presuppose upright, sinless behavior on Israel's part:

> • Our Father, our King, be gracious to us and answer us though we have no good works of our own...Listen to the voice of our supplications and remember for us the

Covenant of our fathers (p. 170).

• Remember Your servants, Abraham, Isaac and Jacob. Look not upon our stubbornness or wickedness or sin. Turn from Your fierce anger and relent of the evil against Your people (p. 176).

• Our Father, our King, though we be without righteousness and good deeds, remember unto us the Covenant of our fathers and the testimony we bear every day that the Lord is One (p. 178).

In the Exegetical Literature

Here, as well, in the literature of the medieval period, we find the dual notion of Israel's backsliding as the cause of her exile coupled with hope for return to the land.

In the perspective of the medieval biblical commentators, notably Rashi, Nachmanides, and David and Joseph Kimchi, the link between exile and return to the land were the commandments God had given to Israel. These exegetes equate exile with Israel's non-observance, on the one hand, and on the other, hope for return rooted in God's unconditional covenant with Israel.

According to Rashi, the land is the place where the commandments are to be observed, and since it is God's gift to the people they must demonstrate their love most completely by carrying out the Divine mandates.[3] Nachmanides expands on this premise by observing that *since Israel was now in exile, it is because of her failure to observe the commandments.* He then proceeds to specify which commandments were not observed. These include the Sabbatical and Jubilee years, forbidden sexual relations, falsehood and the perversion of justice.[4]

But then the other aspect of our dual notion comes into play. In the context of polemics between Christians and Jews during the medieval period, there emerges a clear emphasis on the part of the Jewish exegetes on hope for return to Israel's homeland, indeed, firm confidence and faith in such a future.

Christians claimed that the Jews lack a land and a king as a sign of punishment, to which David Kimchi responded, "We can see that Jesus did not establish himself in Jerusalem. Most of its inhabitants did not follow him. Most of the people who travel there today are evil soldiers." Yet more: Kimchi and his fellow exegetes emphasized that in Israel's current exile, all other people have failed to establish themselves in the land. This fact proved to their satisfaction that God had given the land to the Jews in perpetuity, ultimately destining it to be returned to them. Gentile conquerers have failed to permanently settle the land; Christians have failed to convert the Moslems and both groups constantly threaten one another.[5]

In the end, the land is personified as patiently awaiting the redemption of its exiled children, and eventually that will come about in due time at the will of God. The exegetes reveal a hopeful, even triumphal spirit in their description of Israel's return to the land: Israel will, indeed, be a "light unto the nations."

In his commentary on Genesis, chapter one, Rashi indicates that as Creator of the world, it was God's decision to bestow the land on Israel.[6] Michael Signer utilizes this assertion to describe the perspective of the biblical commentators of their era on our subject. He tells us that the Pentateuch began with the story of creation because, despite the consequence of exile that befalls Israel when it fails to keep the commandments, the covenant between Israel and its God is not exclusively rooted in Israel's obedience to God through the observance of the Law. *Certainly the covenant would never be so dependent on observance of the law that God's ultimate promise to Israel would be nullified. Rather, God acts beneficently to Israel long before commanding any laws at all.* The universality of the creation story is refracted into the particular act of the bestowal of the land upon Israel via the promise to the patriarch Abraham.

Rashi does not present the negative aspect of Israel's exile. For him the Torah is not the narrative of Israel's debilitating exile but of its proud possession of the land. As the covenant is eternal, so Israel's possession of its land is eternal. God cannot be so capricious as to take back what was graciously bestowed from creation's very inception.[7]

In the Kabbalistic Literature

In the medieval period, the Kabbalists developed a daring new perspective on the issue of exile and return. And here we find significant divergence from Deuteronomy's dual notion, which was embraced by Talmudist, liturgist and exegete. Exile was indeed punishment for Israel's sins but it also had positive purpose, and hope for return took on symbolic meaning rather than concrete expectation for return to the land.

On Exile

The exile of Israel represents for the Kabbalists the exile of God as well, as it were. As Israel is in exile from the land, so God is in exile from Himself, from His plenitude, the *shekhina*. If Jewish existence is understood in this conception as broken, the Divine totality is broken as well. This perspective became one of the dominant themes of medieval Jewry.

According to Gershom Scholem, the exposition of the notion by the Lurianic Kabbalah is "the deepest symbol of the exile that could be thought of." To summarize: in the beginning, God was in the process of withdrawing Himself in order to provide room for the cosmos. In His first expansive sending forth of light, that light broke into countless sparks that have become trapped in the material world below; thus God Himself became broken, fragmented and in exile from Himself. It is man's awesome responsibility to rescue his Deity and in so doing to rescue himself. Thus as Israel rescues her Deity from exile, she rescues herself.[8]

In this conception, the experience of exile on Israel's part is a participation in the divine pathos and thus an experience in salvation. Israel's exile is her experience of painful separation from her land followed by rebirth in it. Hence, it became necessary to experience exile so that rebirth and restoration may come about. The notion was extended in the popular mind in that Israel needs to press ever further into the chaos of exile in order to gather the lost sparks of the Deity and return the lost fragments of Himself to Him. Thus we find the Hasidic preludes to selected rituals that are intended "for the sake of the unification of the Holy One Blessed Be He and His *Shekhina* (indwelling presence)."[9]

According to Scholem, *Galut* here acquires a new meaning. Formerly it had been regarded either as a punishment for Israel's sins or as a test of Israel's faith. *Now it is still all this*, but it is also a mission: its purpose is to uplift the fallen sparks from all their various locations.

> This is the secret why Israel is fated to be enslaved by all the nations of the world. In order that she may lift those sparks which have also fallen among them...and therefore it was necessary that Israel should be scattered to the four winds in order to lift up everything.[10]

When this language of the recovery of the lost sparks took root as a significant notion during the medieval period, it continued on into the mindset of east European Hassidism and impacted the Sephardic world as well.[11] It helped explain the meaning of exile.

On Return

As for the Kabbalistic notion of hope for return to the land, the notion took on a mystical character replacing the more concrete desire for return. According to Moshe Idel:

> The most important contribution to the image of the Holy Land made by medieval Jewish literature was afforded by

the *Book of Zohar,* which combined and embellished fragmentary descriptions of the Land found in the antecedent texts, and even invented details which sometimes are in flagrant contradiction to the real geography. *The Zoharic literature created an imaginary "sacred space" with an illusory sacred shrine.* These had an impressive impact on the Kabbalists, especially on those who established the Kabbalistic center of Safed in the second half of the sixteenth century. Even when living in the real Land of Israel, the phantoms of the imaginary accounts were much more influential than such ancient and concrete *loci sacri* as the Western Wall.

To give only one example: Zoharic literature turned R. Shimeon bar Yohai into the chief hero of ancient mysticism; the Safed Kabbalists "discovered" his grave at Meron, near Safed, and it became for them a place of pilgrimage, second only to the remnants of the Temple.

Idel proceeds to explain how the Kabbalists viewed return to the land in this new mystical light. They found a way to live outside the "sacred space." They built their existence around the Holy Land as a living reality without having to uproot themselves in order to live in it. The substitutes for the real effort to reach the concrete land were exegesis and meditation on texts dealing with the land. They preferred to concentrate on literary symbols of the sacred center in place of direct contact with its actual geography. Thus, since contact with the terrestrial land itself was in their minds quite remote, they found contemplation of figurative language more effective as a way to express their hope for return to the land. [12]

CHAPTER SEVEN

THE LAND IN THE MODERN PERIOD

The establishment of the State of Israel in our time must be understood as release of the redemptive forces latent within the Jewish people. If the People Israel acted in history, it was in response to imprisoned redemptive impulses which for a hundred years clamored with rising intensity to be set free. Even the most secular Jew will have to recognize that the messianic idea played as much of a part in the redemptive process as did the rise of European nationalism. However each of us interprets the Messiah idea, it is clear that when the Jewish people returned to Eretz Yisrael, it was in response to a call that issued, not from the Congress of Vienna or the uprisings of 1848, but from the depths of the Jewish spirit.

David Polish
Israel, Nation and People

In rejection and triumph, openly or in disguise, the religious conceptions of homelessness and homecoming continued to direct the thinking of the modern cultural Zionists, political Zionists, non-Zionists, and anti-Zionists alike.

Arnold M. Eisen
Modern Jewish Reflections
on Homelessness and Homecoming

First, there are those who cling to the religious tradition that explains the exile as punishment for Israel's backsliding, that is, for violating the conditions of the Sinai covenant. In addition, in this traditional world the outlook of the kabbalists as to the cause—and purpose—of Israel's dispersion among the nations continued to function in the mindset of many. However, in the modern age, according to this perspective, the Jewish people's suffering in exile had run its course and the time had come to seize upon God's unconditional promise of the land and, at long last, return to it.

Second, there are those who have fashioned a new, secular perspective about the land of Israel. While eschewing Israel's guilt as the reason for her exile, this realm's leading spokesmen have negated the exile in strong, non-theological terms, adopting the return to Zion as a political and national cause. Of course, there remain those, especially in America, who resist this denigration of the diaspora, though we would argue that this view hardly squares with the classical view on the matter.[1] In either case, secularists and affirmers of the diaspora alike could not escape the underlying religious imperative of return to the homeland. Martin Buber has emphasized this point, rooted as it is in the essential nature of Judaism and the Jewish people:

> In the life of the Jewish people no sphere is unconnected with the religious one. Not only is Judaism's specific creativity bound up with its relationship to the unconditional (i.e., God), but so too is its specific vitality. Any distinction between different fields of endeavor, characteristic of most other peoples, is alien to the nature of Judaism; its extra-religious elements are, in one way or another, determined by and dependent upon religious factors. *Ancient messianic dreams live on in the ideologies of Jewish socialists.*[2]

What follows seeks to document and explain these observations.

The Religionists on Exile and Return

For the past two thousand years up to this very day the rationale for Israel's exile has been implanted in the festival prayer service and endlessly recited by Jews throughout the diaspora:

> *Because of our sins we were exiled from our Land, and removed far from our soil.* And we cannot make our Festival pilgrimages to perform our sacred duties in the great and holy Sanctuary dedicated to Your service.
>
> Lord our God and God of our ancestors, merciful Sovereign: Have compassion upon us and upon Your Holy Land. Rebuild it speedily, and enhance its glory. Reveal the majesty of Your sovereignty over us soon; may all humanity witness that You are our Sovereign. Gather the dispersed of our people from among the nations, and assemble our scattered folk from the ends of the earth.
>
> Lead us to Zion, Your city, with song, and to Jerusalem, site of Your Temple, with everlasting joy. For as there our ancestors brought to You the prescribed sacrificial offerings of this day, so will we serve You there, with devotion, fulfilling our duties, wholeheartedly, in accordance with Your will.[3]

Clearly, the retention of this prayer and its repetition by traditionalists in our time reflects continuity with Deuteronomy's dual notion of the conditional and unconditional covenants: backsliding as the reason for exile and hope for return to the land.

A Set of Thinkers

A number of seminal and representative thinkers about the modern Zionist movement embraced the fundamental notion of exile and return framed by Deuteronomy—the notion that persisted among religionists down through the ages.

Rabbi Yehudah Alkalai *(1798-1878).* The collective return to the land, Alkalai proclaimed, "was foretold by all the prophets; even though we are unworthy, Heaven will help us for the sake of our holy ancestors."[4]   Here, as in his other writings, Alkalai stressed the traditional explanation for exile as the result of an "unworthy" people while simultaneously emphasizing the practical need of return based on the promise to the ancestors.

Rabbi Zvi Hirsch Kalischer (1795-1874). Kalischer viewed the exile as a "test" of Israel's faith. She failed that test once and hence had to taste the bitterness of exile. "Throughout the days of our dispersion, we have so suffered martyrdom for the sanctity of God's name," Kalischer wrote, "we have been dragged from land to land and have borne the yoke of exile through the ages, all for the sake of His holy Torah, and as a further stage of the testing of our faith." But the faith of Israel is also being tested, he continued, by "a clear heavenly command to go up and inherit the land and enjoy its good fruit...only a natural beginning of the redemption is a true test of those who initiate it."[5]   Thus exile and return were formulated in traditional religious categories.

Rabbi Samuel Mohilever (1824-1898). Mohilever, in his message to the first Zionist Congress in 1897, wrote, "The basis of *Hibbat Zion* (the Love of Zion movement) is the Torah, as it has been handed down to us from generation to generation with neither supplement nor subtraction. The Torah which is the source of our life must be the foundation of our regeneration in the land of our fathers."

Tolerant though Mohilever was of his non-religious Zionist brethren, in this message and throughout his life and work he quite naturally embraced the traditional religious notion of exile as the result of Israel's backsliding; however, the time had now arrived to work toward return to the land based on the authority of God's promise to Israel's forebears: "Our hope and faith has ever been and still is that our messiah will come and gather all the scattered of Israel, and instead of our being wanderers upon the face of the earth, ever moving from place to place, we shall dwell in our own country as a nation in the fullest sense of the word...this is our faith and hope, as derived from the words of our prophets and seers of blessed memory and to this our people cling."[6]

Rabbi Abraham Isaac Kook *(1865-1935).* Rav Kook was probably the greatest religious traditionalist to espouse the cause of Zion in the modern age. *Eretz Yisrael* was part of the very essence of Jewish nationalism, he contended, bound organically to its very life and inner being and inextricably linked with the religion of Israel:

> As long as the light of the higher Torah is sealed, the inner demand of return to Zion is not aroused with the depth of faith. The arousal that comes as a result of the troubles and persecutions of the nations is but an accidental arousal, of purification. It is capable of firing up weak elements, but the foundation of life must come from the essence of the formal demand of the nation. And this will be magnified and strengthened in proportion to the light of the inner Torah—the depth of its opinions and mysteries— coming alive in its midst with great genius.

What needs especially to be noted about Rav Kook's seminal contribution to Zionist thought was his emphasis on the central role of the land in the Jewish people's mandated pursuit of "holiness." Segregating holiness from the everyday as an independent category of human existence is contrary to nature. Cultivating the spirit through prayer and ritual alone is an imperfect holiness. The separate and independent holiness of the spirit, as opposed to the holiness of the natural life, arose in Israel when the people was removed from its soil and reduced to a truncated religious life. It was then that Jews separated themselves from the life of the passing hour.

True holiness, Rav Kook stressed, requires of Jews and all people the ennoblement of nature—of the simple life, of its health, of normality in *all* human activity—social, political, economic, cultural et al. The national movement of Israel, the return of the people to the land is grounded in this requirement.

As for the exile, "the *very sins which are the cause of our exile* pollute the pristine wellspring of our being, so that the water is impure at the source." But, Rav Kook continued, this condition is beginning to come to an end, "the well is clearing itself until the original purity returns. When that process is completed the exile will become a disgust to us and will be discarded." The messiah will begin to gather in the exiles and the Jew will be enriched by "the greatest giant of humankind, Abraham, who Almighty God called to be a blessing to man"—a blessing Kook understood to be fully possible only when the people Israel was rooted in her own land that God through Abraham promised to His people.[7]

Martin Buber *(1878-1965).* Rav Kook's view about the organic nature of Jewish nationalism as encompassing the life of religion was echoed by Martin Buber, another great figure in the constellation of Zionist thinkers. Buber could not entirely abandon the Deuteronomic notion that "long life upon the land" was conditional on Israel's moral conduct, that non-adherence to the covenant between God and the people of Israel could result in the land "spewing forth" that people.

At the same time, Buber could not abandon Deuteronomy's optimism about hope for the morrow. In the process he embraced Kook's notion of the organic nature of Judaism. "A Jewish nation cannot exist without religion any more than a religious community without nationality," he emphasized. "Our only solution is to become Israel again and to become a whole, the unique whole of a people and a religious community—a renewed people, a renewed religion, and a renewed unity of both." Indeed, for Buber the greatest values of Judaism issued from a marriage between a people and a faith, and only faith in the God who promised the land to His people and continued faith in Him as the Redeemer of His people in exile would enable Israel to return to her homeland.[8]

To summarize: The clear consensus among the leading religionists concerning the land of Israel in the modern age was adherence to the traditional perspective about Israel's exile and return (some directly, some obliquely)—in basic continuity with Deuteronomy's dual notion. Yes, the Sinai covenant was conditional upon Israel's observance and faith. However, the loss of standing with God and the exile never meant that God would ever totally repudiate the people. Israel's election and her title to her land had permanence as enshrined in the unconditional promise by God to Abraham and his descendants down through the corridors of history.

The Secularists on Exile and Return

The predominant view in the non-religious Zionist realm eschews the notion of the exile as judgment of the Jewish people's backsliding, but describes the exile negatively in no uncertain terms on other grounds. They do not see any prospect of a future for the Jewish people outside the land of Israel. From all that has happened in our time to European Jewry, they conclude that anti-Semitism is not merely a passing madness; it is a chronic disease of all western civilization. They maintain that it is delusional to expect the democratic countries—not to speak of the non-democratic ones—to give Jews the sense of security necessary for leading a normal life. The only escape from the debilitating realities of exile is migration to Eretz Yisrael. There are those who dissented from this negative assessment,[9] though if one views the nature of Jewish exile in historical terms, the negative assessment seems far more in conformity with the reality of the Jewish lot in the diaspora.

Despite the openly "secular" analysis about exile and return, the religious impulses behind this perspective were implacably present. These analysts could not but feel the weight of the Jewish religious tradition in a very powerful way. Arnold Eisen has put it this way:

> In rejection and in triumph, therefore, openly or in
> disguise, the conceptions of homelessness and home-
> coming which we have examined (i.e., the religious
> notions) continued to direct the thinking of the cultural
> Zionists, political Zionists, non-Zionists and anti-Zionists
> alike.[10]

The religious tradition could not be escaped; it was the "template," as it were, upon which the modernists forged their secularist notions.

This assessment of the Jewish people's exile and return—nuanced by the faith of Israel in the background—can be described via the works of a number of leading representative Zionist thinkers.

Moses Hess (1812-1875) in his seminal volume, *Rome and Jerusalem*, analyzed the Jewish condition of exile and return in "secular" terms as did most of the leading Zionist thinkers of the nineteenth century. However, in his case, religious perspectives also underlie his point of view. Indeed, he has been called by some "a religious socialist."

The Jewish people, Hess says, must be rehabilitated in their ancient land because of political, economic and cultural reasons but especially because of an anti-Semitism that was incurable. Jews were made outcasts by virtue of their latent distinctive nationality but also because of their faith. He then segues into the core character of Jewish identity. As Arnold Eisen puts it, "The two aspects of Jewish identity (i.e., nationality and religion) were inseparable, Hess argued, and not only in the eyes of the gentiles. Pious Jews throughout the ages had always been, above all, Jewish patriots. The most touching thing about the Hebrew prayers, Hess emphasized, is that they are really an expression of the collective Jewish spirit."[11]

Hess went further in spelling out his notion of Jewish nationalism. "The thought of my nationality," Hess wrote, "was connected with my ancestral heritage, with the Holy Land and the

Eternal City, the birthplace not only of the Jews, but of the belief in the divine unity of life and the hope for the ultimate brotherhood of men." Hess dreamt that the Jewish people, when settled in their land, were destined to carry out their historic function on a greater scale, which was to bring about the redemption of humanity by helping to encourage harmony and amity between nations. The land would enable the Jewish people to develop its life in accordance with the Jewish spirit which, in turn, would enable her to contribute positively to the world. For this to come about, Hess emphasized, Jews need *earth*. Their ideals were not designed for the next world but for *this* world. The Jewish people needs ground under her feet, her own ground, a land on which she can build up an independent, self-determining life; for that and to work on the task of contributing to the world she needs a land of her own. [12]

Here, in the contribution of Moses Hess to the cause of modern Zionism, we have both an underlying and overt religious tradition that motored his basically secular approach to the Jewish condition.

Leo Pinsker (1821-1891), a prominent physician and erstwhile passionate patriot of Russia, turned Zionist under the impact of the pogroms of 1881. His analysis of Jewish exile was profound in its psychological insight. The nationless Jew was a stranger in the lands in which he lived. The world saw him in the frightening form of one of the dead walking among the living. "This ghostlike apparition of a people without unity or organization, without land or other band of union, no longer alive and yet moving about among the living—this eerie form scarcely paralleled in history, unlike anything that preceded it or followed it, could not fail to make a strange and peculiar impression upon the imagination of the nations." [13]

It was a "fear of ghosts, something inborn," Pinsker stressed, that provoked the implacable hatred of the Jew and his persecution on the part of the gentile world. This was an endemic condition that could not possibly be changed. The only solution for the Jew was to have a home in a country of his own, to be reconstituted as a nation like all other nations. The Jews, he said, "have a past, a history, a common unmixed descent, an indestructible vigor, *an unshakable faith*, and an unexampled suffering to show." The Jews must have a land of their own to which "we shall take with us the most sacred possessions which we have saved from the shipwreck of our former fatherland: *the God-idea and the Bible.*"

When Pinsker's age-old idea about the need for a home Jews could call their own, his arresting approach was received with enthusiasm in Zionist circles in Eastern Europe. *His approach included a homeland wherever possible, not necessarily the ancient "Holy Land."* However, he allowed himself to be persuaded by these circles to give Palestine preference as the ideal goal of the masses of the Jewish people. This will, or as Pinsker termed it, "the instincts of the people which does not err," is endemic to the collective mindset of the Jewish masses; it is part of their heart and soul nurtured throughout the generations by their religious literature and historical experience. The magnetic needle of their compass constantly pointed in *one* direction. These are the people who are prepared to take action. These are the real people and only what the real people wants can be realized for their will tends unmistakably toward Palestine. Pinsker added that he personally rejoiced in this decision of the people.

The striking mixture of secular rhetoric about the Jewish condition, along with his allusion to the Jews' *unshakable faith,* to their *God-idea and the Bible,* as well as his acceptance of the manifest reality of the will of the Jewish masses, rooted as it was in their historic faith, point to the religious tradition's undergirding of Pinsker's otherwise secular perspective.[14]

Theodore Herzl (1860-1904), the founder of modern organizational and political Zionism, echoed Pinsker's analysis of the Jewish people's exile and return in secular terms—anti-Semitism and all the rest. Yet his reformulation of "the state idea, that princely dream which had sustained Jews throughout the long night of their history," could not escape the weight of the traditional conception. The continuing power of the "state idea," Eisen avers, "is attested first of all by the imagery and cadences of Herzl's rhetoric and is further witnessed by Herzl's very emphasis upon the idea as Zionism's indispensable inspirational force."[15] In this connection, it is telling that when Herzl came across Moses Hess's *Rome and Jerusalem*, he exclaimed, "Everything about our cause is there." Here, too, we discern the religious "template" for a modern secular Zionist thinker.

Modern Zionists have tended to either deliberately evade or evince lack of awareness of the underlying motor power that drove Herzl's thinking and practical work. Avi Ehrlich has put it this way:

> Biblical Zionism lights Herzl's torch whose lesser light, standing in the foreground, outshines the brighter beam...the culture of landless longing stands closer to us than does the Bible, so its dimmer light joins that of Herzl to obscure the original brilliance.[16]

Ahad Ha-am, the essayist Asher Ginzberg (1856-1927), envisioned the land of Israel as a spiritual center and, as such, the solution to the negative effects of Jewish exile. It would be a source for the regeneration of the Jewish people, a place where morality would be exampled, where the Jew would become a model for what a true Israelite should be. And from this center the spirit of Judaism would radiate throughout the diaspora, giving it new vitality and unity.

Ahad Ha-am departed significantly from the traditional religious notion about the land; indeed, he transformed it. "What for the rabbis had been a faith—a way of life in service to God," Eisen writes, "was for Ahad Ha-am a culture, the product and expression of the Jewish peoples' 'national spirit.' The object of allegiance had shifted; the 'god-term'—the root of one's standard of conduct, the object of one's ultimate loyalty—had become the Jewish people itself." The function of the land, then, was secularized in that this working out of the Jewish people's national spirit was its primary function.

Yet here, too, lurking behind the notion of the land as a spiritual center, is the Jewish religious tradition. Ahad Ha-am could not escape it. In criticizing Leo Pinsker for suggesting that a homeland for the Jews could well be in a location other than Palestine, Ahad Ha-am declared, "The deep love for the land of our forefathers was foreign to him (i.e., Pinsker), a love which is unconditional which we—"raised on" (חֲנִיכֵי) the Bible and the Talmud—feel in our hearts from early childhood."[17] But more: though Ahad Ha-am substituted peoplehood and its culture for Judaism's life in service to God, yet he was faithful to the biblical-rabbinic notion that a Jewish homeland was fundamentally a means to a higher end which was the moral regeneration of the Jews in exile. Indeed, the religious notion of the "Holy Land" as a spiritual entity served as the "template" for Ahad Ha-am's מֶרְכָּז רוּחָנִי, "Spiritual Center."

A. D. Gordon (1856-1922) was the apostle of labor in the land as the path to a normal, complete existence as a nation. Life not rooted in the soil was a barren existence which was the essence of exile: parasitic in the extreme. Gordon's language was replete with reference to the Jewish tradition. Only work on the אֲדָמָה (ground, earth) of the Jewish people's national אֶרֶץ (land, territory) could make it whole again. These and other references to biblical, rabbinic and kabbalistic texts regarding redemption from exile and fulfillment as a people by return to ancestral soil illustrate the religious wellsprings of Gordon's idealistic/practical Zionism.[18]

Gordon considered immersion in the soil of the land a religious act though not in the traditional sense of religion as a regimen of ritual activity. It was the "feeling" of faith, rather than the fixed forms which resist change, that was the crucial factor in Jewish renewal. Nonetheless, the faith of Israel was the template upon which Gordon grafted his fundamental affirmations about the land and his modern Zionist ideology.

David Ben Gurion was, of course, the secular Zionist par excellence. He rebelled against the Jewish tradition, negated the exile in no uncertain terms and advocated the building of the land of Israel by means of socialism. And yet when Ben Gurion argued for his cause, he appealed to whomever would listen to open the Bible and recall Jeremiah's emotional rationale for Israel's land, or Joshua's coming into the land, or the prophet Isaiah's wrestling with the role of the place in Israel's life. He invoked the Jewish people's "pioneering mission to all men" and its "great and eternal moral truths and commandments." The ingathering of the Jews from exile and their rehabilitation on their own land would be a boon to the entire world. Indeed, Ben Gurion could not help but be thrown into the hands of Rav Kook and the religionist minions.[19]

In sum, the secularists' notions of exile and return either could not evade or did not choose to evade the Jewish religious tradition in making their cases for Zionism. From Hess to Pinsker to Herzl to Ahad Ha-am to Gordon to Ben Gurion—and we might add to most of the secular Zionist thinkers of the modern period—such indeed was the case. They fused their vision of renewal with the tradition, rooting the transformation of the Jewish enterprise in it in order to wrest the legitimacy that the religious tradition conferred.

In the end, the religious perspective on the Land of Israel as the "template" for the secular perspective might be encapsulated by this statement of *Chaim Weitzman*, first President of the State of Israel:

> The Balfour Declaration is not our mandate; the Bible is our mandate.

PART TWO

THE MEANING OF "HOLY" LAND

In this part we set out in search of a second major theological notion about the land of Israel: the nature of "holiness" in general and how it applies to the sanctity of Israel's land in particular.

─────────

The perspective we here propose is as follows:

When we focus on the essence of each of the previous chapters, and examine them as a whole, we discern a common thread, a basic theological thought-line. It is this: the land, in the many and different contexts in which it is discussed, is perceived in terms of the relationship between God and Israel. The land derives its fundamental character and importance from the nature of that relationship. Its role and function, its goodness and vitality, all stem ultimately from the special connection of Israel to God—and not from any particular property of "sanctity" inherent in that particular place.

Israel is expected to be an *am kadosh*, a "holy people," and anything and everything having to do with the land is rooted in and flows from that reality. Thus, in a sense, the status of the land, fundamental and central as it is in Israel's scheme of things, is derivative of the people's relationship to its God. Indeed, Israel's connection to the place is basically and ultimately rooted in the prior and primary relationship between God and His people as set forth in the Abrahamic and Sinaitic covenants. Flowing from that relationship is the expectation on Israel's part of "holy action," her behavior as a "holy people" on the land. And so it is by virtue of this basic thought line that the land may be referred to as "holy."

What follows seeks to spell out this perspective. Thus, in Chapters Eight, Nine and Ten (to be discussed) the essence of the idea of land sanctity is located. Chapter Eleven proceeds to summarize them, along with the same notion implicit in Chapters

One through Four. Additional data detailing "conferred holiness" is presented.

This all, then, will have delineated what we believe to be the meaning of "Holy Land" and specifically the scriptural notion of the Land of Israel as such.

CHAPTER EIGHT

THE LAND AS A GOOD LAND

And He brought us into this place and gave us this land flowing with milk and honey. Behold, now I bring the first of the fruit of the ground which You, O Lord, has given me (Deut. 26:9-10). Regularly the Israelite thanks God for the good land given him for his use and enjoyment.

The land in Deuteronomy, as we have seen, has theological and historical dimensions: it is God's gift to Israel, sworn to the patriarchs. However, it is also a physical, concrete geographical entity in which people live and out of which they draw sustenance. Thus it is seen in natural terms as well. As a result of this perspective, a consistent idea emerges: the land is an אֶרֶץ טוֹבָה (a good land). It is good because its physical features provide not only for life and growth, but for satiety and wealth. It is the source of well-being. It is the basis for blessing and security. This picture is the ground for yet another set of ideological affirmations.[1]

The place is depicted in various ways. Some representative texts:

- *It is good because of its natural qualities:* "For the Lord your God is bringing you into a good land, a land of brooks of water, of fountains and springs, flowing forth in valleys and hills, a land of wheat and barley, of vines and fig trees and pomegranates, of olive trees and honey, a land in which, without scarcity, you will eat bread, in which you will lack nothing, whose stones are iron, and out of whose hills you can dig copper. And you shall eat and be full, and you shall bless the Lord your God for the good land He has given you" (8:7-10).

- *It is good because it is a land of milk and honey*: "Look down from Your holy habitation, from heaven, and bless Your people Israel and the ground which You have given us, as You swore to our fathers, a land flowing with milk and honey" (26:15).

- *It is good because of its abundance of water.* "For the land which you are entering to take possession of is not like that of Egypt, from which you have come, where you sowed your seed and watered it with your feet, like a garden of vegetables; but the land which you are going over to possess is one of hills and valleys, which drinks water from the rains of heaven, which the Lord your God cares for; the eyes of the Lord your God are always upon it, from the beginning of the year to the end of the year" (11:10-12).

- *It is good due to the efforts of the previous occupants:* "And when the Lord your God brings you into the land which He swore to your fathers, to Abraham, to Isaac, and to Jacob, to give you, a land with great and goodly cities, which you did not build, and houses full of all good things which you did not fill, and hewn-out cisterns which you did not hew, and vineyards and olive trees which you did not plant..." (6:10-11).

Indeed, in our book's varied depictions of this territory as good it does so in hymn-like fashion; it is a source of all blessing because of its ideal natural qualities; it is described in terms that suggest the place as a kind of "paradise."

Now the student of biblical texts is aware that the praises heaped on the land here are, in significant measure, out of touch with the reality about the territory of Canaan. They appear to surpass the object of the praise, as a comparison with the many biblical references elsewhere about persistent drought and famine in the land show. Indeed, we know Canaan to be small in size and to have a paucity of natural resources. Presumably, then, the Deuteronomist was writing from the perspective of one who was seeking to "make points" theologically rather than presenting a purely objective depiction of the land's natural qualities. What are the theological points Deuteronomy is making?

1. The Good Land: Replica of Celestial Models.

Mircea Eliade on Sacred Space

The land, as we have seen, is depicted as a kind of paradise—a perfect place, a source of all blessings. The background for this picture, providing a clue to the quintessentially good place described, can be found in the studies of Marcea Eliade about sacred space.[2]

One of the outstanding characteristics of traditional societies, Eliade maintains, is the opposition they assume between their inhabited territory and the unknown and undefined space that surrounds it. The former is "our world" and everything outside it is a kind of "other world"—a foreign, chaotic space, peopled by strangers. Man takes possession of a heretofore unknown, foreign, chaotic territory by establishing a living relationship with it: making it his home, clearing uncultivated ground, building houses, burying his dead, erecting altars to and experiencing the deity, fighting on and dying for the territory. In a sense, man thereby "creates" his world; but for this creation of his to be efficacious, it must reproduce the work of the gods; that is, man must transform it symbolically from "chaos" to "cosmos" through a ritual repetition of the cosmogony, the work of the gods in their creation of their heavenly world.

An example of this is the Vedic ritual for taking possession of a territory. Possession becomes legally valid through the erection of a fire altar consecrated to Agni. In what way is this altar built? It is, in fact, nothing but the reproduction, on a microcosmic scale, of the creation. The water in which the clay is mixed is assimilated to the primordial water; the clay that forms the base of the altar symbolizes the earth; the side walls represent the atmosphere. And the building of the altar is accompanied by songs that proclaim which earthly region has just been created. Here is a clear example of a ritual that validates taking possession of a territory by reproducing the work of the gods.[3] Thus, to settle in a territory is to consecrate it; it is a decision that involves the deity. For this newly created human universe is always a replica of the paradigmatic universe created and inhabited by the gods.

And so, since in the religious imagination the celestial models for the land and the sacred objects on it were fashioned by the deity, these models are, by definition, quintessentially good. Hence, man's work with and on the land—in imitation of these models—render the land itself and the objects man fashions not only sacred, but good.

Biblical Space

The Patriarchs Take Root in the Land

The experience of the patriarchs on the land of Canaan fits the pattern of land settlement, possession and validation as depicted by Eliade. Indeed, the patriarchs established a concrete relationship with the place that included a set of visions and ritual acts involving the deity; this in their mindset and of their progeny, validated its possession and established it as a holy and good land down through the generations. Listen to the scriptural data (all citations are from the book of Genesis):

- "Abraham settled in the land of Canaan" (13:12) and had, at one point, "dwelt in the land of Canaan ten years" (16:3). Isaac spent his entire life in the land and Jacob his for many decades. Both Abraham and Isaac amassed a good deal of wealth (13:6, 26:12-14). Abraham and Isaac dug and re-dug wells for their herds (21:30, 24:18, 26:18, 26:22-25).

- All three patriarchs named places in the land: Beersheva by Abraham (21:31), Rehovot well by Isaac (26:22), Bethel by Jacob (35:7). Abraham purchased a burial plot for Sarah (23:17-20) where the patriarchs and their wives were eventually buried

(49:29-32). Jacob purchased land from the children of Hamor (33:20).

- All of Abraham's children and grandchildren were born in the land of Canaan—Ishmael (16:15), Isaac (21:2), the children of his wife, Keturah (25:1-4), Jacob and Esau (25:24-26), all of Jacob's thirteen children (chs. 29-30). Jacob's son Benjamin was born near Ephrat (35:16).

- All three patriarchs fought and struggled with fellow inhabitants of the land. In fact, Abraham, with a sizeable set of retainers, engaged in an armed battle with a group of kings who took his nephew Lot captive (ch. 14).

- According to the scholarly consensus, Abraham came into Canaan at approximately 1800 BCE and the Israelites went down to Egypt at ca. 1600 BCE. During this 200-year period, according to the scriptural data outlined but briefly above, the Israelites struck deep roots in the land of Canaan. Further, it has been surmised that not all the Hebrews actually migrated to Egypt but many actually remained rooted in the land and greeted their fellow Hebrews to Canaan following their exodus from Egypt.[4]

- Finally, in parallel to Eliade's construct concerning visions and ritual acts involving the deity, we have Abram's vision at Shechem in which God promised his descendants the land (12:1-7); Abram's vision after leaving Lot, who settled in Sodom when the land was again promised to him and his offspring, after which Abram built an altar to the Lord in Hebron; Isaac's vision at Beersheva where the promise was reiterated and he built an altar where he invoked the name of the Lord (26:25); Jacob's dream at Bethel where the promise was again given and where Jacob took the stone he had put under his head and set it up as a pillar and poured oil on top of it (28:10-19).

Thus, following Eliade's formulation regarding sacred space, we can say this: since the patriarchs in fact established a measure of rootedness in Canaan and invoked the Deity in the process, the land begins to be considered a good land; the notion gains fuller expression in later scripture with particular emphasis in Deuteronomy.

Canaan, Jerusalem, Temple

Eliade, in applying the concept of celestial models to biblical space, puts it this way: "Whatever the extent of the territory involved, the cosmos that it represents is always perfect. An entire country (i.e., Canaan), a city (i.e., Jerusalem), a sanctuary (i.e., the Temple in Jerusalem), all equally well represent an *imago mundi* (an image of the world). Treating of the symbolism of the Temple, Flavius Josephus wrote that the court represented the sea (i.e., the lower regions), the Holy Place represented earth, and the Holy of Holies represented heaven[5]. It is clear, then, that the *imago mundi* is repeated in the inhabited world. Canaan, Jerusalem, and the Temple severally and concurrently represent the image of the universe. This reiteration of the image of the world on smaller and smaller scales constitutes one of the specific characteristics of the religious mindset in traditional societies."[6]

To be sure, the notion of a heavenly Jerusalem as the model for the earthly Jerusalem is not specifically mentioned in our biblical texts; it is, rather, a later rabbinic concept inferred from various biblical sources (see Tractate *Taanit* 5a; Midrash *Tanhuma* on Sidra *Pekuday*, 132:1 and on Sidra *Tzav*, 9:12; cf. Baruch 4:3). It is Eliade, in his depiction of the ancient notion of sacred space, who includes the city of Jerusalem (as well as the entire land of Canaan) along with the Temple as copies or reflections of their celestial archetypes. This depiction flows from Eliade's assertion that "every Temple or palace, and by extension, every sacred town and royal residence, is assimilated to a 'sacred mountain' and thus becomes a center." Thus, according to Eliade, it is not only the mountain on Mount Zion in Jerusalem but the land of Israel in its entirety that is sacred in the biblical mind. In fact, the idea of a "holy land" that is so startlingly dominant in the religion of Israel in all periods is most likely an extension of the universal idea of the holiness of the Temple or mountain, which, in the religious imagination, were fashioned after celestial models. And since celestial models by definition are good, so are those elements after which they are modeled—good.

Biblical Models

The Bible's employment of celestial models for earthly building tasks such as the revelation of a blueprint (תַּבְנִית) for the human builder of a worship locale, has deep Near Eastern roots. For example, in the third millennium the Sumerian king Gudea of Lagash was shown in a dream the plan for the sanctuary of Ningirsu, which he was told to build.[7]

Similarly, for Israel the models of the Tabernacle, of the sacred utensils, and of the Temple itself, had been created by God, who revealed them to His people, to be reproduced on earth. For example, God says to Moses, "And let them make Me a sanctuary that I may dwell in their midst. According to all that I show you concerning the pattern of the Tabernacle, and of all its furniture, so you shall make it" (Ex. 25:8-9). "And see that you make them after the pattern for them, which is being shown you on the mountain" (Ex. 25:40).

When David gives his son Solomon the plans for the Temple buildings and everything about them, he assures him, "All this (I give you) in writing from the hand of the Lord, which He made me understand—all the work to be done according to the plan" (I Chron. 28:19). This appears to indicate that David was aware of the celestial model created by God from the beginning of time. This is what Solomon affirms: "You told me to build a Temple on Your sacred mountain and an altar in the city which is Your dwelling place, a copy of the sacred Tabernacle prepared by you from the beginning" (Wisdom of Solomon 9:8).

Additional ground for such a claim can be found in the Bible in its conception of the nature of man in relation to the Deity. Says God, "Let us make man in our image, after our likeness... So God created man in His own image—b'tzalmo—in the image of God He created

him—*b'tzelem Elohim bara oto*" (Gen. 1:26-27). And the Psalmist
(8:5-6) appears to spell out what those verses in Genesis mean when
he sings, "What is man that You are mindful of him, and mortal man
that You have taken note of him, that You have made him a little less
than God and adorned him with glory and majesty." Perhaps here,
too, is a hint that man, fashioned as he is in the image of God,
partakes of some of His goodly (godly) characteristics.

Goodness Qualified.

It is, of course, clear that perfect goodness cannot be ascribed to
any place or object a man fashions. The earthly city of Jerusalem,
which in the religious mind was fashioned after the heavenly
Jerusalem, was only an approximate reproduction of its transcendent
model; it could be polluted by man because it was involved in time as
the heavenly model was not. Similarly the Temple in Jerusalem:
"This building now built in your midst is not that which is revealed to
Me, that which was prepared beforehand here from the time when I
took counsel to make paradise, and showed it to Adam before he
sinned" (II Baruch 4:3-7). Nonetheless, something of the
quintessential goodness of the heavenly model after which man
fashions "his world" can be said to "rub off," as it were, on his earthly
world. For this is what biblical man seems to claim when he asserts
that his earthly world and the specific objects he fashions within it
are fashioned after heavenly models. In his mind, since the Deity's
models are reflected in man's earthly midst, the earthbound objects
partake of the goodness of the celestial models.

And so, when Deuteronomy portrays Israel's land as such a good
land, a place of such perfection and source of all blessings, this
characterization appears to be a reflection of the theological notion of
celestial models.

2. The Good Land Versus the Non-Land

Canaan is seen as a good land with special clarity when it is
contrasted with the desert land. As Johannes Pedersen put it in a

summary statement of the subject, "Through the powerful descriptions which the prophets give of the non-land, we get perhaps the strongest impression of what the good land, the land of man, is."[8]

As we have seen, Canaan is depicted in glowing terms. Its natural condition and resources are rich and abundant. The opposite of the land of man is *desert-land*. It is the place "where there is no seed, no figs, no vines, no pomegranates, neither is there any water to drink" (Num. 20:5). In the desert good plants do not grow; its soil is full of stones and salt, covered with nettles, thorns and thistles (Is. 5:6, 7:24; Zeph. 2:9). "Terrible" the Israelites call the desert; it consists of waterless wastes, inhabited by fearsome creatures such as serpents and scorpions (Deut. 8:15). From there comes the fiery, all-consuming storm, not the mild winds that bring rain and fertility (Jer. 4:11).

Thus for the Israelite, the desert appears as the very opposite of the ideal place; he knows only its terror. The Bedouin speaks of the desert in positive terms, of his love for the free, unbounded expanses. The Israelite who himself came from the desert no doubt looked upon it at one time in a similar way; a trace of this view is found during a later period in the Rechabites for whom the life of the desert was the ideal one. But this was not the prevailing view of the average Israelite during the time of his settled life on the land.

Indeed, for the Israelite the wilderness is the place of the curse. Wicked demons are at work there (Lev. 16:10); but for human beings, it is uninhabitable. There are no houses and lodgings in it, only the bellowing of wild animals. The prophetic imprecation on Edom (Isa. 34:9-15) is a description, point by point, of a cursed realm, where the blessing is lacking. The wilderness is a realm of chaos because the law of life does not operate there. The desert, we are told, is "without form and is void," the characteristic Hebrew expression for chaos, the dark, the lawless, the empty. He who wanders there may suddenly be led astray for there is no road; how can a road leading to a goal be found in a place whose essence is disorder and confusion?[9]

In light of this clear and specific contrast between "the land of man" and the "desert-land," a contrast that ancient man in general and the Israelite in particular saw and profoundly experienced, Israel's place as portrayed in Deuteronomy comes into even sharper focus: the land is a good land indeed!

3. The Good Land: Given To Israel By God In History

Deuteronomy insisted that the goodness of the land belonged to the spiritual and historical order of things. The book puts it this way: "Beware lest you say in your heart, 'my power and the might of my hand have gotten me this wealth.' You shall remember the Lord your God, for it is He who gives you power to get wealth; that He may confirm His word which He swore to your fathers, as at this day" (8:17-18). Repeatedly and emphatically it is made clear that Israel did not build the cities and houses or plant the vineyards and olive trees. These are a part of the inheritance that Israel receives (Deut. 12:9), a term frequently used by Deuteronomy to express the notion that God has given the land as a gift within history.[10]

This perspective that sees Israel's place as divinely given brings every aspect of the material and economic aspects of life into the sphere of religion. There is no distinction between the material and spiritual realms. Material possessions are linked to Israel's covenant with God; hence, everyday life is stamped with the seal of God's holiness. Thus Deuteronomy may be regarded as teaching a "holy materialism."[11]

The Pagan vs. Israelite Notions

Among Israel's pagan neighbors, on the other hand, the belief prevailed that there was a direct and intimate relationship between a territory and the deities who were worshipped on it. The land could be used only when these "divine landlords" were propitiated through tithes and offerings. To be sure Israel, in some measure, shared such beliefs.[12] But Deuteronomy, for the most part, rejected the notion that the land itself was filled with divine power, that its goodness was due to God's immanence in it, as if there was an indwelling of God Himself in the land. Israel, in fact, had not always possessed this place, but had gained possession of it through a process of acquisition that God Himself had directed (Deut. 7:1-2, 9:1-3). Thus there was no magical or mythological association between Canaan and the people of Israel. Israel came to possess it through certain historical events. Everything that gave it legal and religious significance was governed by a sense of history, by a consciousness of events that had brought land and people together.

This relationship between the God of history and the natural land is adumbrated in another context by Yehezkel Kaufmann.[13] Kaufmann analyzes the great stress Deuteronomy puts on the centralization of the cult in Jerusalem. Deut. 12:2 forbids worshipping God at "every place," on the "high hills and under every leafy tree." This ban, Kaufmann argues, was not only motivated by the fact that these were pagan cult sites, or the fear that such worship would lead to paganism, but also by the view that this very manner of worship was pagan: "You shall not do so for the Lord your God" (Deut. 12:4, 30 f.) Pagan land sanctity is rooted in nature and may, therefore, be found everywhere. Israelite land sanctity, on the other hand, is a creation of the will of God; it originates in an historical election of a people and in a revelation of God's word in time.

History Prevails

The ancient tabernacle was a portable sanctuary unconnected with any sacred site, indicating that the deity could be worshipped anywhere. Later, throughout Israelite life in Canaan down to the time of Josiah, the popular idea of the inherent holiness of place and consequently worship at rural altars was acquiesced in. Nonetheless, tension between the two concepts was dormant rather than dead. The idea that the land in general, and specific sites in particular, were holy, savored strongly of natural sanctity. The biblical narratives sought to overcome this pagan savor by dating the holiness of sacred sites to patriarchal times, explicitly providing thereby an historical rather than a natural basis for their sanctity. In time, however, a more militant concept came to the fore: Deuteronomy's total exclusion of the local sanctuaries. The historical ground for the holiness of place here prevails.

E. von Waldow makes essentially this point from a different perspective.[14] He takes the position that Israel adopted in significant measure the ancient Canaanite notion that the deity was immanent in the land when she changed from a nomadic to a sedentary life. In this notion the belief prevailed that the gods from within the ground, as it were, give the blessing to the soil and make it good. However, Israel creatively transformed this notion; she described it in categories unknown to the Canaanite world of thought. The God of Israel who is, indeed, the owner of the land is the God of history. That understanding is clearly reflected in Deut. 6:10-11 f., where it is stated that God brought Israel into the land that He had promised to the patriarchs, a locale with "great and goodly cities," etc. Here the goodly gifts of nature are related to God as the Lord of history.

The Harvest Credo

This sense of history relating to the natural land is part of the ancient credo in Deut. 26:5-10. It is spoken by the worshipper upon bringing the first fruits of his harvest as an offering in acknowledgement of his debt to God for the gift of the land. The credo summarizes the main historical events of Israel's origins—the wandering patriarch, the experience of Egypt, the exodus—and concludes, "And He brought us into this place and gave us this land flowing with milk and honey. And behold, now I bring the first of the fruit of the ground, which you, O Lord, hast given me" (vv. 9-10). Here the Israelite, at regular, public intervals, indicates that it is God, at specific points in time, who saved Israel; a central aspect of this saving activity was His giving the people this good land for their use and enjoyment. This recognition elicits appropriate gratitude.

And so, in the theological mindset of scripture, the land of Israel is a good land indeed.

CHAPTER NINE

THE LAND AS POSSIBILITY AND AS PERIL

Here we probe for the details of potential blessing on the land, and identify the aspects of peril it presents. We thus delineate the manner in which Deuteronomy portrays both sets of elements presented to Israel—as challenge and as choice. [1]

In Deuteronomy's view, the land is that physical setting in which Israel can live the good life. On it the fields yield their produce and human and animal life multiply. Fulsome nourishment is available; there is no lack. One can eat and be satisfied and enjoy nature's blessings. The land can be a permanent dwelling place wherein roots may be struck. It is a place where the people can feel secure. In it long life is possible and goodness abounds. It offers rest to a people weary of war and wandering. It is a place wherein community can be experienced and God worshipped.

While the land can be all these good things, there looms also in Deuteronomy the sense that this place may be a problem, indeed, perilous for Israel's future as a people. There is the consciousness that just as place opens up the possibility for the blessings of a good life, it contains within it as well seductive elements that can open the way to the people's eventual banishment. Deuteronomy knows that as a landed people Israel can choose a life that yields to the seduction of the place; she can opt for a new definition of self that blurs the past and misinterprets the present, and thus endangers the future when the territory could be lost, the people decimated and politically annihilated.

We now examine this dual perspective.

I. The Land as Possibility

Deuteronomy presents three basic elements that constitute the positive possibilities for life on the land: it can be a home, a place of rest, and a locus for a good life. [2]

What characterizes a "home"?

Our texts use characteristic language for describing a home: יָשַׁב ("sitting") signifies settling down in a place; יָרַשׁ ("possess") connotes a place taken physically and made one's own; and נַחֲלָה ("inheritance") indicates an established dwelling place. These terms limn a domain in which man can live normally and naturally.

Pedersen[3] refers to this as "human land" where the blessing resides, in contrast to the cursed land of the wilderness where only jackals and wild beasts make their home. As pointed out by Mircea Eliade[4] in his analysis of sacred space, man creates his world out of the unknown, undefined, chaotic space that surrounds him by taking "possession" of it, "by establishing a living relationship with it, making it his home by clearing uncultivated ground, building houses, burying his dead, erecting altars to and experiencing the deity there, fighting and dying for the territory," in sum, by putting one's own clear, distinctive stamp on the place. These are the things that make the promised land a possible home.

What characterizes a "place of rest"?

Deuteronomy holds out the possibility for Israel of a surcease of war, a tranquil existence. The term מְנוּחָה ("rest") is linked with the struggle to be free of enemies. She could have the power to be victorious in war and be independent of the surrounding nations. The promise is held out that Israel would not be a vassal of another country, but free to govern her own life. We are not to think of this rest only as "peace of mind," or as partaking of a particular "spiritual" quality. Rather, it is an altogether tangible peace granted to a nation plagued by enemies and weary of wandering. It seems to be the supreme benefit of landedness: "you will dwell in safety" (Deut. 12:10). It is the gift which guarantees the enjoyment of all the other natural blessings bestowed upon the place. It appears that the term מְנוּחָה "expresses the ultimate gift that God bestowed on Israel in granting the land."[5]

But more: in the context of the move to centralize the cult in Jerusalem (12:10-14), rest appears as a precondition. Safety is needed to enable Israel to worship its God in the prescribed manner. The idea of regular pilgrimages from all over the country to the central shrine mandated by Deuteronomy presupposes an open and secure countryside through which people are not afraid to travel. It presupposes order and regularity so that the cultic rhythm could be maintained. And so, rest is perceived as the all-encompassing blessing. von Rad puts it this way: "The life of the chosen people in the 'pleasant land,' at rest from all enemies round about, the people owning their love for God, and God's blessing His people—this is the epitome of the state of the redeemed nation as Deuteronomy sees it."[6]

What characterizes the "good life"?

In addition to the natural blessings with its material abundance, there are other factors that can make for the good life on the land.

• *There is the capacity to multiply.* The stability of a settled life enhances the capacity to reproduce. Barrenness is a curse, fertility is a blessing. This is consistent with the biblical view that to have many children is a desideratum of the first order and a coveted blessing, a notion undoubtedly connected with survival needs and group maintenance in the face of natural scourges and enemy attacks. Pedersen expands on this by tracing the desire for progeny to man's need that his soul persist and grow through his sons. His soul spreads in his sons and their sons, and the more numerous they are, the greater the soul becomes . Progeny is not what comes after, is separate from a man; it is man himself who multiplies, lives on, and thus defies death while growing and expanding across the generations.[7]

• *There can be freedom from illness and disease.* Obviously, Israel had not been immune to the diseases that plagued ancient societies. These illnesses are designated by the roots חלה and דוה. The root חלה connotes a state of weakness and exhaustion in which the vital powers of a person have been sapped. דוה reflects the mental effects of physical weakness—anxiety and a feeling of indisposition. The magnitude of living in good health becomes clear when one reflects upon the biblical and extra-biblical allusions to illnesses and plagues of all sorts that beset ancient man.[8] Yet God can bring healing; He gives the capacity to the ill to recover from illness and to ward off disease and thus resume a life of physical normalcy.

• *There is the chance for a long life.* לְמַעַן יַאֲרִיכֻן יָמֶיךָ, "that your days may be prolonged" (Deut. 5:16) is an oft-repeated promise. An ideal life in ancient Israel could only be a long life; in order for man to realize his destiny, he must have time. The predominant view in the Bible is that man's life is restricted to life in this world. The relationship between God and man is also limited for the most part to this world since the dead stood outside God's concern (Ps. 88:6, 11-13).[9]

The hope in Israel was for a man to die "in a good old age" as did the patriarch Abraham (Gen. 15:15, 25:8), as did Isaac, who was "old and full of days" (Gen. 35:29), having lived out in peace man's allotted span.[10] Dying young or "in the midst of one's days" was considered a divine punishment. Scriptural as well as extra-scriptural evidence point to the many natural disasters that decimated entire populations, with the consequences particularly severe on the very young and old. In view of this, the possibility of living a long life in a stable environment which Deuteronomy postulates takes on greater intensity and heightened significance. A long life is, indeed, a blessing, a vital ingredient for appreciating the good life on the land.

- *There is potential for the consciousness of the less fortunate.* The experience of living in the land is linked to a consciousness of the less fortunate in society, those without a territory of their own. For example, a master who is discharging his Hebrew slave at the end of six years is told to share with this slave his (the master's) "cattle, threshing-floor and winepress." He is told to furnish him liberally in proportion to the blessing with which God has blessed him (15:14). Recollection of Egyptian slavery (15:15) brings Israel back to the time when she could call very little her own. In bringing them to the land, God has blessed His people with the abundant goods of life. In principle all are equal partners in the enjoyment of this wealth. Through the vicissitudes of life, "have nots" emerged who must be regarded with compassionate concern by the "haves."

Hence, every opportunity is seen by Deuteronomy as a means of distributing God's blessings more equitably. Indeed, one of the book's dominant concerns is the inclusion of the landless people in the cult festivals and yearly offerings in order that they might share in the enduring blessings of the domain and rejoice in them. These are the man and maid servants, the Levite, the stranger, widow and orphan (12:12, 14:26, 16:14, 26:11). There is deep concern (14:29, 26:12) that they too "shall eat and be satisfied."

A Possibility, Not a Guarantee

Thus the element of possibility in the land is emphasized in Deuteronomy. Yes, the place could be Israel's home, a place of rest and a locus for the good life, but this was but a possibility—not a guarantee or forgone conclusion. Indeed, these blessings are not immediately achieved. The land becomes a dwelling place only after a series of initial stages are over. Thus the crossing of the Jordan, coming into the territory, inheriting it, dispossessing the Canaanites, are all prelude to possessing the territory and then to settling down in it. "To dwell in safety" (12:10) is the final stage of the extended process. A "place of rest" is not an immediate achievement but a hope for the future. And, finally, an expectation Deuteronomy sets forth:

dwelling in the land which God gives, an achievement all by itself, is
not the end all and be all of Israel's existence. Rather, it affords Israel
the opportunity, in tranquility and security, to be responsive to her
God and to His direction for her life. It is to be viewed as a state of
heightened spiritual possibility.

II. The Land as Peril[11]

Yes, the land has the possibility for blessing—but it also can be a
source of peril. What are the perils of landedness?

Israel's temptation is to forget

Deuteronomy's repeated warning, הִשָּׁמֶר לְךָ פֶּן תִּשְׁכַּח אֶת ה' אֱלֹהֶיךָ
"take heed lest you forget the Lord your God" (8:11)—is rooted in the
realistic fear that guaranteed satiation is the enemy of memory.
Being sated is a phenomenon of the present and evokes a sense of
self-sufficiency. It means to settle for how things are and to forget
how things were. To forget means to imagine that not only was life
always so, but that life will always be so.

The object of Israel's forgetfulness is God, the Lord of history. We
read: "Beware, lest you forget the Lord who brought you out of the
land of Egypt, out of the house of bondage" (Deut. 6:12)..."who led
you through the great and terrible wilderness" (8:14-16). Land is not
a place without a context; it is a place for recalling slavery and exodus
and desert and manna; it is a place for remembering that slaves were
freed, nourished, and made heirs to a land given by God whose
willingness and power transformed this people. To forget God means
to forget this transformation as well as the covenant relationship in
which God's gifts were given and for which Israel's gratitude and
fidelity were expected (Deut. 26:5-10).

Deuteronomy knows that as a landed people Israel can be
tempted to escape from history, from her experience with her God.
She may well prefer the sameness, the sureness, the familiarities of
the present to recollecting the precariousness of the historical past.

But for Israel to forget her history with God means to forget how she came into her land, that this domain is a gift from the hand of a beneficent Giver; it means to forget that Israel is addressed by this Giver, and if she feels that she is not being addressed, then she need not answer. Such forgetfulness along with its consequences are not acceptable, for Israel's task in the world is not to be complacent and self-indulgent. Thus Deuteronomy announces an ultimate contingency for Israel: she can lose the land, for those who wish territory without memories will perish.

Another specific and vital dimension of forgetting God is "by not keeping His commandments and His ordinances and His statutes..." (8:11).[12] The commandments are seen in Deuteronomy as the way by which Israel remains on the land, and at the same time remains with God. Observance of the Law means obedience to God and honoring the Sinaitic covenant. A life without Law is a life without obligations and tasks. The commandments reflect the One who commands. To neglect the laws is to forget God.

Another peril is the glorification of self[13]

We read: "When you eat and are full and have built goodly houses...and when your herds and flocks multiply and your silver and gold have increased and all that you have has prospered, then your heart will be lifted up and you forget the Lord your God...Beware lest you say in your heart, 'my power and the might of my hand have gotten me this wealth.' You shall remember the Lord your God, for it is He who gives you power to get wealth..." (8:11-18).

Here Deuteronomy is keenly aware that Israel can be seduced by all the good things into imagining that she herself made it all happen. She can be tempted to mistake the real source of her security and choose to replace trust in God who promised and bestowed the place with trust in her own self-sufficiency. Such a choice changes who Israel is and alters the basis for her existence on the land. With such an attitude she is no longer the receiver of gifts but the controller and manager of material things. Thus the true Giver of the things that make up the good life is obscured and Israel has deified herself.[14]

Deuteronomy cautions against this peril and offers instead a higher, nobler understanding of the state of possessing the good things of life: the source of wealth is in a power vested not in Israel but in God who meets her need (8:15, 16), and whose will it is to fulfill the destiny set out for her—"for it is He who gives you power to get wealth in order to fulfill His covenant which He swore to your fathers as of this day" (8:18). Success and prosperity are not ultimately rooted in human ingenuity; they are, rather, blessings bestowed by God.

Yet another element of peril is apostasy

An oft-repeated Deuteronomic term is אֱלֹהִים אֲחֵרִים ("other gods"); these were the indigenous Canaanite deities: Baal, Dagon, Astarte, Anath, Asherah. They are a source of peril for Israel. Negation of them is expressed in various ways. Do not: "go after other gods" (6:14, 8:19); "serve them" (8:19, 11:16, 12:30); "bow down to them" (8:19, 11:16); "let your heart be deceived" (11:16); "go astray" (11:16); "ensnared to follow them" (12:30); "inquire about their gods" (12:30).

These terms reflect both an inner disposition and overt action, by which Israel becomes apostate. Deuteronomy knows that having a territory can be a problem for faith in God.

In living the good life on the good land, Israel needs an appropriate theology. She can heed "other gods" whom she believes will legitimer her pursuit of satiation and help secure the means by which to attain it. This kind of belief sees the source of blessings in the territory itself—in the fields, in the hills, in the sky above; other gods abound who "take credit" for these blessings and may be manipulated to secure them. Israel's God, however, will not tolerate competing loyalties. He is a "jealous God" who insists on exclusive loyalty (6:15).[15] This loyalty has its basis in God's dealings with

Israel (Deut. 5:6, 6:12). God's election of Israel is the source of that people's existence, the basis for slaves becoming free and a wandering people becoming landed. All of this was bestowed upon her as a gift of God. The way to retain that gift is to stay exclusively loyal to the Giver of the gift, in gratefulness and obedience. "Other gods" are not legitimate options.

What Are the Resources With Which to Withstand the Perils of Landedness?

If Israel succumbs to the temptations of the land—to forgetting her past and her God, to self-glorification and apostasy, she then paves the way for her own demise. The question may here be raised: is the people left to face these perils without resources of any kind? Are there any weapons with which to arm herself in order to combat these very real dangers? For Deuteronomy, though the perils are great, yielding to them is not inevitable. There is a vision here that in the land, faithful people can resist the temptations that abound, and need not perish. What are these resources?

Memory

This is Israel's chief resource. She must remember. And memory for her is important apart from the substance of that which is remembered. Remembering is an historical activity. It acknowledges movement and change. It is a reflection of how it was, how it is, and how it can be. It maintains distances and linkages. For her it recalls a time prior to the gift of the land: when a slave in Egypt, when a wanderer in the desert. If this history is recalled, Israel will also recollect the way in which she received the land, and will be led to acknowledge its Giver. A land filled with memories is vital, for it then becomes the repository of identity and commitment. And so, memory is a major resource with which the people can withstand the land's temptations—and remain in it (7:18, 8:2, 16:12).

Observance of the commandments

We read: "Beware lest you forget the Lord your God by not

observing His commandments…" (8:11). From this we may infer that by observance of the laws, Israel will keep afresh the remembrance of the Lawgiver and His claims.

Walter Brueggemann focuses specifically on three Torah laws and how they mould the consciousness of a covenant community. [16]

The first is the prohibition against images (5:8). Images, "being the controllable representations of our best loyalties and visions," reduce God to manageable size and "domesticate" Him; images never change; they remove land and people from history. Thus images are "off limits" to a people who would remain in history.

The second is that Israel is to observe the Sabbath of debts, an institution that affirms that in a covenanted place, there is a limit to buying, selling, owning, collecting and managing. When debtors are released by their creditors every seventh year, it is an affirmation that people are due dignity, respect, and freedom, and that people, like land, cannot ultimately be managed or owned. It is an affirmation that security is not guaranteed by acquisition or ingenuity.

The third is that Israel is under mandate to care for brother and sister who have no sustenance afforded the landed in the community. These are the poor, the widow, the orphan and the Levite. As participants in the covenant and in its promise of the land, they may not be forgotten. They do not have power, but they have dignity. Hence the numerous laws in Deuteronomy and elsewhere concerning compassionate concern for them (e.g., 15:1-11, 12:18, 22:1-4; cf. Lev. 25:25-55).

Loyalty to Israel's system of worship

Israel must maintain a fierce cultic loyalty to God. Deuteronomy calls for a fidelity that not only rejects all other gods, but which, in a positive sense, attaches itself exclusively to the Lord in the strongest kind of allegiance. Israel's form of worship can be the source from which memories derive, through which gratefulness is expressed, and in which joy is experienced (Deut. 26:11). Through the prescribed worship, the people can protect itself from the lure of the foreign cults.

Summary

In this chapter we have noted how Deuteronomy presents Israel with a total view about life in the land. It can be a home, a place of rest, a locus for a good life. But she can also be tempted to forget her God, glorify herself, lapse into apostasy—perils that can be combatted by memory of her journey with God in the past, observance of her God's commandments, and loyalty to her system of worship. Which of these alternatives will she choose? As Deuteronomy sees it, the destiny of Israel depends on her response to that question.

CHAPTER TEN

ISRAEL AND THE "NATIONS" IN THE LAND

As we have noted, the book of Deuteronomy records how the land can come to Israel as a result of God's promise to the patriarchs and their descendants. Israel is now in a position to take possession of the land. However, this involves dispossessing the people already living there. It is to this issue of dispossession that we now turn our attention.

Deuteronomy is replete with passages calling upon the Israelites to alternately dispossess the Canaanites, to settle in the land among the natives as a dominant force, to extirpate their religious way of life. Note several representative texts:

- The Lord your God will dislodge those peoples before you little by little; you will not be able to put an end to them at once, else the wild beasts would multiply to your hurt. The Lord your God will deliver them up to you, throwing them in utter panic until they are eliminated (7:22-23).

- Hear, O Israel. You are about to cross the Jordan to go in and dispossess nations greater and more populous than you...He will subdue them before you that you may quickly dispossess and eliminate them as the Lord promised you (9:1-3).

- When the Lord your God has cut down the nations whose land the Lord your God is giving to you, and you have dispossessed them and settled in their towns and houses, you shall set aside three cities in the land that the Lord your God is giving you to possess (19:1-2).

- You shall surely destroy all the places where the nations who you shall dispossess served their gods upon the high mountains and the hills and under every green tree (12:2).[1]

Some Preliminary Observations

The task set forth in this chapter is to respond to the following question: How did Deuteronomy rationalize Israel's occupation of the land of Canaan at the expense of the people who were its prior inhabitants? This is an issue which must be candidly faced; Israel's conception of her God and her own ethic are at stake.

Before embarking on scripture's thinking on the subject, there are three observations we need to make, to wit:

First, Deuteronomy's statements about elimination of the Canaanites was an objective *and not an actual historical occurrence.* Martin Noth points out that at the time of Israel's settlement in Canaan, she was able to gain a footing in the land without turning out the older Canaanite inhabitants from their properties. Concerning the subsequent period, Noth indicates that Israel did not, in fact, expel them: "The Canaanites remained in the land and, generally speaking, were able to continue unimpeded with their own way of life and with their possessions undiminished."[2] We suppose also that the Canaanites remained in place down to the time of Josiah. If such were not the case, why should Deuteronomy be so insistent on their elimination? Assuredly, the historical situation presupposes an existing native population, a situation to which Deuteronomy is clearly addressing itself.

To be sure, the Albright school of archaeologists/historians (John Bright, George Ernest Wright, Paul Lapp, et al.), supporting in general the conquest account in Joshua 1-12, has pointed to the archaeological evidence that indicates a definite pattern of destruction of Canaanite cities during the late Bronze Age (the latter part of the 13th century BCE, precisely Joshua's time). This is an

alternative view to that of Noth. However, even if we accept the basic
thrust of the Albright school about the initial period of settlement,
this would not alter the view that the Canaanites were never largely
dislodged from Canaan—then or later. The biblical text simply does
not permit such a conclusion. To cite but a few of these texts among
many others: [3]

> • ...Be most resolute to observe faithfully all that is written
> in the book of the teaching of Moses, without ever
> deviating from it to the right or to the left and without
> intermingling with *these nations that are left among you*
> (Joshua 23:6).

> • The Lord was with Judah, so that they took possession of
> the hill country; but they *were not able to dispossess the
> inhabitants of the plain* for they had iron chariots (Judges
> 1:19).

> • The Benjaminites did not dispossess the Jebusite
> inhabitants of Jerusalem; so *the Jebusites have dwelt with
> the Benjaminites in Jerusalem to this day* (Judges 1:21).

> • ...They [the Israelites] followed other gods, *from among
> the gods of the peoples* around *them*; they provoked the
> Lord (Judges 2:21).

*Secondly, there is considerable evidence that Israel had a bad
conscience about the objective of expropriating the land either by
conquest or settlement.* The Bible consistently records the effort to
justify her thought and actions. Thus, even in the context of Israel's
practical affairs, she clearly was dealing with a major moral issue of
which she was conscious. Indeed, the value of life and the perspective
that humans were created in God's image were integral to her own
religious teachings, and these were very much a part of the biblical
mindset as it confronted this issue. Let's look at the texts:

In Josh. 24:13, Israel is reminded that she did not develop the
land herself. In Josh. 24:8, the land is called unequivocally the land

of the Amorites. Similarly, in Judg. 11:19 ff., the consciousness that Israel had dispossessed a people of its land is clear: it had avoided doing so in the case of the Moabites and Edomites (Judg. 11:17-18). According to 2 Sam. 7:23, the conquest of Canaan was made possible only through "great and terrible things" wrought by God in driving out a nation and its gods. In Num. 33:50ff., the sole justification for the occupation is that God has seen fit to give Israel the land; the initial price of occupation is high in destruction (33:52). In Deut. 9:4 ff., a reason for God's gift of the land is offered: it is "because of the wickedness of these nations that the Lord is driving them out before you": the conquest is, thereby, justified. The same justification appears in Deut. 18:9-14, in which the offensive practices of the nations are described. "Can we also detect a need for justification in Ps. 44:3?" W. D. Davis asks. It is God, not the sword, who gave Israel the land; here it is as if the conquest were divorced from Israel's own volition. As late as the turn of the first century BCE, the "bad conscience" about the conquest and the need for a justification of it remains (1 Macc. 15:33).[4]

Other Nations in History

To grasp more fully the uniqueness of this "bad conscience" phenomenon on Israel's part and her need for self-justification, one needs to contrast the phenomenon to the posture of other nations in the annals of history as to how they came into possession of their lands. Invariably this came about by either displacing or subjugating the prior inhabitants by various forms of force and violence, and then imposing their own language and culture and religion on the native peoples whose lands they engulfed. To cite but a few such instances:

- The Normans who invaded Italy in the 5th century CE and subjugated the native Romans.

- The ethnic Germans who displaced the native Celts by various invasions in the 5th century CE and thus fashioned the character of the German nation.

- The nomadic Magyars who subdued the native Moravians in Hungary in the 5th century CE.

- The ethnic Franks who invaded France in the 6th century CE and displaced the native Gauls.

- The warrior Vikings who launched a series of violent raids from the sea on Norwegian, Swedish and Danish lands in the 9th century CE and imposed their ways on the native peoples.

- The English and other adventurers who appropriated the lands of the Australian aborigines.

- The English colonists in the 17th century CE who came to America and expropriated the lands of the native Indians.

Indeed, this has been the pattern of nation formation throughout history. The above is but cursory data that does not include the previous history of the nations mentioned. These, in turn, came into being as a result of displacement or domination of peoples already living on their lands as a result of various forms of forceful incursions. Nor does this picture include similar phenomena of ancient peoples such as the Egyptians, Assyrians, Babylonians in biblical times or the later Greeks and Romans and Byzantines, all of whom molded the characters of the peoples and nations into whose lands they entered in less than peaceful fashion.

In few such instances does history record evidence of a bad conscience that prompted justification on moral grounds on the part of these nations. It is only biblical Israel—burdened with the moral sensitivity of a "holy nation"—who has thereby felt the need for justification.

And, parenthetically, we would add a phenomenon of profound irony: armed with the biblical data, the descendants of the various nations mentioned, while overlooking the history as to how *their* nations and *their* character came into being, yet quite forcefully place Israel before the bar of justice![5]

Thirdly, in Jewish tradition the Bible is seen through the prism of rabbinic thought and literary interpretation. Hence, one looks to rabbinic Judaism for normative and definitive perspectives on given subjects. Indeed, the rabbis do not base their views on a literal reading of the Bible. Instead, Jewish thought and practice are based on how the Bible is interpreted in the oral law, which is contained in the Midrash, Mishna, and the Babylonian and Jerusalem Talmuds.

Thus, examination of the rabbinic sources on the subject of Israel's relations with the Canaanites in the land shows that Deuteronomy's notion about their dispossession was not only but an objective (and not an actual historical event), but even the objective was effectively interpreted out of existence.

Maimonides, for example, takes the position that people who think that God is asking Israel to commit genocide misinterpret both the Bible and Jewish law. He then proceeds via an extensive examination of talmudic and midrashic texts to uncover the authoritative Jewish view on the subject. The essence of his exposition is this:

> No war is declared against any nation before peace offers are made to it. This obtains both in an optional war and a war for a religious cause, as it is said: 'When you draw near to a city to fight against it, then proclaim peace unto it' (Deut. 20:10). If the inhabitants make peace and accept the seven commandments enjoined upon the descendants of Noah, all of them shall be spared (*Mishna Torah, The Book of Judges, Laws Concerning Kings and Wars* 6:1).

This dictum, Maimonides stressed, applied both to the "seven nations" as well as to Amalek; a peace offer must be made in order to avoid warfare. He proceeds to refute contrary views in the Talmud quoting Joshua's offer of peace to the Canaanites before embarking on the incursion into the land of Canaan. Various other rabbinic sources are cited to support the view that warfare with the Canaanite nations was not a legitimate undertaking, thus radically altering the Deuteronomic objective of dispossessing them.

Why does Maimonides stress this? Because he understood that Judaism and the Bible, as understood by the rabbis, stand for an affirmation of ethics, as he writes: "There is no vengeance in the commandments of the Torah, but compassion, mercy and peace in the world" (*Laws Concerning the Sabbath*, 2:3).

After citing a range of subsequent rabbinic responsa which concur with the views of Maimonides, Avi Sagi notes, "Maimonides' (and the rabbis cited) moral interpretation is in accordance with the spirit of the Torah and its fundamental premises regarding human justice, premises that should come into play in our behavior toward all human beings."[6]

The Classical Rationale

Since it is the stated purpose of this book to allow the biblical materials to speak for themselves, in terms of their own time and clime, we proceed to an examination of Deuteronomy's rationale for Israel's objective of dispossessing the Canaanite people from the land promised to the ancestors and their descendants.

Who are these Canaanite people? We refer here to the so-called "seven nations" who lived in Canaan on the western side of the Jordan River, into whose territory the Israelites moved (ca. 1225 BCE), settled in and predominated from approximately the thirteenth to the sixth centuries BCE. A representative enumeration of them is found in Deut. 7:1:

> When the Lord your God brings you into the land which you are entering to take possession of it, and clears away many nations before you—*the Hittites, the Girgashites, the Amorites, the Canaanites, the Perizzites, the Hivites*, and *the Jebusites, seven nations* (שִׁבְעָה גוֹיִם) greater and mightier than yourselves...[7]

How, indeed, did Deuteronomy justify Israel's desired occupation of this land at the expense of these people who were its prior inhabitants? There emerge from our texts three explanations.

1. Not Israel's Virtue But the Nations' Wickedness

The nations were to be driven from Canaan because of their wickedness and their abominable practices. Note these key passages:

- Not because of your righteousness or the uprightness of your heart are you going in to possess their land; but because of the wickedness (בְּרִשְׁעַת) of these nations the Lord your God is driving them out before you (9:5).

- You shall not learn to follow the abominable practices of those nations...because of these abominable practices (הַתּוֹעֵבֹת הָאֵלֶּה) the Lord your God is driving them out before you (18:9-12).

- You shall eliminate them—the Hittites, and the Amorites, the Canaanites and the Perizzites, the Hivites and the Jebusites—as the Lord your God has commanded. That they may not teach you to do according to all their abominable practices which they have done in the service of their gods (20:17-18).

This rationale for the dispossession of the Canaanites is not confined to Deuteronomy. In Gen. 15:16 we read that in the context of the Abrahamic covenant, Abraham is told that his descendants will not be able to take possession of the promised land until the fourth generation "for the iniquity of the Amorites is not yet complete." In other words, the existence of the Canaanites on the land was tied to their behavior. Lev. 18:24-25 is quite explicit about this: "Do not defile yourselves by any of these things, for by all these the nations I am casting out before you defiled themselves. And the land became defiled, so that I punished its iniquity and the land vomited out its inhabitants." [8]

Now, what specifically constitutes this "wickedness," these "abominations"? Again our texts tell us:

- You shall not do so to the Lord your God (i.e., follow the mode of worship of the nations), for every abominable thing which the Lord hates they have done for their gods; for they even burn their sons and daughters in the fire to their gods (12:31).

- You shall not learn to follow the abominable practices of those nations. There shall not be found among you anyone who makes his son or his daughter pass through the fire, anyone who practices divination, a soothsayer, or an augur, or a sorcerer, or a charmer, or a medium, or a wizard, or a necromancer (18:9-11).

The Bible elsewhere attests to the prevalence of child burning as part of the cult amongst the nations. [9] We are told of the action of the King of Moab as recorded in II Kings 3:27 in which the king took his eldest son "and offered him as a burnt offering upon the wall" to gain the favor of Chemosh, the god of Moab; this was done when the Moabites were in dire straits during a battle with the united forces of northern and southern Israel in the mid-ninth century. Though Moab is not one of the "seven nations," this episode shows that child sacrifice took place in the area. This is also indicated by the fact that the Israelite King Ahaz had adopted the practice for which he was castigated: he burned his son "according to the abominable practices of the nations who the Lord drove out before the people of Israel" (II Kings 16:3).

The various forms of divination as indicated above (Deut. 18:9-11) are also widely attested to outside of our Deuteronomic source. Samuel considers divination a rebellion against God (I Sam. 15:23).

The Philistines called upon their priests and diviners when seeking to learn what to do with the ark of the Lord that was in their territory (I Sam. 6:1-2). There was a "Diviners' Oak" in Shechem (Judg. 9:37). Micah prophesies the elimination of sorcerers and soothsayers from Israel's midst (Micah 5:11).[10]

The basic objection of biblical faith to the variety and profusion of magical superstitions and practices among the Canaanites (and Israelites) was the view that God's will cannot be learned via force or coercion by human means; God cannot be tricked or manipulated into revelation. He will make Himself known when and how He himself chooses, i.e., by His herald, the prophet, whose word shall be clearly spoken and clearly understood—in contrast to the devious and mysterious world of the occult.

The Extra-biblical Data: Pagan Practice

There is extra-biblical evidence that confirms the decadence of the nations that was rooted in religious thought and practice. Indeed, Canaanite mythology and cult were characterized by a fundamental immorality, which inevitably led its followers to a life of immorality.

William F. Albright describes in detail the thought and practices of the Canaanites. [11] He gives as one of the explanations for the pronounced—often catastrophic—decline of Canaanite life and culture between the sixteenth and thirteenth centuries BCE, "the extremely low level of Canaanite religion, which inherited a primitive mythology and had adopted some of the most demoralizing cultic practices then existing in the Near East" (BANE, p. 452). The description of Canaanite religion that follows is not merely of what was practiced during the Late Bronze Age, i.e., 16th-13th centuries B.C.E; so much of its pagan character persisted throughout the subsequent period down through the seventh century BCE. Among these practices were:

• *Human sacrifice*, which was long since given up by the Egyptians and Babylonians. The Phoenicians and Carthaginians, for example, sacrificed children to the god Kronos at times of grave national danger or calamity, a practice that was felt to possess extraordinary efficacy in averting disintegration (II Kg. 3:27).

• *Sacred prostitution of both sexes*, which was apparently not known in native Egyptian religion though widely disseminated in Mesopotamia and Asia Minor. A characteristic feature of the Canaanite fertility cult was sacral sexual intercourse by priests and priestesses and other specially consecrated persons intended to emulate and stimulate the deities (Asherah and El, Anath and Baal in the Ugaritic myths) who bestowed fertility.

• *The vogue of eunuch priests* (kumru, komer), which was much less popular in Mesopotamia and not found in Egypt. Part of the Canaanite mythology was El's self-emasculation as well as the castration of his father. Thus the phenomenon of Canaanite eunuch priests who emulated this act of their god, in order to explain the withering vegetation, the infertility of the earth, of man and of beast.

• *Serpent worship*, to an extent unknown in other lands of antiquity. One of the favorite creatures of the Canaanite goddess Anath was the serpent because of its reputed fecundity (*FSAC*, p. 234). Thus worship of the snake in the Canaanite cult.

• *Holy marriage* in a sacred place with a female representative of the deity.

The Extra-biblical Data: Pagan Thought

From a description of cultic practices Albright proceeds to pagan thought. "The brutality of Canaanite mythology, both in the tablets of Ugarit and in the later epitome of Philo Byblius, passes belief; to find even partial parallels in Egypt and Mesopotamia one must go back to the third millennium BCE" (*BANE*, p. 453). Some examples of this Canaanite mythology:

The most important active figure of the Canaanite pantheon was Baal. He is the storm-god, but also is king of heaven and earth, thus the head of the pantheon. Anath is Baal's virgin sister, but also his consort. In one epic myth, while Anath was in the form of a heifer, Baal raped her "77 – even 88 times." In another myth, Anath was bathing on the shore of the sea at Hamkat. Baal went for a walk—and raped her, "leaping her as the sacred ram (of Amun) leaps, forcing her as a...forces...." Baal fell ill because of this, but Anath came unexpectedly to his rescue: "Anath, the Victorious, a man-like woman, dressed as a man but girded as a woman, went to the sun-god, her father." Ra replied at some length stressing Baal's folly and ending, "It is punishment for his folly, since he...had intercourse with her in fire and raped her with a chisel" (*YGC*, pp. 128-129).

Anath is represented as having slaughtered mankind from "the rising of the sun" to "the shore of the sea." Apparently the slaughter delighted her, since "her heart rejoiced and her liver exulted" over the massacre:

> Beneath her were heads like balls,
> Above her were hands like locusts.
> She plunged her knees into the blood of warriors,
> Her thighs into the blood of youths. (*YGC*, p. 130)

When Anath found the dead body of Baal, we read in a Canaanite tablet:

> While Anath walked along, lamenting
> The beauty of her brother (--how fair!)
> The charm of her brother—how seemly!
> She devoured his flesh without a knife
> And drank his blood without a cup. (*YGC*, p. 131)

Connection Between Thought and Behavior

The above limns something of a portrait of the endemic decadence of the Canaanite cult and mythology. What is of particular significance is the cause-and-effect relationship between this cult and mythology and the immoral behavior of the Canaanites. The cult practiced by humans encased and adumbrated the action and thought of the gods (the mythology) with the result that similar human action and thought inevitably followed.

How was this so? The Canaanite pagan believed that his ritual played a vital influential role in the life of the gods; his cultic activities were felt to directly affect the ways of the gods or activate transcendent forces for the good of the gods and for the good of his human world. Indeed, the human celebrant participates in the divine mysteries, suffers with the gods, mourns their deaths, triumphs in their resurrections. As Yehezkel Kaufmann puts it, much of this ritual "is based on the idea that man merely *imitates* what has proven to be efficacious in the case of the gods." [12] Thus, for example, the gods and the goddesses could be persuaded to give their blessings of rain, grain, wine, oil, and other benefits by ritual fertility acts performed by male and female prostitutes serving in the Temples.

Yet more: some Canaanite ritual activity also served to explain certain harmful phenomena in the natural world. For example, in Canaanite mythology an earthly drought was explained via the god of vegetation emasculating himself. So, to account for withering vegetation, eunuch priests emasculated themselves in imitation of the god.

And so, *when in Canaanite cultic practice and mythology the behavior of the gods (as illustrated by Albright) is as immoral as it is, so inevitably is the behavior of their human imitators.* Martin Noth encapsulated this perspective this way:

> "For the Israelite tribes, who were used to the strict discipline of a patriarchal society, all this (Canaanite) moral laxity was contemptible and shocking. It was, no doubt, bound up to some extent with the special character of the Canaanite cult to which the Israelites, with their devotion to the demands of a stern deity, were especially antagonistic." [13]

The Biblical Perspective: The Link of Morality to Consequence

From the perspective of the Bible, how is such a system of thought and practice depicted above to be looked upon?

According to Nahum Sarna, [14] a fundamental biblical understanding is that the way people function in the moral realm determines what eventually happens to them. People cannot expect to flout the moral law without being accountable to God. The story of the flood (Gen. 6-8), for example, assumes a system of morality applicable to the whole world and when it is transgressed the Supreme Judge will not permit the transgression to go unchecked. Man cannot undermine the moral basis of society without endangering the very existence of civilization. In fact, society by its own corruption actually may be said to initiate a process of inevitable retribution. The sins of the generation of the flood are subsumed under the term *hamas* (חמס), the definition of which is "lawlessness," "violence." For these transgressions God holds society accountable.

Another example is the Sodom and Gomorrah narrative (Gen. 18-19). The people of these places "were very wicked sinners against the Lord." Their kind of sin is soon vividly illustrated by the conduct of the Sodomites at the arrival of the visitors at Lot's house. Here we find them violently demonstrating their hostility to the stranger and lusting to indulge in unnatural vice. The sweeping condemnation of the Sodomites is contained in the following passage:

> Then the Lord said, "The outrage" (זַעֲקָת) of Sodom and Gomorrah is so great, and their sins so grave. I will go down to see whether they have acted altogether according to the "outcry" (הַכְּצַעֲקָתָהּ) that has come to me" (18:20-21).

The connotation of the roots זעק / צעק indicates the anguished cry of the oppressed, the agonized plea of a victim for help in some great injustice. The sin of Sodom was, then, of a grievously moral nature.

The prophet Ezekiel, centuries later, speaking in God's name sums up its iniquity: "Behold, this was the guilt of your sister Sodom. She and her daughters had pride, surfeit of food, and prosperous ease, but did not aid the poor and the needy. They were haughty, and did abominable things before Me; therefore, when I saw these, I removed them" (Ezek. 16:49-50).

Sarna juxtaposes the flood and Sodom and Gomorrah episodes this way:

> As with the Flood, the Sodom and Gomorrah narrative is predicated upon the existence of a moral law of universal application for the infraction of which God holds all men answerable. The idea that there is an intimate, in fact, inextricable, connection between the moral condition of a people and its ultimate fate is one of the main pillars upon which stands the entire biblical interpretation of history. The theme is central to the Flood story, basic to the Sodom and Gomorrah narrative and fundamental to the understanding of the book of Jonah (3:8).

It is this perspective that constitutes one vindication of God's action in dispossessing the Canaanites before the incoming Israelites. The biblical understanding of the nexus between the moral behavior and the ultimate destiny of a nation applies not only to the "nations" but to the people of Israel as well as to the Assyrian and Babylonian nations at a later stage in history. Indeed, it was integral to the prophetic consciousness, receiving full expression, for example, in the teaching of Amos (1:3-2:8).

2. Israel: "A Holy People to God"

A second rationale for Israel's obtaining the land from the hands of the Canaanites is rooted in the notion of Israel being perceived as a "holy people" with a special task in the world—a task for this particular people based in a specific place, and unimpeded by restraining forces embodied in another people in that place.

Israel's relationship to the Canaanites can be illumined by her conception of herself as a firm, coherent, distinctive whole. As Johannes Pedersen has pointed out, to ancient Israel a people was not a collection of human beings more or less like each other; it was a "psychic whole," a kind of "ideal quantity." The "people" is not visible; all common experiences are merged into the common soul and lend it shape and fullness. It is an independent collectivity with an identity that transcends any of its individual members. It has its own historical past; within it are patterned interrelationships between its individual members in the present; it has a concept about its future. [15]

And, as W. Robertson Smith maintains, the deity has his part and place in what Smith calls this "natural society" equally with men; thus, every social act has a reference to the deity as well as to man, for the social body was not made up of men only, but of gods and men. In this vein, Emile Durkheim asserts that the basic characteristics of all religion—including the godhead—are rooted in the collective nature of society. [16]

Outside this firm and distinct collective entity that is Israel stand all the other peoples. Israel recognizes these peoples with their peculiarities and gods, but, as strangers, they were "unclean" in the eyes of the Israelites. Instinctively they were looked upon as such because they stand outside of Israel's collective soul. And so, when a people yearns to fulfill the natural need to preserve its own inner character and identity in this context, difficulties emerge.

Tension

Where and when the worlds of Israel and the other peoples meet, tension arises that leads to explosions, wars in which the people fight to maintain their psychic whole. At times, the tension can be relieved when the peoples enter into a relationship with each other by concluding covenants; they thereby assimilate something of each other's soul; this is what happens when Israel adopts Canaanite ways. Indeed, even the least connection creates a relationship between the two distinct collectivities and the forces contained in them. Thus, for example, he who lives in a foreign country must enter into a connection with strange gods. This is what David fears in the effort of his enemies to banish him from his homeland when he rails at Saul: "...For they have driven me out this day that I should have no share in the heritage of the Lord, saying, 'Go, serve other gods'" (I Sam. 26:19).

For the Israelites in Canaan the question of the relationship to the non-Israelites was especially acute because they lived side by side with them. Entering into an intimate relationship with the Canaanites through covenants, through intermarriage, through commerce, through breaking bread, through the gamut of normal people-to-people relationships meant—necessarily and inevitably—adopting their ways and absorbing their spirit, including the mythology and cultic practices that went with them. Jon Levenson has described this condition:

> A covenant with the Canaanites will oblige Israel to recognize the pantheon of these new allies. But to do so is to grant legitimacy to the other gods, in fact, to absorb them into the institution of (Israel's) covenant, which until now has involved only one deity, the Lord.
>
> To the nation whose God is its suzerain, every god is a suzerain, a potential paramour with whom the slightest contact harbors the ominous capacity to destroy the covenant. Hence the fear of following after other gods, a fear certain to be realized where one brings the others into his home through intermarriage. (Thus) the prohibition of polytheism.[17]

Now, we know that during the periods of the Judges and the Kings, Israel, to a greater or lesser degree, followed the natural course; she concluded covenants with the Canaanites and thus took into her collective life something of the substance, the soul and spirit, of these peoples—including their gods. But the era of Josiah became a propitious time, and the Deuteronomist draws the line: the honor of God does not permit Israel's union with other gods; Israel is "a holy nation," that is, a nation set apart for God, and must abstain from everything that might prejudice its subordination to Gods' sole authority. Indeed, Deuteronomy emphasizes a diminished readiness for Israel to amalgamate with the nations—because doing so would hold her back from fulfilling her special function in the world.

The Need for Separation

Conscious of Israel's special calling, Deuteronomy realized the necessity of drastic separation from all current paganism, which clearly meant a radical separation from the people who were its practitioners. It understood, at its historical point in time, the terrible results of a tolerant syncretism, an amalgamation with the surrounding nations that inevitably brought their gods and cult and decadent life into Israel's collective life. Indeed, aspects of the Deuteronomic theology were developed after the destruction of the northern kingdom and in light of that catastrophe. The northern kingdom had tolerated assimilation and was therefore destroyed. Now Judah was on the same course, and Deuteronomy knew that such a course could destroy the southern kingdom as well (Deut. 7:4) and thus wipe out Israel's special calling in the world.

Deuteronomy understood that only a concrete, functioning people, with its collective character and spirit intact, with a clear and undiluted notion of its unique God, could carry out what Israel considered to be her role in the world.

A Model Society Requiring Territory

The notion of a people equipped to carry out its role as a holy people with a mission in the world has been emphasized in another way—this in addition to the perspective delineated above about the need of Israel's separation from those who would deter efforts to pursue that mission.

Jacob Petuchowski has told us that whatever modern Jews may feel about *the separation of Church and State, there can be no doubt that the thought of such a separation was completely alien to the Hebrew Bible.* On the contrary, the Hebrew Bible itself is, at one and the same time, both the record of God's revelation and the constitution of the ancient Hebrew Commonwealth.

The Biblical concept of the "Promised Land" was more than the concept of a haven of refuge for a horde of liberated Hebrew slaves from Egypt. Between the Exodus from Egypt and entry into the Promised Land there was the Revelation at Sinai, there was God's Covenant with Israel, making Israel "a kingdom of priests and a holy nation." It has frequently been noted that, whereas in Christianity, God's Covenant is with the saved individual, the Covenant in Judaism is with the redeemed *people.*

Biblical Israel was to be a model society, its political no less than its cultic life was to be lived with reference to the Law of God. *But model societies cannot exist in a geographical vacuum. They need a territory on which to establish themselves.* And, according to the Bible, Canaan was to serve as that territory. It was the land which the Lord swore to the Patriarchs to give unto their descendants.

This model society on Canaanite soil was not to exist for Israel's benefit alone. According to the second chapter of the Book of Isaiah, all nations were to turn to it, saying: "Come ye, and let us go up to the mountain of the Lord, to the house of the God of Jacob. And He will teach us of His ways; and we shall walk in His paths. For out of Zion shall go forth instruction, and the word of the Lord from Jerusalem."

We would add to Petuchowski's assertion about the political and religious life being part of a model society the other facets of human life that are equally a part of such a society: the social, economic, cultural, financial and military. These facets, too, need a concrete physical territory on which to seek to implement the ideals in the context of the *Sturm und Drang* of the real world.[18]

3. By Whose Authority?

Israel's appropriation of the land can be understood from a third perspective. The Bible itself and the aggadic interpretation of the Bible seek to develop both in Israel and the nations of the world an understanding of the intended Canaanite dispossession from the land for what it was: an event initiated by God for His own ends. Among the many instances of deities bringing a people into a land where it is to settle (e.g., Amos 9:7), God's leading of Israel into Canaan is of central importance, for, in contrast to the pagan nations, it is only Israel who knows, while it is being led, that it is the one and unique God, Creator of the world, its Lord and Redeemer, who is leading her. Indeed, Israel enters the land because she is being led by this God and is serving His will.[19]

The full gamut of our Deuteronomic texts delineates in unmistakable terms the central, active, determinative role of God in the process and purpose of Israel's intended conquest of the land. The terminology and general thrust of these texts give ample evidence of this:

> God chooses the combatants "for His own treasured possession" and because of Him they constitute "a holy people" (7:6); God is the leader of Israel's forces (9:3); God is "in the midst of the people" (7:21); "the Lord will throw them in great confusion" (7:23); God assures victory and dispels the people's fears (7:17-20); God Himself fights for Israel (7:1-2).

These texts, in addition to the others in Deuteronomy, point clearly, in Israel's faith, to God as the ultimate authority for the entry-into-Canaan enterprise; God, out of His love for Israel, gave her the land as a gift (6:10-11), and He grants them the land in fulfillment of His oath to the fathers (9:5).

The Midrash sees it this way, as well, as it discerns a fundamental biblical concept about the relationship of God to the land and hence to Israel's and the nations' relationship to it. The question is asked in the Midrash as to why the Torah does not begin with the instructions for the new month, which are, after all, the first commandments in the Torah; rather, it begins with the creation story. Psalm 111:6 is quoted in reply:

כֹּחַ מַעֲשָׂיו הִגִּיד לְעַמּוֹ לָתֵת לָהֶם נַחֲלַת גּוֹיִם

He has shown His people the power of His works, in giving them the property of nations.

And the midrash proceeds, "For should the nations of the world say to Israel, 'You are robbers, you have conquered the lands of seven nations,' they [Israel] can point out to them that the entire earth belongs to the Holy One Blessed be He; He created it and He can apportion it to whom He wills. According to His will He gave you the land and according to His will He has taken it away from you and given it to us." In other words, in giving the property of nations to Israel, God was, in effect, according to the rabbis, telling of "the power of His works," that is, that He created the earth and He could, therefore, transfer it to whom He willed.[20]

In the words of Martin Buber:

> Now, this does not at all mean that all invasions of other lands are to be considered equally justified because they are willed by God or that all acts of violence of one people against another are justifiable. The essential point articulated in the above midrash is that Israel heard the will of the Lord of the world, the Creator of all the earth, at the beginning of her expedition to Canaan, and conquered the land in the perfect and well-founded faith that it was accomplishing His will.[21]

This idea that the land is controlled by God the Creator is not a concept read into the Bible by the later rabbis; it is, rather, a fundamental biblical notion, very old and of much historical significance in ancient Israel. In his discussion of the evidence in biblical literature of Israel's "bad conscience" about the act of expropriation, W. D. Davies, based on von Rad's premise about the ancient notion of "the Lord's land," assembles the biblical data from Deuteronomy and elsewhere that confirms the idea with the same inference that the above-quoted midrash drew: "Since the land is controlled by God and is His to dispose of, He can thus promise it to Abraham." [22]

The Authority

As indicated, Israel sees its appropriation of Canaanite territory as having happened because she acted under authority and in confident knowledge of its authorization. This conviction of Israel's *did not arise after her settlement in the land*—as a "rationalization" of a deed of greed, as a way, after the fact, to justify in theological terms her very human and selfish need for *Lebensraum*. According to Albrecht Alt, God's promise of land to Israel was an original element of the pre-Mosaic cult of the God of the fathers. It was, thus, a very old tradition: the God of the patriarchs had already promised possession of the land to the ancestors of Israel when they lived in tents on the edge of the settled territory, a fact that is quite clearly shown by the "covenant of the pieces" (Gen. 15:7-11, 17-21), which has come down to us from that time almost intact. [23]

And so, we may affirm that the will of Israel's God was at work very early, very actively and in quite determinative fashion in the life of the people. She truly believed that God was the originating and ultimate authority in connection with her settlement of the land. This revelation of God's will about the land, Israel's faith in that revelation, and the action that followed from that faith are what make Israel's claim quite distinctive both "religiously" and historically.

We close this chapter with the trenchant lines of Martin Buber on this perspective.

At all times there have been peoples who have given divine labels to their passions, and interpreted the acts of violence born of their own greed for possessions and power as commanded by their divinities; at all times there have been peoples whose actions and self-apprisement were (cast by them as) most honest and pure. And yet, so far as we are able to judge from the records, no other people has ever heard and accepted the command from heaven as did the people of Israel. So long as it sincerely carried out the command it was in the right, and is in the right insofar as it still carries it out.

Israel's unique relationship to its land must be seen in this light. Only in the realm of perfect faith is it the land of this people. But perfect faith does not mean faith in oneself, in one's own rights or one's own *Lebensraum* or anything of that kind, but faith in the Commander and the command, in the Giver of the commission and in His commission. Where a command and a faith are present—in certain historical situations conquest need not be robbery; but conquest is not by any means a historical necessity, for God is the Lord of history, not history the Lord of God.[24]

CHAPTER ELEVEN

THE LAND AS A "HOLY LAND"

Here we bring together a set of key elements in this book that lead us to an understanding of the notion of "Holy Land" in scripture. This notion is further illumined by other peoples around the world in search of the meaning of their places which they believe partake of sanctity.

––––––––––––

The only time the actual term "holy land" occurs in the Bible with reference to Canaan is in Zechariah 2:16:

וְנָחַל ה' אֶת יְהוּדָה חֶלְקוֹ עַל אַדְמַת הַקֹּדֶשׁ וּבָחַר עוֹד בִּירוּשָׁלָיִם

And the Lord will allot to Judah his portion in the *holy land*, and He will choose Jerusalem once more.

Thus the designation "holy land" in this chapter is not based on scripture's specific linguistic usage, on a pattern of language that directly labels the territory of Canaan as "holy." Rather, we use the term here, as throughout this book, in a relational sense. That is, sanctity is inferred or, as we will later seek to demonstrate in some detail, it is conferred by factors external to the land.

The Ground for "Holiness" Specified

As we have pointed out,[1] the idea that the land is holy in a direct sense, that is, God's indwelling, is rooted in another theological strand in the Bible. Deuteronomy, for the most part, diverges from that view because it borders on pagan mythology. Rather, it is because of Israel's relationship with God in covenant and the expectation of "holy action" on the place, her action as a "holy people," that the place may be considered a "holy land."

The essence of various chapters in this book testify to that Deuteronomic notion, to wit:

- *The Land as Gift (Chapter One)*

The land is a gift of God to Israel. The people have not earned it by virtue of its own labors or character, but due to God's gracious will. Israel possesses the place because of God's predetermined decision that she have a home. Israel responds with the first fruits of the harvest as a token of her appreciative and loving relationship with God.

- *The Land as Oath (Chapter Two)*

The land to be possessed by Israel is destined to be hers because of a divine oath in history by which God bound Himself by His word to Israel's founding fathers—Abraham, Isaac and Jacob. All Israelites through the ages are recipients of this place because of that special relationship.

- *The Land and The Law (Chapter Three)*

The land is the sphere in which Israel does what God requires, in which, therefore, the obedience of the people shall be visible. It is thus the instrumentality through which the terms of the special relationship between Israel and her God are carried forth. It provides the resources for the people to stay connected to its God.

- *Integration of the Covenants (Chapter Four)*

The promise of this territory to the early patriarchs was given without conditions concerning Israel's behavior and is a permanent one; however, the realization of that promise, Israel's actual possession and retention of the territory, does depend upon her observance of the laws stipulated in the Sinai covenant.

- *The Land as a Good Land (Chapter Eight)*

The place is depicted as so very good in order to emphasize that the God of history also controls nature, and Israel shares in this control because of her special relationship with God.

- *The Land as Possibility and Peril (Chapter Nine)*

The land as home, place of rest, the setting for the good life affords
the opportunity to be responsive to God's direction for Israel's life.
The place's blessings are evidence of His favor. On the other hand,
the place given out of love, in the context of a covenant in which a
special relationship is established between a people and God, can be
wrenched from that people if it breaks that covenant by not living up
to its stipulations.

- *Israel and the "Nations" in the Land (Chapter Ten)*

Israel can possess this land from the hands of the Canaanites because
she is a "holy nation" with a purpose in the world. Only an actual,
functioning people in full control of the apparatus of her
environment could act out that purpose. Only a polity with its
collective character and spirit intact, with a clear and undiluted
notion of its unique God and His demands for Israel, could carry out
its God-ordained role.

In sum, there exists a distinctive relationship between God and
the people of Israel which is the basis of that people's existence,
character and destiny. This fundamental condition stamps the land
with its character, importance and function in the life of the people
Israel and the world—and is the basis for attributing to it the quality
of "holiness."

The Land in the General Theological Framework of Deuteronomy

Does the above fundamental theological statement mesh with the
overarching outlook of Deuteronomy? Is it consistent with its general
theological thrust? We believe the answer is in the affirmative. We
seek to demonstrate this by outlining below the perceptions of a set
of scholars as to what the general outlook of Deuteronomy is, and
how its treatment of the land fits into the overall framework of the

book. In each case we will amplify and supplement the views of these scholars in light of what we perceive to be one of Deuteronomy's fundamental theological understandings about the land.

Ronald Clements.[2]

Deuteronomy's overriding purpose, Clements maintains, was to show the nature of God and the ways in which men, women and children in Israel could enjoy communion with Him. In face of the profusion and confusion of religious beliefs and practices then current amongst the people, the Deuteronomist sought to stiffen the mental and moral fiber of Israelite citizens by providing them with a clear understanding of God and of the unique relationship that bound them to Him.

For all its national and political status, Israel is not like other nations, but is regarded as quite distinct from them. This is very clearly indicated: "For you are a people holy to the Lord your God (כִּי עַם קָדוֹשׁ אַתָּה לַה' אֱלֹהֶיךָ); the Lord has chosen you to be a people for His own possession (עַם סְגֻלָּה), out of all the peoples that are on the face of the earth" (Deut. 7:6).[3] The phrase "a people holy to the Lord your God" discloses the uniqueness of Israel: her citizens are different from the citizens of other nations because the former have a connection with the Lord as their God; Israel is holy by virtue of the specially strong bond that binds her to God. The concept of Israel's holiness is related by Deuteronomy to the belief that a covenant exists between God and Israel made at Mount Horeb (Sinai), in which Moses acted as mediator. This provides the point of union between God and His people. And this is a basic presupposition of all that Deuteronomy has to say.

The election of Israel was an act of divine grace. Hence Israel was a people in great debt to God. God, in His love, has given to His people innumerable gifts so that the primary motive for the people's obedience to Him should be gratitude for what He has given. First among these gifts is the land of Canaan, which is a major theme of

Deuteronomy's speeches of exhortation. The land is integral to Israel's election because for Israel to be a nation it had to enjoy full political control over this territory. People and land belonged together since the possession of this domain was the badge of their nationhood.

What we hear Clements saying here is that the land is a means to an end: it is God's way of actualizing Israel's nationhood, which was an indispensable prerequisite for the fulfillment of her role as a source of blessing to all the families of the earth. It is thus clear that the function of the land derives from the relationship between God and Israel.

Gerhard von Rad.[4]

According to von Rad, Deuteronomy sets the Israel of Josiah's time in the uncertain situation between election and fulfillment. Though the highest heaven and the whole earth belong to God, God turned toward Israel's ancestors and promised them and their posterity by oath the land of Canaan. Alone of all the nations, He elected Israel, and He did so not because Israel was an imposing people but because of His love for her.

A primary expression of this election was God's promise of the land and rest from enemies round about that this place would bring for Israel. It is a land of an entire united people; it is a good and rich and fertile place, one that God continually watches over. It is, indeed, the all-sufficient prerequisite for the welfare of the people of God. But, continues von Rad, "it would be a mistake to take the land as the real subject of the Deuteronomic preaching. The constant logic of all these addresses is rather this: since the Lord has shown you such faithfulness in all these matters, it is your duty to love Him in return and to keep His statutes and judgments. In other words, this preaching is a summons to obedience."

It is apparent that what von Rad is saying is that the land is seen here as a central element of God's "faithfulness" to Israel, as the place in which she can find a home and rest and goodness and prosperity. The land is thus part of that which should motivate Israel to love God, to follow His commands, to be faithful to Him—in grateful response to His blessings freely showered on her. Here again the idea comes through that the land derives its role and significance from the prior and primary relationship between God and Israel.

Joseph Hertz.[5]

The central declaration of all the Deuteronomic oratory, Hertz asserts, is that God is One and that humans must be wholly His, that God is righteousness and faithfulness, mercy and love. The God proclaimed by Deuteronomy stands in relation to Israel not merely as Judge or Ruler, but as Friend and Father. Therefore, a whole-souled love and devotion to God is expected, expressed in the basic command to the people: "And you shall *love* the Lord your God with all your heart, and with all your soul, and with all your might."

Hertz does not discuss the role of the land in this context. However, we can with confidence deduce this from his analysis: if the basic thrust and purpose of Deuteronomy is to affirm the nature of the intimate connection between God and Israel, then the land (among other things) is an instrument in that relationship through which to help this people work out its task of heartfelt love of God. The place is one element to be sure, but a basic element nevertheless.

George Ernest Wright.[6]

Wright notes the primary exhortation of Deuteronomy as the intense and all-absorbing loyalty that Israel owed to the Lord, who alone is God. The chief emphasis of the book is thus on the grace and power of God, which should elicit from Israel the corresponding response of love, obedience and reverence.

God's gracious acts, including His giving of the land, are of such a nature that Israel's corresponding loyalty should be expressed in the realm of emotions that exist between devoted friends. Thus the centrality of the *Shema* (6:4-5): to love God with the complete devotion of one's whole being; it is love based on trust and gratitude and should be the chief concentration of one's existence; it should issue in an obedience that is willing, cheerful and uncompelled; this love is indeed the mainspring of the whole community life.

Israel is an elect nation. God directs the destiny of the nation, which is especially clear in His gift of the land, for it is He who directs the wars of Israel to His own ends. The Holy War idea illustrates the intense conviction in Deuteronomy of God's purposive and powerful activity in the nation's history. The land was to be readied for the elect nation.

Why should this territory be so readied? The implication is clear: in order that Israel may be constituted as a nation so that God's purpose for her in the world could proceed toward fulfillment. Thus here again the territory is perceived as an instrumentality for the implementation of God's ends for Israel. Indeed, the land's function stems from the special relationship between God and Israel.

Martin Buber.[7]

The basis for Israel's appropriation of the land is that it was an event intended and carried out by God for His own ends. Israel enters the territory because she is being led by Him and is serving His will. Without this fundamental belief neither Israel, nor its history, nor its unique relationship to its territory can be understood. At the time of Abraham she heard God promise the place to his descendents; at the beginning of the Exodus from Egypt she again understood that it was her God who was leading her from bondage to the promised land; in her belief she affirmed that God created heaven and earth, that the whole earth was His, and therefore He could take the land from the Canaanites and assign it to Israel.

The essential point of the above is that Israel heard the will of the Lord and took possession of the territory in the perfect and well-founded faith that she was accomplishing His will. Thus this basic faith of Israel in her God and in His will for her is the root of her connection with the territory. Buber focuses his point this way: "Only in the realm of perfect faith is it the land of this people. But perfect faith does not mean faith in oneself, in one's own rights or one's own *Lebensraum* or anything of that kind, but faith in the Commander and the command, in the Giver of the commission and in His commission."

Buber's assertion here is that faith in God and in His stated role for Israel is a presupposition of her entitlement to the land. Thus, the relationship between God and Israel, both in time sequence and thought process, *precedes* the matter of Israel's relationship to the land, is a *prior requirement* for Israel's legitimately coming into possession of it. The land derives its purpose from a pre-existing relationship: God's command to His people and His people Israel's faithful response.

On Conferred "Holiness"

Up to this point, what has emerged from our analysis of the Deuteronomic texts and the general theological framework of the book is that the land can be said to be invested with sanctity as a result of Israel's relationship with her God. We now take this matter a step further in an effort to amplify the notion of holiness being conferred on a place by people in encounter with God and/or the memory of that encounter. How can we be helped to think about such a notion in general? And specifically how does the phenomenon apply to the people of Israel and its land?

The Bible

The notion is attested to by a set of representative biblical incidents:

• In Genesis 28:16-17, Jacob is en route to Haran where he has a dream about a ladder reaching from earth to heaven with angels ascending and descending on it and God standing beside him, promising offspring, land and blessing. Jacob is deeply moved and exclaims, "Surely God is present in this place...how awesome is this place (הַמָּקוֹם הַזֶּה); this is none other than the abode of God and this is the gateway to heaven."

• In Exodus 3:5, Moses is at Mount Horeb/Sinai, where he encounters a burning bush that is not being consumed. There he hears the voice of God, who commands, "Remove your sandals from your feet for the place (הַמָּקוֹם) on which you stand is holy ground (אַדְמַת קֹדֶשׁ הוּא)." Moses is then told by God of His compassion upon the Israelites in Egypt and of Moses' task to lead them from their slavery to freedom.

• In Joshua 5:15, Joshua is in Jericho, where he encounters a "captain of the Lord's hosts" standing before him who he greets warily at first. Realizing that the figure is a messenger from God sent to help in capturing Jericho for Israel, Joshua asks the messenger what he wills, to which Joshua is told in words similar to the ones Moses heard at the burning bush, "Remove your sandals from your feet, for the place where you stand is holy" (כִּי הַמָּקוֹם אֲשֶׁר אַתָּה עֹמֵד עָלָיו קֹדֶשׁ הוּא).

From the above accounts it is apparent that the different locales in which Jacob, Moses and Joshua experienced the deity *became* sacred places as a result of their experiences. In discussing the burning bush encounter, for example, Robert Wilken tells us this: "What makes the place holy is the theophany at the burning bush, and the bush could be located anywhere, or more accurately, wherever God appeared."[8] Such also are the encounters of God with Jacob en route to Haran and Joshua at Jericho. *It is human experience with God in history that confers holiness on a place.*[9]

The History

Historical events have played a key role—if not *the* key role—in accounting for the sanctity of place, in this case, the city of Jerusalem. Robert Wilken[10] examines the issue from this historical vantage point. He points out how the city of Jerusalem became a holy city. Originally one of Canaan's city-states, it gave no signs of glory or grandeur. Only after it was conquered and subdued by King David in the tenth century BCE did it become an Israelite city. And only after David brought the Ark of the Covenant that had been housed in Shilo into Jerusalem did Jerusalem become a holy place. The Ark was the central sacred object of the twelve tribes, the symbol of God's presence in the midst of Israel. Therefore, holiness *now—not before*—was deemed to be present in the city. Further, it was later when the Ark was deposited in the inner sanctuary of the Temple built by King Solomon, that God's presence was deemed to be securely established in Jerusalem. *Thus this sacred city of the Bible was a creation of the Israelites.* Here is a clear example of human "holy action," as it were, conferring sanctity on a place.

This phenomenon of conferred holiness is analyzed by Robert Cohn in similar fashion. He tells us that the prominent role of Jerusalem in biblical times as political and cultic center of Judah and in post-biblical times as a focus of Jewish territorial and spiritual aspirations makes it easy to forget that *this sacred center was not always sacred or a center for Israel.* A Jebusite fortress belonging to none of the tribes, Jerusalem in pre-monarchial days was a foreign enclave in the midst of the Israelite land of settlement. To appreciate the transformation which rendered this site God's "holy mountain, beautiful in elevation, the joy of all the earth" (Ps. 48:3), we must consider the geographical focus of those early days.

Not one but a multiplicity of centers characterized the settlement period. Each clan or tribe or group of tribes had its shrine. Dan in the north, Shechem, Gibeon, Gilgal, Bethel in the center of the country, and Hebron and Beersheba in the south, for instance, could claim theophanies or various sacred objects which attracted the allegiance of the surrounding inhabitants. Although many such sites were undoubtedly inherited from Israel's Canaanite predecessors, legend transformed them in the name of the Lord and He was invoked and worshipped in them.

Clearly, none of these centers was the political or cultic locus of order which Jerusalem eventually became...When King David came to power he seized upon the plan which was to end the "center vacuum." Seven years after being proclaimed king in Hebron, he captured Jerusalem in an apparent bloodless coup and made it his personal possession, the "City of David" (2 Sam. 5:7). It soon became the capitol of an expanding empire, new home for the ancient Ark (2 Sam. 6:16), and under Solomon, the site of the "house of the Lord." *In one master stroke, David transformed a foreign (Jebusite) hamlet, elevated his capitol above tribal rivalries, and harnessed the power of the revered tribal sanctum to sanctify the new city.*[11]

The Talmud and Aggadah

Sanctity Via Observance of the Rules

The Mishna articulates a similar thought line from the ritual point of view. Precisely because it was the land to which the law most applied, the place gained in sanctity. [12]

> There are ten degrees of holiness. The land of Israel is holy. Wherein lies its holiness? In that from it they may bring the Omer (Leviticus 23:10), the first fruits (Deuteronomy 26:2) and the two loaves (Leviticus 23:17), which they may not bring from any other land.

Seven additional laws are then enumerated, laws that can only be observed in Israel's land. Here the Mishna is associating holiness of the land with Israel's fulfillment of a variety of prescribed laws (which we describe as "holy action"), and it is this action that confers sanctity on the place. W. D. Davies puts it this way:

> In each case—in the reference to the land, the walled cities, the wall of Jerusalem, the Temple Mount, the Rampart, the Court of Women, the Court of the Israelites, etc.—*it is the*

*connection with an enactment of the law that determines
the degree of the land's holiness.*

And Davies adds an illuminating point about the applicability of
the law to the land in this Mishna that assures its special holiness.
The implication is that Jewish sanctity is fully possible only in the
land; outside of it only strictly personal laws can be fulfilled, that is,
the moral law, sexual law, Sabbath law, circumcision, dietary laws,
etc. Of necessity, outside the land, the territorial laws have to be set
aside. The exiled life is therefore an emaciated life. Thus the laws
applicable only to the land of Israel afford more opportunity to
confer sanctity on it.[13]

Sanctity Via Human Intentionality

After noting in detail the elements pertaining to agricultural work
and produce outlined in Mishna Kelim 1:6-9 cited above and found
elsewhere in scripture, Richard Sarason points to these as central to
the relationship between the God of Israel, the Land of Israel and the
people of Israel. He cites the singular attention the Mishna devotes
to the *role of human action and intentionality in this construct.* In
this, both territory and people are intersecting categories in the
rabbinic mind.

The rules are directed exclusively to "native" Israelite society at
home in her domain. They express a dynamic unity among the God
who controls the land and rules over the people, the people who live
on God's land and render God service through their work on the
place, and the land that is under God's special providence and
nourishes the people if they obey God's law.

Since, for the Mishna, the agricultural and other rules required
for observance in the land apply only to the territories' Israelite
inhabitants, *the sanctity of the land would appear to be relative to
that of the People Israel; the Israelites, by inhabiting and working
the land, would actively complete the land's consecration.*

In his concluding comment on this subject, Sarason appears to echo the observation of Davies about the laws applicable only to the Land of Israel affording more opportunity to confer sanctity on it:

> The various Mishnaic rulings...maintain that through study of God's Torah and observance of God's commandments, the God of Israel can in fact be served by Jews anywhere and everywhere, but *fully and perfectly* only in the Land of Israel where additional land-bound commandments obtain, as Scripture ordains.[14]

Sanctity in the Fullest Sense

This notion that the fullness of Jewish life can be realized only in the Holy Land has long since been emphasized by the Rabbis:

The perspective of *Rabbi Moses ben Nahman (Nachmanides)* has been articulated by Moshe Idel this way:

> Dwelling in the Land of Israel becomes for Nachmanides not only a religious obligation but the single way *to attain perfect Jewish life*. The performance of the commandments in the Diaspora is, in Nachmanides' view, a mere preparation intended to enable their true performance in the Land of Israel. Moreover, the Promised Land, being the only proper forum for *a full religious life, the Jews must live in their own land* even if this aim can be achieved through non-peaceful means. Nachmanides considers this effort as one of the religious obligations incumbent upon every Jew and not a matter to be postponed until the Messianic era.[15]

Sanctity Via the Whole of Life

Martin Buber retells the story in the Aggadah about the Rabbis who go abroad to study and, no doubt, for other noble reasons. However, as soon as they arrive at the frontier, they are so taken by the thought of leaving the land that they weep, tear their clothes and return home with the cry, "Dwelling in the land of Israel outweighs all the commandments in the Torah"—an allusion to Deuteronomy 11:31-32 and 12:28, in which the fulfillment of the commandments and settlement in the land are linked. Says Buber:

> This reference to the Bible explains the ultimate meaning of the Rabbis' cry: *the true and perfect fulfillment of the commandments is possible only in the whole life of the people that settles in the land of Israel.* Therefore, the settlement is the precondition of the true and perfect fulfillment of the commandments and thus it alone outweighs them all for it alone makes the fulfillment of the others possible.[16]

Sanctity: Criteria

There is another rabbinic formulation about the land, which indicates that human action confers (or does not confer) sanctity on Israel's place. The Talmud establishes criteria for the holiness of the land.[17] The principle is קְדֻשָׁה רִאשׁוֹנָה קִדְּשָׁה לִשְׁעָתָהּ וְלֹא קִדְּשָׁה לְעָתִיד לָבֹא, "the first sanctification of the land (in Joshua's time) was meant "for its time" and was not permanent. According to Maimonides, Joshua's sanctification of the territory was temporary in nature; it was abrogated upon destruction of the first Temple in 586 BCE and the subsequent exile because he came into possession of the territory by conquest. In contrast, the second part of this principle is קִדְּשָׁה לִשְׁעָתָהּ וְקִדְּשָׁה לְעָתִיד לָבֹא, "the second sanctification sanctified for its time and sanctified for the time to come." This means that the second sanctification of the land (in Ezra's time) was meant both for its time and future time, i.e., was permanent; this was because Ezra came into possession of the territory not by conquest but via a peaceful return of the exiles from Babylonia. According to Maimonides, this rabbinic principle is the definitive law (הֲלָכָה).[18]

Now, leaving aside the issue of whether or not the land's holiness was temporary or permanent in the above construct, it is apparent that the rabbis viewed the human actions of Joshua and Ezra (who acted in response to what they considered to be God's will) as the factors that bestowed holiness on the land of Israel.

Anthropology and Psychology

Jonathan Z. Smith[19] makes essentially the same point about the conferral of sanctity on place from an anthropological perspective. In order for land to be one's very own, one must live together with it. It is when man dwells in relationship with his land that he transforms the place into the place of his people. It is history that makes the land truly *mine.* "It is that one has cultivated the land, dies on the land, that one's ancestors are buried in the land, that rituals have been performed in the land, *that one's deity has been encountered here and there in the land, that renders the place a homeland, a land of man, a holy land.*" Smith goes on to say that it was not just that the land was promised to Israel by God; it was also fought for and died for and was won. And it is the fighting and especially the dying that adds significantly to the other factors which, taken together, "*confers on the land its sacrality.*"[20]

Ben Zion Bokser[21] has captured the essence of this notion. In what sense can a land be "holy"? he asks. He responds that the land is a setting where man implements his designs and purposes. These enter into his culture and can either taint or hallow his domain. When, for example, Adam rebelled in the Garden of Eden, the earth was cursed along with him. When the flood destroyed the generation of violence in the time of Noah, the earth was destroyed as well. Conversely, "when the people of a land adopt holiness as an ideal, the land is also touched with sanctity."

Every religion has a roster of holy places where special events reminiscent of its central faith have occurred and where these events can be recalled by constant re-living and re-experiencing. "In the case of Israel, the entire land of Canaan became a holy place because it was the physical setting for Israel's effort to build a holy nation in the image of the ideals set forth in the Covenant... *The land was an integral part of the culture created in it, and because holiness was the dominant ideal of that culture, the land itself became tinged with that holiness."*

Louis Jacobs[22] has made this point from the psychological point of view. He tells us that the location of divinity in certain spots belongs to a primitive mode of thought. While there are traces of the idea in the Bible, Judaism nonetheless teaches that God is omnipresent and that He transcends the universe. Yet Judaism knows, too, of places especially hallowed: the synagogue, the Temple site, Jerusalem and the land of Israel as a whole. For modern Jews the most refined understanding of the idea of sacred places is not in the semi-magical way of seeing God as "present" in one place rather than another but in terms of psychological association. "The land of Israel," Jacob asserts, "does have, according to the *halakhah*, more 'holiness,' *kedusha*, than other lands but this should be interpreted in terms of the richer associations it has with the men who found God there. The land in which the patriarchs lived and the prophets taught is the idea which should be stressed. The same applies to the other sacred spots. Superstitious reverence for a particular piece of soil in itself should be rejected."

Jacobs then via analogy says that the Hebrew language is, similarly, the "holy tongue" not because it is God's special language. Historically considered Hebrew is an ancient Semitic tongue with the strongest affinities to other Semitic languages such as Aramaic and Arabaic and was not originally spoken only by the Israelites. Hebrew is the "holy tongue" by association, because it is the language of the Bible, the form in which the covenant between God and Israel first was expressed, the instrument by means of which the seers and prophets of Israel poured out their hearts to God, the key with which to unlock the spiritual treasures of the Jewish people.

How Place is Conditioned by Human Beings: Two Further Illustrations

The following two examples might help us understand more clearly the manifest phenomenon of how people affect the character of a place—one that emerges yet again from scripture, and a second via a contemporary illustration. The point of this is to show by analogy that when the action involved—in our context—"holy action" on the part of a "holy people," it is that human action that confers sanctity on the place on which it takes place.

Land Locales: In Leviticus 18 a series of prohibitions of sexual abuses ends with an appeal to the people not to defile themselves with these abominable customs. "Do not defile yourself in any of those ways, for it is by such that the nations...defiled themselves. *Thus the land became defiled* and I called it to account for its iniquity (vv. 24-25). The same fate will threaten Israel if it becomes unclean and *makes the land with which it has been united unclean* (v. 28). In Deuteronomy 24:4, *the sinful people brings guilt on the land.* Numbers 35:33 requires a murderer be brought to justice *lest the blood he shed "pollutes the land."* Jeremiah accuses Israel of having polluted the land through her whoredom (3:9). Isaiah cries, "*The earth is defiled under its inhabitants* because they transgressed teachings, violated laws, broke the ancient covenant. That is why a curse consumes the earth" (24:5-6).

Clearly these utterances are based on the belief in a direct connection between humans and the earth—a connection based on the nature of human behavior. Man is subject to the God who gave them both the rules and the land upon which to live them; *hence his behavior has a direct influence—for good or for bad—on the earth itself. Indeed, the earth is conditioned by human action.*

Locals for Music and Worship

Imagine a large and totally bare room. It has only a floor, walls and ceiling. It is completely empty: no seats, no stage, no accoutrements, no people. Subsequently, people affix seats on the ground floor and in a three-tiered balcony in which some 2,000 people sit. A stage is erected for a 50-piece orchestra with a conductor at the podium; they are performing a Beethoven symphony. The heretofore totally bare and empty room is now a concert hall!

Alternately: imagine a totally bare and empty smaller room. It is subsequently occupied by some 500 people at a Shabbat religious service sitting in newly installed seats; an ark in which a revered Torah scroll containing "the Word of God" is installed; a rabbi is explaining Torah and a cantor and choir are leading the liturgy. The heretofore bare and empty room is now a synagogue!

The above two bare and empty spaces were not a concert hall or synagogue before human initiative took place there, were they?

Now consider this: the above concert hall has retained its accoutrements but is now empty—no audience, no orchestra, no conductor, no Beethoven. The synagogue remains furnished but also is empty—no congregants, no rabbi, no cantor, no choir, no liturgy. Yet when one enters the empty concert hall, one senses an aesthetic aura evoking the sound and feel of music. And when one enters the empty synagogue, one experiences a sense of reverence, assumes a posture of respect, hears the echo of prayer.

Why is this so? It is because of the *memory*, the awareness in one's mind and heart of what took place in times past in those spaces—of the orchestra and conductor, of the rabbi and cantor who functioned there. It is *recollection* of those activities that conferred the aura, the feelings one experiences even when the concert hall and synagogue are empty. We might put it this way: one *imagines* that a conductor is orchestrating a Beethoven symphony or that a rabbi and cantor are leading prayer in these places and thus the aura and reverential experience.

People confer character on a place. Israelite people experiencing the transcendent on Israel's place confer sanctity on it.

Misreading the Cultic Notion About Holiness of Land

From the preceding we have seen that the idea of the sanctity of the land of Israel is based on the primary relationship between God and Israel and not on an internal relationship of God with the land independent of Israel. We have also noted the general principle wherein the essential character of a place—holiness and otherwise— is determined by people conferring that holiness/character on it rather than these being endemic to the place. Indeed, these findings argue with the cultic notion. We contend that the phenomenon of conferred holiness we have explicated explains why *the cultic notion is actually a misunderstanding of the true nature of the sanctity of land.* What follows seeks to demonstrate this.

The Cultic Notion

As pointed out in Chapter Two and earlier in this chapter, the cultic notion has mythological characteristics. *It conceives of God Himself dwelling within the land,* as it were. God is holy and His presence (כָּבוֹד) is holy and generates holiness, and so the land is holy and must be maintained unmarred and undefiled out of reverence for His presence. God's territorial base is on earth—on Mount Zion in Jerusalem as the site of His Temple, "His abode" (בֵּית ה׳) in the land (Isaiah 2:2 and Micah 4:1). The prophet Isaiah declared: וָאֶרְאֶה אֶת אֲדֹנָי יֹשֵׁב עַל כִּסֵּא רָם וְנִשָּׂא וְשׁוּלָיו מְלֵאִים אֶת הַהֵיכָל, "I beheld my Lord seated on a high and lofty throne, and the skirts of His robe filled the Temple" (Isaiah 6:1). The survivor in Lamentations 2:1 is grief-stricken over the Babylonian destruction of Judean sovereignty and the defilement of God's Temple and cries out: וְלֹא זָכַר הֲדֹם רַגְלָיו בְּיוֹם אַפּוֹ, "He did not remember 'His footstool' on the day of His wrath." God consents to being met by His people at the physical tent of meeting at Shilo and Shechem. King Solomon invites the Lord to dwell on earth: בֵּית זְבֻל לָךְ מָכוֹן לְשִׁבְתְּךָ עוֹלָמִים, "in a stately house, a place where You may dwell forever" (I Kings 8:13). [23]

According to this perspective, the land is conceived of as holy

irrespective of any human activity on it or experience with it. It has a
life of its own, as it were. It is forcefully and vividly personified, as in
Leviticus 20:22-26, which portrays the land as itself ejecting the
Israelites when they are unfaithful to the commandments. Implicit
in this is the notion of the place in action, that the Lord Himself
inhabits it and causes the action. This is the import of Numbers
35:34: "You shall not defile the land in which you live, *in the midst of
which I dwell*" (אֲשֶׁר אֲנִי שֹׁכֵן בְּתוֹכָהּ). Harvey Cox has described this
notion that views nature as semi-divine:

> Pre-secular man lives in an enchanted forest. Its glens and
> groves swarm with spirits. Its rocks and streams are alive
> with friendly and fiendish demons. Reality is charged with
> mystical power that erupts here and there to threaten or
> benefit man.[24]

When a number of scriptural passages emphasize the
centralization of the sacrificial liturgy, limiting it to one shrine only,
they phrase the rationale for the move in terms of the presence of
God there. Hence, even when the Hebrews were in exile in Persia,
they prayed in the direction of Jerusalem in the hope that their
supplications would be heard by the deity there (Daniel 6:11). In this
way Jerusalem retained its sanctity regardless of whether the Temple
was standing and regardless of whether the supplicant was there
physically. The city is thus sacred because God is present there; it is
His "abode," His "throne," His "footstool," "the place where He
dwells forever."[25]

The Notion in the General Atmosphere

The conception of the deity dwelling in specific places has its
analogues in non-Israelite cultures around the world. This appears
to indicate that the notion was part of the Israelite religious mindset
and practice in common with other religionists—past and present. It
would seem, therefore, that embrace of the notion stemmed from

shared human religious impulses and concepts of the deity. To cite but a few examples:

Greece

Vincent Scully in his monumental *The Earth, the Temple, and the Gods* has summarized the results of his studies about ancient Greek temples:

> I tried to show that all important Greek sanctuaries grew up around open altars which were normally sited where they are because *the place itself first suggested the presence of the divine being. Indeed, its natural forms were regarded as embodying that presence.* The Temple when finally built embodied it also, now in terms of the human conception of the divinity. Between the two kinds of shapes a fundamental counterplay developed, seen most richly in the late archaic and classic periods, which created an architectural balance of tensions between the natural and the man-made.

Scully explains that the core reason for these locales being considered hallowed places was because they were favorable to the contemplation of the sky, which was an essential component of religious experience. Thus he proceeded to explore "the holiness of the earth" in his work, quoting an Homeric hymn: "...well-founded Earth, mother of all, eldest of all beings, Mother of the Gods, wife of starry Heaven."[26]

René Dubos supports Scully's thesis about the sanctity of place in his examination of the subject:

> Canterbury Cathedral, which was built on the site of a pre-Saxon monument, became a Christian shrine which has remained a focus of English life ever since. The same can be said, of course, for all the important religious and ceremonial sites of Asia and Europe—the hallowed places

which in French are appropriately designated *hauts lieux*
of civilization. The sanctity of place is as old as man's
association with the caves of Altamira and Lascaux.
Christianity never displaced completely the religion of
nature; rather it built its own temples on sites where
worship had been practiced from time immemorial.[27]

This phenomenon also obtained with regard to the local Israelite
shrines in the land, those in Shechem, Shilo, Gilgal et al., which were
originally sacred sites among previous pagan worshippers. This
accounts for Deuteronomy's proscription of these places in favor of
centralizing worship in Jerusalem as we have pointed out above.

Peru

In a report titled "Their Gods Resided There," published in the
Los Angeles Times, we're told that more than 20 Inca sites on
mountaintops in the Peruvian Andes were discovered during a four-
year period by Johan Reinhard, an American anthropologist and
mountain climber. The Incas who labored up these mountains, some
higher than 20,000 feet, *were worshipping the mountains and the
gods that they believed dwelled in and on them.*

At least 50 such mountaintops with Inca ruins, remains and
artifacts indicative of active worship had been found on peaks from
southern Peru to central Chile:

> The Incas and even peoples of the Andes before them
> thought the mountain gods determined the weather and
> controlled the springs, rivers and underground water
> sources vital to their harvests and animals. Offerings and
> sacrifices—sometimes human—made in the sacred places
> on the peaks were attempts to assure good weather,
> adequate rainfall and abundance of crops and herds.

Reinhard proceeds to document this mountain deity worship on
the famous Machu Picchu and far beyond.[28]

Kenya

In another report, titled "Kenyan Home of God is Melting," we're told that from a tree-shaded plateau facing Mt. Kenya the worshippers gaze anxiously at its melting ice cap and wonder: Is God dead? The melting has been causing serious environmental devastation.

For those Kenyans who still practice tribal religions and revere Mt. Kenya as the home of god, the environmental alterations have triggered a crisis of faith.

> "This is where God lives and it is being destroyed," said one older Kenyan whose community continues to make sacrifices to the deity they believe resides on Mt. Kenya. He worries that the disappearing ice is a sign of God's fury. "God is very angry, and if things don't change, I fear he might abandon us forever."

The report goes on to describe the reasons for Mt. Kenya having become a sacred place, and the forms of worship and sacrifice to the god who inhabited the place in the long past and into the present.[29]

Bahrain

In 1983, a 4,000-year-old temple was discovered on the island state of Bahrain, located off the coast of Saudi Arabia. The temple was described as the greatest monument of the ancient Dilmun civilization. According to the archaeologist Helmuth Andersen of Denmark, who supervised the excavation, the temple was believed to be dedicated to one of the three principle Sumerian deities—*Enki, the water-dwelling god of wisdom.*

A chamber for sacrifices to the god containing a central altar was located. Adjacent to it was a flight of carved steps leading down to Enki's pool, a deep stone-walled well built over one of the numerous underground springs of which Enki was also the god and *where he was believed to live.*

In these springs, which still supply contemporary Bahrain with much of its drinking water, lies one of the cornerstones of the Dilmun civilization. "With bounteous supplies of water from beneath the rock," Andersen said, "Bahrain was in ancient times an oasis of fertility in an otherwise desolate region. It was thus natural that the god ruling this vital source of water should be the principle deity of the Dilmun people."[30]

An Attempt to Modify the Cultic Notion

Jon Levenson attempts to blunt the clearly anthropomorphic implication of the mythic notion about the sanctity of place in the biblical context.[31] In his depiction of "The Temple as Sacred Space" he begins by saying that the idea of the presence of God on the "cosmic" mountain (i.e., the Temple on Mount Zion in Jerusalem as well as in this locale's surrounding environs) "is problematic especially to modern minds, for it implies a dimension of divinity which seems hopelessly primitive to anyone of philosophical sophistication...A God who is spatially limited is, in some minds, no God at all, or at least one of whom the term 'cosmic' seems inappropriate." He points to the biblical tradition itself, which appears to critique the notion of God being present spatially:

> The Lord is near to all who call upon Him, to all who invoke Him in truth (Psalm 148:18). For what great nation is there whose God is near to it as the Lord our God is wherever we call upon Him (Deut. 4:7).

The Psalmist here appears to be saying that the presence of God does not depend on one's location, but upon one's willingness to call to Him from a stance of truth. And the Deuteronomist goes further, implying that God's ubiquity differentiates Him from the would-be gods of the nations who are not able to draw an answer to the call of the heart because they are somehow spatially confined.

Despite this caveat, Levenson contends that the cultic and historical notions of the land's sanctity *are essentially not in conflict with each other.* He begins to do so by seeking to qualify the idea of God dwelling in a specific physical place on earth. When various scriptural passages portray the Lord as inhabiting the central shrine in Jerusalem, "it is not the case that the Lord dwells in the sanctuary in a literal anthropomorphic sense; rather, it is that he places his *essence, his nature, his signature*—there. This presence dwells (שכן) there in the sense of setting up a tent (מִשְׁכָּן). God's presence is not gross and tangible, but subtle and delicate, like the presence of a *traveler* at his favorite camping spot."

Levenson continues: The Lord (in the above sense) *is* localized in the Temple as portrayed in parts of scripture, but He is also ubiquitous, simultaneously inhabiting the whole world:

> The fact is that the Temple and the world, God's localization and his ubiquity, *are not generally perceived in the Hebrew Bible as standing in tension.* It is not that God grants his presence in the earthly Temple at the expense of other locations. Rather, his presence there is an aspect of his universal presence.[32]

In our view, despite Levenson's strenuous and subtle effort, the idea that God—even his "essence," his "nature," his "signature," "a traveler at his favorite camping spot"—inhabits a specific physical locale partakes of a mythic pagan notion. It does suggest anthropomorphism, perhaps not literally, as Levenson contends, but perilously close to it nonetheless. Such a notion does not represent Deuteronomy's dominant perspective.

The Dominant Deuteronomic View

In Deuteronomy the idea of God inhabiting place *is* expressed. Though articulated in a minor key, we hear the notion's echo. When, for example, the passage in 12:5 emphasizes the centralization of worship at a single place, limiting the sacrificial liturgy to one shrine only, the rationale offered is that the Lord's presence was there. The presumed intention of this innovation was to eliminate the local shrines, which viewed the deity as inherent in those places. Yet paradoxically, here the Deuteronomist, by insisting that the people come to the shrine on the three pilgrimage festivals "to appear before the Lord" (6:16), *does appear to locate God spatially.*

God's Name – Not God Himself

However, this notion is powerfully negated by other evidence in Deuteronomy's own text. Indeed, discomfort with localizing the Lord in Jerusalem and the Temple is manifest. In times of religious syncretism when the exclusiveness of "the Lord" was called into being, Deuteronomy emphasized a program of strict concentration on a pure notion of the deity. Here we meet with striking statements about the Lord's *name. The Lord put his name* at the one place of Israel's worship, that he might "dwell" there:

> • Look only to the site that the Lord your God will choose amidst all your tribes as His habitation, *to establish His name there* (12:5).

> • Then you must bring every thing I command you to the site where the Lord your God will choose *to establish His name* (12:11).

> • If the place where the Lord has chosen to *establish His name* is too far for you, you may eat (of your offerings) to your heart's content in your settlements (12:21).

In numerous other passages both in Deuteronomy and in passage reflecting the Deuteronomic influence, we hear the same emphasis on God's name—not God Himself—dwelling in a place. Examples: II Sam. 7:13, I Kings 5:19, I Kings 9:3, II Kings 21:4, II Kings 23:27, Jeremiah 7:12, II Chronicles 33:4. Indeed, the Lord Himself is in heaven (Deut. 26:15), but His name "lives" at the place of worship.

Deuteronomy is obviously attacking the older and more popular idea of the Lord's immediate presence at the place of worship and is substituting for it the theological differentiate between the Lord on the one hand and His name on the other, a severance that is carried through to the point of spatial separation.[33]

Events, Ubiquity

The notion of locating God in a specific place is further powerfully negated by other evidence in Deuteronomy's own text. The second commandment (Deut. 5:8) implies more than the prohibition of images; it implies rejection of all visible symbols of God, of the tendency to believe that He can be experienced in a particular place. Abraham Joshua Heschel has put it this way:

> The fundamental insight that God is not and cannot be localized in a thing was emphatically expressed at a moment in which it could have easily been forgotten: at the inauguration of the Temple in Jerusalem. At that moment, Solomon exclaimed: "But will God in very truth dwell on earth? Behold, heaven and the heaven of heavens cannot contain Thee...how much less this house that I have built!" (I Kings 8:27). God manifested Himself in *events* rather than *things*.[34]

Further, the dominant Deuteronomy forcefully proclaims God's ubiquity. In the worshipper's confession of obedience as he offers a tithe in his own locale he prays:

> הַשְׁקִיפָה מִמְּעוֹן קָדְשְׁךָ מִן הַשָּׁמַיִם וּבָרֵךְ אֶת עַמְּךָ אֶת יִשְׂרָאֵל
> *Look down from Your holy habitation, from heaven*, and bless your people Israel and the land which You gave to us, as You swore to our ancestors, a land flowing with milk and honey (26:15).

God does not dwell on the earth but in heaven; He views the earth and people from on high with His blessings and promises. Moreover, in Deuteronomy 4:7, the people are told that their God is forever close:

> For what great nation is there that has a God so close at hand as is the Lord our God whenever we call upon Him?

Again the text avers that, unlike pagan gods, Israel's God is physically removed while, at the same time, one can experience Him *whenever* one reaches out to Him. And we add, from *wherever* one reaches out to Him: when Israel dwells in a strange land she does not lose her relationship with God. In 4:29 we read:

> If you search *there* for the Lord your God, you will find Him, if only you seek Him with all your heart and soul.

Belden Lane has articulated this overall position:

> Entry to a sacred place is always a matter of one's dynamic relationship with God alone. There is no unchangeable quality of holiness seen to reside statically in any given place. The site is not revered because of what it is in itself. While elements of scripture did adopt certain aspects of mythical space, Deuteronomy viewed Israel as ultimately uncomfortable with the notion of primeval power being permanently possessed by a given locale. God was continually calling them, not back to a mythical *Urzeit* when a particular site was set apart as sacred, but to a non-spatial reality discovered in faithfulness to God.[35]

Non-anthropomorphism

Heinrich Graetz, as well, has emphasized the non-anthropomorphic nature of the Judaic perspective on the land. Shlomo Avineri has summarized Graetz's view. He tells us that at the moment Judaism entered history, it appeared as a protest, a negative force, a revolt against paganism; and this revolt is considered by Graetz the main historical characteristic of Judaism. Paganism is the cult of Nature, while Judaism appears as the Spirit, the antithesis of Nature, and hence representing a more developed phase of historical development. *Pagans, according to Graetz, saw Nature in its broader meaning as an immanent force acting out of its own power.* Even among the Greeks, with their sublimated notion of nature, god remains forever idealized nature, even in its highest stage of development where it is stripped of every animal and plant form and becomes humanized. The Olympian gods remain, just like ordinary mortals, subservient to the blind force of Tyche, the goddess of fortune.

To Graetz, Judaism is the exact obverse of this relation. *The divine and the natural are separated, and nature becomes an* object *of divine activity*; nature is even considered as being created by God *ex nihilo*. God is omnipotent and is not Himself ruled by nature It is before God that man is responsible for his actions. Judaism thus signifies man's emancipation from matter, and human responsibility becomes a possibility.

Paganism is thus an immanent religion of nature, Judaism a spiritual religion of the transcendental. Pagan art is steeped in nature, and is expressed in its being mainly figurative art, whereas Jewish art is poetic, verbal. Pagan man *sees* the deity in natural, physical form and molds it accordingly, whereas in Judaism one *hears* God. He appears as being mediated through consciousness and spirit. "Pagans saw nature in its broader meaning as an imminent force acting out of its own power. Judaism protested this notion, making it its central idea and main historical characteristic."[36]

The Role of Memory

Gerhard von Rad has emphasized that though the cultic notion of sanctity of the land informs much of the Pentateuchal legislation, "it nowhere appears in the Hexateuchal narrative on anything like an equal footing with the dominating historical perception." This also is the view of Yehezkel Kaufmann concerning the Hebrew Bible's general attitude about paganism that Israel encountered in its territory. Paganism's cultic character, which pictured the deity in mythic terms, gave way in Israel to the historical conception of the deity, which notion Kaufmann saw "as sovereign and self-sufficient."[37] We concur with von Rad and Kaufmann.

It is the activity of human beings, their experiences with God in the land, which renders the place "holy." And it is *the collective memory of those experiences*—on or off the land in history—that continued and continues to constitute the source of the land's sanctity. It is the memory of Israel's patriarchs' experience with God on the land in hoary antiquity; of the Israelite tribes inhabiting the place guided by a demanding yet loving God; and it is the memory of King David bringing the Ark of the Covenant to Jerusalem; of King Solomon completing erection of the Temple and placing the ark in the inner sanctuary; of the colorful ritual conducted by the priests and Levites at the Temple with its sacred instruments and sacrifices; of the three pilgrimages to Jerusalem by the Israelites; of the farmers' first fruits (*bekurim*) offering; of the great prophets walking the streets of the land's towns preaching God's word.

The role of history recalled as the way to understand the land of Israel as holy land has been articulated by Louis Jacobs this way:

> We find it hard to accept the view that Eretz Yisrael is a divinely promised land in a direct sense, because we have become accustomed to the dynamic view of Jewish history, including sacred history
>
> On this view we need to be no less devoted to the land of Israel as the Holy Land, or indeed, as the Promised Land, provided we understand the holiness and the promise as conveyed through the historical experiences of our people. We would tend to see it as holiness and promise through association rather than divine fiat; through the fact that in this land and in no other did God reveal Himself to the prophets; that here and nowhere else did Israel see God on the throne with the seraphim singing "Holy, Holy, Holy"; that here Amos taught us justice and Hosea love and compassion; that here Rabban Yochanan Ben Zakkai and Hillel and Akiba made the mighty attempt at translating prophetism into a wondrous way of life whose power has not abated....

> This land and no other has become sacred to Jews and a
> central feature of Jewish religion because of the
> tremendous associations between land and people and God
> through a history of three thousand years.[38]

This notion of the Holy Land being such by historical association
has been similarly formulated by Harry Emerson Fosdick. During a
visit to then Palestine in the mid-1920s, he came upon the coastal
city of Acre (Acco). It was a desolate place, yet he tells us that one
needed to understand that spot "not by sight but by insight," by
reminders of its ancient glory and storied history.[39]

Martin Buber knew that "all real living is meeting," that the place
of meeting serves always as the trigger of memory, the occasion for
hope. The physical locale forms the palpable context around which a
people's story grows. And it is *the remembered place* that excites and
directs the imagination in its effort to understand the people's
experience with its land—past and present—whether physically at the
place and elsewhere no matter how far away.

Abraham Joshua Heschel connects Buber's notion of the intimate
connection between place and memory to Israel's relationship to her
place. He emphasizes the compelling role of memory about Israel's
life on the land. He asserts that after the destruction of Jerusalem,
the city did not become a relic of the distant past; it continued to live
as an inspiration in the hearts and minds of the people. Zion itself
became a recurring theme in the liturgy, at the wedding ceremony, at
the circumcision rite, in the grace after each meal, in the Amida
prayer three times every day, in the prayers for dew and rain.

> We are a people in whom the past endures, in whom the
> present is inconceivable without moments gone by. The
> vision of the prophets lasted a moment, a moment
> enduring forever. What happened once upon a time
> happens all the time. Abraham is still standing before the

Lord seeking to save Sodom and Gomorrah (Genesis
18:22). Nathan the prophet is still standing before David
the king and saying, "You are the man" (II Samuel 12:7).[40]

In sum, the relationship of Israel to her land was based on her
relationship to her God and the recollection, near and far, of that
encounter on her place. *It was the memory of "holy acts" that
occurred in the place on the part of a people summoned to become a
"holy people" that rendered it "holy land."* It was not God Himself
inhabiting the land that constitutes its sanctity even as God does not
inhabit an empty synagogue sanctuary or an orchestra conductor an
empty concert hall, except in the people's memory of what other
people made happen in those places. *The cultic notion mistook the
memory of God interacting with people on the land for His actual
dwelling in it.*[41]

Conclusion

Here, then, is another of Deuteronomy's fundamental theological
notions about the land of Israel. However, based on the alternative
notion about the sanctity of the land depicted in this chapter and
elsewhere in scripture and rabbinic thought, in the final analysis, one
could never be sure about what makes a place sacred or not. Such is
the paradoxical character of the divine-human encounter caught in
the flux of space and time. Yet, we submit this statement by Belden
Lane as our conclusion to this subject:

> What we humans seek at last in the spiritual quest is not
> the ability to discern vast, numinal qualities inherent in the
> sacred place itself. What we seek at last is God alone—the
> God who consents to be met within the context and
> meaning of any given place, made accessible by the
> religious imagination. Often as not, it is the experience of
> meeting which gives meaning to place, not the attributes of
> place which are able of themselves to occasion meaning.[42]

SUPPLEMENTS

- **The Land: What Geographical Entity?**

- **Additional Analyses of the Relationship Between the Abrahamic and Sinaitic Covenants**

- **The Land of Israel: What is "Holy" Land and What is Not: The Rabbinic Perspective Amplified**

- **The Use—and Misuse—of Biblical and Rabbinic Data About the Land**

- **The Jewish People and the Land of Israel: A Union for Service to Humankind**

- **What Binds Diaspora Jewry to Israel?**

- **Religion and State: The Ongoing Tension**

ſ

SUPPLEMENT I

THE LAND: WHAT GEOGRAPHICAL ENTITY? [1]

The term "land" is used more times throughout this work than we dare to count. It is our basic subject. It is necessary, therefore, to define clearly the specific geographical entity involved.

———————

When we have talked about "the land" in this book we have been referring to the established territory of "the land of Canaan" at the time Israel came into the region during the second half of the 13th century BCE. This "Canaan," with more or less clearly defined boundaries, had been under Egyptian domination during the 14th and 13th centuries BCE. It had, in fact, been transformed into a political concept and had become the official name of the Egyptian province that included (what later became known as) Palestine and southern Syria.

The biblical description of the borders of "the land of Canaan" at the time of the conquest defines the exact same area of the above Egyptian province the borders of which we know independently from extra-biblical sources. Indeed, the Bible's delineation matches perfectly the boundaries of the Egyptian district of Canaan during the second half of the 13th century to such an extent that the biblical sources could be seen as constituting a sort of definitive deed and testimony for the Israelite tribes which considered themselves the rightful heirs of Canaan. [2]

The political and ethnographic situation of "the land of Canaan" and, of course, the territory's borders, changed with the occupation of the Israelite tribes and other peoples and with the cessation of Egyptian authority in Canaan. Also, the term "the land of Israel" came into use with the Israelite occupation; and the significance of that term changed as the borders throughout the period of the monarchies continuously changed depending upon the given historical situation. *However, the ancient boundary delineation which existed in the country when the Israelite tribes under Joshua came was not forgotten in the biblical tradition; its echoes continue to the end of the kingdom period.* Indeed, these boundaries cannot be explained in light of the political or ethnic conditions in the later Israelite period.

For example: the Israelite boundary never in fact extended as far north as the biblical boundary delineation indicates; it never passed north of Sidon on the Phoenician coast even during the reign of David. Another example: Gilead (the area occupied by the tribes of Reuben, Gad and the half-tribe of Manasseh) was always an integral part of the Israelite population and remained within the boundaries of the kingdom of Israel during most periods, yet it is specifically excluded in the biblical boundary sources. A final example: Bashan (the area north of Gilead and to the east and north of the Sea of Kinneret) was never really occupied for a significant length of time by Israel during her period in Canaan; yet this area is included in the biblical boundary sources.

Thus, in summary conclusion of the above, we can say this: *the boundaries that define "the land" are, in fact, the ideal ones established initially in the consciousness of Israel at the time of her entry into the land during the 13th century.* They are the boundaries of "the land of Canaan" of which territory Israel felt herself to be the rightful heir. This geographical entity remained the ideal down through the biblical period, including the era of the book of Deuteronomy, despite the actual changed facts of history. [3] This is "the land" of which we have spoken throughout this book.

The Specific Boundaries

The basic biblical description of the borders is in Numbers 34:1-12. There are two other passages that parallel the above list: Joshua 15:1-4 for the southern boundary, and Ezekiel 47:15-20 and 48:1, 28, in which the same list is used to describe all the borders as expressed in terms of geographic concepts of that prophet's own day.

See the map that follows this section, and follow along with this description:

The Southern Boundary: Begins at the southeastern edge of the Dead Sea. It proceeds southwest past Tamar, to the Ascent of Akrabbim, past the wilderness of Zin, which is north and alongside of Edom. It then continues to the southwest to a point south of Kadesh-barnea, which is on the southern edge of the Negeb and north of the Wilderness of Paran. (For further identification purposes: this Kadesh-barnea is about 50 miles south of Beersheba and about 75 miles north of Ezion-geber at the Gulf of Aqabah.) Here it proceeds through Hazar-addar and then turns northwestward to Karkaa and on to Azmon.

From here the boundary continues on its curve to the northwest on to "The Great Sea" (i.e., the Mediterranean) following the "Brook of Egypt," the great Wadi el-Arish, which is the natural geographical boundary between Palestine and Egypt. (For further identification purposes: this Brook of Egypt is about 30 miles south of Raphia and about 50 miles south of Gaza.)

The Western Boundary: "The Great Sea," i.e., the Mediterranean.

The Northern Boundary: Begins at Mount Hor on "The Great Sea," which mount is perhaps one of the northwestern summits of the Lebanese range about 15 miles north of Byblos and 15 miles south of Tripolis. It proceeds eastward to the city of Lebo-Hamath (modern Al Labwah, north of Baalbek in Lebanon, about 20 miles south of Riblah), which was situated between the Orontes and Litani rivers in a region forested and only sparsely settled in antiquity and which served in all periods as a natural boundary in the middle of the Lebanese Beqa (valley).

From Lebo the boundary continues eastward to Zedad (modern Sadad in Syria), which is situated on the edge of the desert and proceeds to the next two desert oases to the east—Ziphron and Hazar-enan. (For further identification purposes: the above boundary line is about 40 miles north of modern Beirut in Lebanon, 55 miles north of Damascus in Syria, and 70 miles north of Dan in Israel.)

The Eastern Boundary: This is the most difficult border to establish; its upper portion is a subject of conjecture because the biblical texts are unclear about the boundary's direction from Hazar-enan to the Sea of Kinneret. Yohanan Aharoni conjectures that it comes down southwestward approximately along the Yarmuk Valley skirting Ain to the north and the Yarmuk river to the south, and proceeds on to the southeastern edge of the Sea of Kinneret; thus, this boundary included Bashan (in which the Golan Heights area taken by Israel in the 1967 Six-Day War with Syria is located).

From the Sea of Kinneret the boundary follows the Jordan River to the northern part of the Salt (Dead) Sea, so that Gilead and the southern sectors of Transjordan are excluded from the limits of the land. The Salt Sea itself to its southernmost point completes the eastern boundary. Here we return to the boundary's original starting point.

THE BORDERS OF THE LAND OF CANAAN
This map is taken from the volume by Yohanan Aharoni,
The Land of the Bible: A Historical Geography, p. 64.

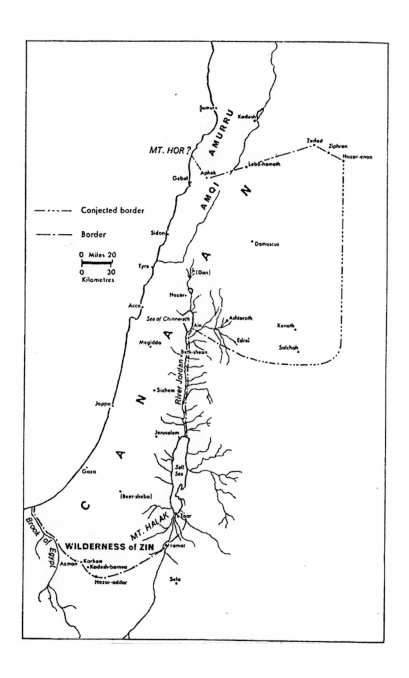

SUPPLEMENT II

THE UNCONDITIONAL CHARACTER OF THE ABRAHAMIC COVENANT: CHALLENGE AND RESPONSE

In Chapter One, "The Land as Gift," we documented the notion that the promise of the land to Abraham was given without conditions. Harry Orlinisky has seen the matter differently, arguing that strings were indeed attached. What follows presents Orlinsky's views and our disagreement with them. We thus maintain that an objective reading of the texts involved leads to the affirmation that the covenant with Abraham is, indeed, unconditional.

———————

Harry Orlinsky has analyzed the contract ("covenant" is its theological term) between God and Israel as reflected in the experience at Sinai, in the prophets, psalms and other areas of scripture. He documents the notion of this covenant's *conditionality* with telling detail and, in our view, accurately as our own Chapter Three, "The Land and the Law," demonstrates. (See his article "The Biblical Concept of the Land of Israel," in Hoffman, ed., *The Land of Israel: Jewish Perspectives*, p. 28ff). He prefaces his case this way:

> In accordance with the covenant between God and each of the patriarchs and with the people Israel, which both parties to the contract vowed to fulfill, God gave Israel the land of Canaan. This is not a gift, something that is given voluntarily and without compensation, a present. The Hebrew Bible regarded the covenant as a case of *quid pro quo*, an altogether legal and binding exchange of obligations and rewards for each of the two contracting parties.

> If God became Israel's Deity and no other people's, and if
> He gave to Israel, and to no other people, the land of
> Canaan, Israel in turn had to accept and worship God alone
> and no other deity, powerful and attractive as so many of
> the deities flourishing at the time appeared. This solemn
> agreement on the part of God and Israel was no gift, with
> no strings attached—no more on the part of God than on
> the part of the patriarchs of Israel; on the contrary, it was a
> normal and valid case of give and take common to every
> kind of contract into which two parties voluntarily enter,
> with strings very much attached (p. 42).

He then proceeds to the applicable biblical passages.

The problem is that Orlinsky begins his analysis with the covenant with Abraham seeking to show that the notion of conditionality *begins* with Abraham, Isaac and Jacob. Indeed, he makes no distinction between the Sinai and Abraham covenants; to the contrary, he cites in detail the texts of the patriarchal covenants in an effort to show that they, too, were given with "strings attached."

We contend that Orlinsky has forced meaning into these texts that do not allow the contention that they represent conditions that Israel was required to accept. Such, indeed, is the case with the Sinaitic covenant but most assuredly not with the Abrahamic.

Orlinsky's Citations and Comments—And Our Responses

• *The Covenant with Abram*

Orlinsky: With the appearance of Abra(ha)m son of Terah on the scene, this universal covenant was supplemented by a more limited and specific but no less everlasting contract, one that involved God on the one hand and Abraham and his household and heirs on the other. As put by the biblical writer (Gen. 12:1-4):

> (1) The Lord said to Abram: Go forth (*lekh-lekha*) from
> your native land and from your father's house to the land

that I will show you. (2) I will make you a great nation, /
And I will bless you; I will make your name great, / And
you shall be a blessing: (3) I will bless those who bless
you, / And curse those who curse you; All the families of
the earth / Shall bless themselves by you. 4) And Abram
went forth (*vayelekh*) as the Lord had spoken to him... 5)
When they arrived in the land of Canaan... (7) The Lord
appeared to Abram and said, "I will assign (*eten*) this land
to your heirs (*lezarakha*)." And he built an altar there to
the Lord....

Thus Abraham agreed to God's proposition, and they entered into a
contract with one another. If God had not made this binding offer to
Abram, or if Israel's progenitor, after due consideration, had decided
not to accept it, there would have been no contract, and consequently
no Bible and no Land of Israel. No force and no threat—no kind of
pressure—induced either party to offer or to accept this contract.

Our comment: In the first place, even a cursory reading of the
above text indicates that God did not present a "proposition," "a
binding offer" to Abram. The text contains no conditions Abram was
required to adhere to. Presented here is an unambiguous promise
about Abram's future and that of his progeny on the land.

Secondly, to assume that the fact that Abram went forth from his
then home to Canaan as he was commanded means that "Abraham
agreed to God's proposition," and that Abraham and God "entered
into a contract with each other" is a claim our text does not support.
Moreover, what is the basis in our text to support the assertion that
Abraham gave "due consideration" to the contract?

Thirdly, to assert, as Orlinsky does, that had there been no
*mutually agreed upon contract between God and Abraham there
would be "no Bible and no Land of Israel"* is a grand assertion that
also does not emerge from the text. Abraham is the recipient of a

divine promise in an unfolding drama conceived by God and willed by Him in which Abraham was to play a pivotal role. God's choice of him and blessings bestowed upon him and his posterity flow freely and are not attached to "propositions" that could frustrate or imperil God's will.

• *The Covenant Renewed with Isaac*

Orlinsky: This contract was renewed between God and Abraham's son Isaac. As recorded in Gen. 26:2-4, the Lord appeared to Isaac in Gerar, in the territory of King Abimelech of the Philistines, and said:

> (2) ...Do not go down to Egypt; abide in the land *(shekhon ba'arets)* which I point out to you. (3) ...I will be with you and bless you; to you and your heirs (*ki lekha ulezarakha*) I will assign (*eten*) all these lands [or regions, territory; *aratsot*], fulfilling the oath that I swore (*et hashevu'ah asher nishbati*) to your father Abraham. (4) I will make your heirs as numerous as the stars of heaven, and I will assign to your heirs *(venatati lezarakha)* all these lands, so that all the nations of the earth shall bless themselves by your heirs.

Isaac accepted this proposition; as the text has it succinctly:

> (6) So Isaac stayed (*vayeshev*) in Gerar.

Our *comment:* Again an objective reading of this text reveals not even a hint about any conditions God is imposing on Isaac. It is obviously not a "proposition," an offer being made to Isaac to accept or reject. Further, the fact that Isaac stayed put in Gerar and did not go down to Egypt as God commanded could just as well be interpreted to mean that it was an act of obedience in keeping with Isaac's passive character. To view Isaac's act as entering into a binding agreement with God is a stretch our text does not sustain.

• *The Covenant with Jacob*

Orlinsky: Essentially the same statement is made, e.g., in Gen. 28:13ff., when God appeared in a dream to Jacob, who was on his way from Beersheba to Haran, and said to him:

> I am the Lord, the God of your (grand)father Abraham and the God of Isaac: the land on which you are lying, to you I will assign it and to your heirs (*ha'arets...lekha etnena ulezarekha*). (14) Your descendants shall be as the dust of the earth; you shall spread out to the west and to the east, to the north and to the south. All the families if the earth shall bless themselves by you and your descendants. (15) I will protect you wherever you go and will bring you back to this land. I will not leave you until I have done what I have promised you.

This is supplemented by Jacob's plea to God, made on the way back from Haran to Canaan and in dread of the confrontation with his brother Esau (Gen. 32:10ff.):

> (10) Then Jacob said: O God of my (grand)father Abraham and God of my father Isaac, O Lord, who said to me, "Return to your native land and I will deal bountifully with you." ...(12) Deliver me, I pray, from the hand of my brother, from the hand of Esau....

Our *comment:* Yet again, a close reading of God's statement reveals no strings attached, requirements to which Jacob was obligated to adhere. Also the fact that Jacob appealed to God's promise to his (grand)father, Abraham, at a point of danger in his life, could well mean that he was hopeful for God's protection from his hostile brother. It is a stretch, indeed, to imply, as Orlinsky presumably does, that Jacob's plea indicates his agreement to a covenant with God. The above text resists such a stretch.

• *The Covenant with Jacob - Again*

Orlinsky: Isaac's son Jacob is said to have had the same experience with God and the covenant that his father and grand-father did; Gen. 35:9ff. offers one of several statements to this effect:

> (9) God appeared again to Jacob, on his arrival from Paddan-aram, and He blessed him. (10) God said to him:

> > You whose name is Jacob,
> > You shall not be called Jacob any more;
> > But Israel shall be your name....
> > (12) The land that I assigned
> > to Abraham and Isaac,
> > To you I herewith assign it;
> > And to your heirs to come
> > I assign the land.

And so Jacob too entered into the covenant with God, a contract sealed by the erection of a sacred stele accompanied by a libation offering:

> (13) God parted from him at the spot where He had spoken to him. (14) And Jacob set up a pillar at the site where He had spoken to him, a pillar of stone, and he offered a libation on it and poured oil upon it. (15) And Jacob gave the site, where God had spoken to him, the name Bethel.

Our comment: Finally, nothing in God's statement to Jacob here even remotely suggests any requirements to be adhered to. Moreover, Jacob's erection of a sacred stele upon which he offered a libation could well mean his way of expressing appreciation for God's promise. To assert, as Orlinsky does, that the stele act means that "Jacob too entered into the covenant with God" is an effort to enter into Jacob's mind, to speculate about his intention without any basis in the text.

From all the above, it becomes clear that Orlinsky's unwillingness to recognize the distinction between the Abrahamic and Sinaitic covenants has led him to a misreading of the texts of the promises to the patriarchs. The contents of Chapter One in this book, both in its analysis of the relevant texts and its presentation of additional data relevant to the subject has, we believe, demonstrated this.

Yet more: The biblical understanding of the promises' unconditionality is a perspective that has ever been called upon at various moments of Israel's rebellious history to assure her title to the land as well as to keep alive her hope for a future on it. To base Israel's relationship to the land solely on the conditional covenantal promise is to rob Israel of such title and hope. Scripture does not allow such a perspective, for when do human beings not fall short of what is expected of them?

SUPPLEMENT III

THE LAND OF ISRAEL: WHAT IS "HOLY" LAND AND WHAT IS NOT: THE RABBINIC PERSPECTIVE AMPLIFIED

In Chapter Eleven's discussion of the land as "Holy Land," we noted briefly a basic rabbinic formulation of the subject. Because of its special importance from the *halakhic* point of view, we include here that formulation in detail.

————————

There can be little doubt that the Jewish people, like all other peoples, has an intrinsic right to a homeland. There is no gainsaying that Jews have a call on their own corporate existence in their own physical territory with their own language, culture, religion and collective consciousness. This is their right based on their very humanity, their history, their tradition. And it must be emphasized: the religious dimension of the Jewish claim to the land, however attenuated that claim may at times have been, is a fundamental given in Jewish thought. Out of that given there emerged with growing power the entirely legitimate impulse for political and geographical sovereignty which is clearly manifest throughout biblical and rabbinic literature and in the life of our own times.

But this claim and right must not be anchored in a false reading of the Jewish religion. The Bible and Jewish law must not be misconstrued in the often frenzied pursuit of legitimacy, in the effort to make the case for the details of Jewish territorial nationhood. To do so is to exhibit a self-serving agenda; it is to reveal the masking of an underlying political agenda with a religious cast; and it is most assuredly counterproductive.

Alas, such has been the case in some circles both before and since the assassination of Yitzhak Rabin, prime minister of the State of

Israel. Jewish law has been misrepresented by overeager opinion-dispensers about the peace process in which the government of Israel has been engaged and about which portions of the land should or should not be relinquished in that process. At the heart of these agitated discussions is the presumed position of the *halakha*, Jewish law, with regard to the concept of *kedushat Eretz Yisrael*, "the holiness of the Land of Israel." A basic principle in Judaism, this concept has been consistently and "authoritatively" invoked to justify positions about relinquishing or retaining parts of the land. What follows seeks to explain.

Halakhic Issues Affected by the "Holiness" of the Land

Jewish law deals with concrete issues of life, with patterns of action, with specific choices to be made. The issue of the "holiness of the Land of Israel"—its character and geographic applicability—illumines and determines in rabbinic discourse such life situations and actions. Since the status of many areas within the historical boundaries of the Land of Israel with regard to *kedushat Eretz Yisrael* is far less clear than others, the resolution of these issues (i.e., which areas are sanctified and which are not) in the affirmative or in the negative will determine the answers to be given to the following questions:

1) According to the Talmud[1] and the Midrash[2] residence in the Land of Israel constitutes fulfillment of a biblical commandment. Question: Is this commandment fulfilled by one who dwells in Gaza, Beersheba, Ramallah, Jericho?

2) If either a husband or a wife wants to emigrate to or from *Eretz Yisrael* and one or the other refuses to go along, the rabbis rule that the spouse is obliged to acquiesce; failure to do so is grounds for divorce.[3] Question: To which area does this dictum apply: Nablus (Schechem), Nazareth, En-gedi, Bethlehem, Meron?

3) According to the Talmud,[4] relinquishing real estate within the

boundaries of *Eretz Yisrael* to a non-Jew either via a sale or gift is prohibited. Question: May real estate in Ashdod, Haifa, Tiberias, Jerusalem, Beth El be sold or given to a non-Jew?

4) Are the "laws contingent upon the land"[5] such as observance of the Sabbatical and Jubilee years, voluntary giving (*terumah*) and tithing (*maaser*) applicable in Safed, Acco, Modiin, Ashkelon, Tel Aviv, Gezer?

5) According to Maimonides[6] an inhabitant of *Eretz Yisrael* is forbidden to leave the Holy Land except for a limited number of specific purposes, such as: to study Torah, to marry, for business. Even then he must return. Though given permission to leave, this is not the "pious" thing to do. Question: May a resident leave any of the following cities: Hebron, Arad, Metullah, Eilat, Bet Shemesh?

What is the basis in the *halakha* upon which these questions can be answered? To determine this we need to identify the fundamental and authoritative principle embedded in Jewish law with regard to *kedushat Eretz Yisrael*. What criteria have been established that enables us to arrive at an authoritative definition of the "holiness" of the land?

"First" and "Temporary" Sanctifications vs. "Second" and "Permanent" Sanctifications

The land was sanctified twice by historical events—in the time of Joshua and in the time of Ezra; these are termed the "first" and "second" sanctifications.[7] The first was deemed temporary and the second permanent.[8] This construct was codified by Maimonides in his *Mishna Torah*.[9] The contexts of these rabbinic positions are the status of "sanctification"—its presence or absence—in order to determine where and whether or not various laws connected with the land such as those catalogued above were to be observed.

• The first consecration of the land took place when, after years of wandering in the desert following the exodus from Egypt, Joshua led the *olay mitzraim*, the "emigrants from Egypt," into Canaan, conquered it and settled the Israelite tribes in various parts of the territory.[10] This took place at approximately 1225 BCE.

• The second consecration took place when Ezra led the *olay bavel*, the "emigrants from Babylonia," back to the land after an extended period of exile following the destruction of the first Temple in 586 BCE. He, along with Nehemiah shortly thereafter, settled amid the returnees in Jerusalem and the Judean environs.[11] This took place at approximately 450 BCE.

The *halakha* makes a distinction between the original sanctification of the Land of Israel in the days of Joshua and its re-sanctification by Ezra following the Babylonian captivity. The underlying concept is encapsulated in the Talmudic principle, *kedushah rishonah kidshah le-sha-atah ve-lo kidsha le-atid lavoh*,[12] "the first sanctification (in the days of Joshua) was only for 'its time,'" but was not permanent sanctification." Joshua's consecration was temporary in nature and was abrogated upon the destruction of the first Temple and the attendant exile.

By contrast, Ezra's sanctification is depicted in this way: *kidshuah kedusha she-niyah ha-omedet le-olam le-sha-atah ule-atid lavoh*—the land the Babylonian exiles occupied "they sanctified via the second sanctification which stands permanently, for 'its time' and for all time to come."[13] This consecration remained in effect not only during the period of the Second Commonwealth but was permanent in nature; it was not abrogated by the subsequent destruction of the second Temple.

A number of reasons have been advanced by a variety of scholars in explanation of the disparity between the sanctification by Joshua, which was temporary in nature, and by Ezra, which was permanent.

1) Maimonides in his *Mishna Torah*[14] explains that since the original Jewish settlers in Joshua's time imbued the territory with holiness by virtue of the very act of conquest, their sanctification

remained in effect only until the land was lost through conquest. Ezra's consecration, on the other hand, was not brought into effect by an act of conquest, but by virtue of *hazakah*, by the returnees taking possession in peaceful fashion, and hence did not lapse.

2) A series of explanations in the same vein as Maimonides are articulated in the rabbinic literature. One indicates that Ezra's possession of the land was via divine beneficence and not conquest and therefore its sanctification did not lapse. Another argues that since Joshua never had the intention of peacefully acquiring the land, his sanctification lapsed. Yet another asserts that holiness achieved through conquest lapses through conquest while when achieved through peaceful means is permanent. Still another avers that since Ezra's sanctification was a "verbal" one it cannot be abrogated. And yet another explanation for the disparity asserts that conquest can be nullified since it is effected by force without the consent of the previous proprietors; the possession of Ezra cannot be nullified since it was carried out with the consent of the rulers of Persia.[15]

3) Rabbi Samuel Ashkenazi[16] articulates an incisive explanation that reflects a fundamental biblical principle: *the fulfillment* of the promise of the land was *conditional*.

There was a clear condition attached to the grant of the land to the people of Israel: they need to adhere to the Torah's laws. According to the Psalmist, "He gave them the lands of the nations, and they took possession of the fruit of the peoples' toil, *to the end that they should keep His statutes and observe His laws.*"[17] This condition was not met and that is why the first Temple was destroyed. What was the specific reason? Because, the Talmud tells us, the people of Israel were guilty of murder, sexual immorality and idolatry.[18] And this is why the gift of the land of Israel was annulled and the land's sanctity abrogated.

On the other hand, the second Temple was destroyed for another reason: because of *sinat hinam*, baseless hatred, which was widespread amongst the people—and not because they did not observe the fundamental practical tenets of Torah. This enmity between brothers was indeed a serious matter but at the time the Jews did basically keep the laws. And so, since they did observe the conditions they were obligated to, Rabbi Ashkenazi contends, the sanctity of the land did not lapse.

Distinction Between the Two Sanctifications

Based on the many and varied rationales outlined above, it becomes clear that there is a substantive distinction between the first and second sanctifications. It is this: *The territories peacefully settled in Ezra's time are permanently sanctified; the territories captured in Joshua's time but not re-settled in Ezra's era are not sanctified for all time.* And according to Maimonides in the *Mishna Torah*, this is the definitive *halakha*.[19]

The Geography of Sanctification in the Times of Joshua and Ezra

We come now to the crucial heart of this analysis: the actual areas that Joshua and Ezra took into their possession. This data will, in turn, provide the basis for answers to the questions of Jewish law posed at the beginning of this section, and for other significant implications.

1) *In the Time of Joshua...*The ideal or what we might call theoretical boundaries of the land at the time of Joshua's conquest are outlined in Numbers 34:1-12 and Joshua 15:1-4.

The southern boundary begins at the southeastern edge of the Dead Sea, continues in a southwesterly direction to south of Kadesh-barnea, curving to the northwest along the "Brook of Egypt" (i.e., Wadi el-Arish) into the Great Sea (i.e., the Mediterranean).

The western boundary is the Great Sea.

The northern boundary begins at Mount Hor on the Great Sea

(north of Byblos) proceeding eastward through Lebo-hamath, Zedad and Ziphron to Hazar-enan (northwest of Damascus).

The eastern border begins at Hazar-enan proceeding southward and curving westward (south of Salecah) to the southern edge of the Sea of Kinnert (south of Ain). The border follows the Jordan River to the northern edge of the Dead Sea which, at its southern shore, completes the eastern boundary. Here we come full circle.[20]

These were the borders of the "Land of Canaan," which during this period was an established province of Egypt. According to Yohanan Aharoni, the borders of this province detailed in extra-biblical sources are exactly the same as those outlined in Numbers 34:1-12 above. The actual sphere of the Israelite conquest and control in Joshua's time was more limited.[21]

2) *In the Time of Ezra*...The boundaries of the land at the time of Ezra's immigration from Babylonia are based on both biblical data and extra-biblical materials.[22]

The southern boundary begins at En-gedi on the Dead Sea, continuing westward to Beth Zur (north of Kiriath-arba/Hebron) and on to Keilah.

The western boundary proceeds from here northward through Azekah to Gezer.

The northern boundary proceeds from Gezer to Baal-hazor (north of Beth El and south of Shilo and Shechem) to Jericho (south of Gilgal) and then curves southward to the northernmost point of the Dead Sea.

The Dead Sea constitutes the eastern boundary and at the point it touches En-gedi we've come full circle.[23]

Among the evidence of the extent of Judea during this period are the seal impressions on storage jars on which appear the name "Yehud" or "Jerusalem" in various forms often accompanied by a symbol of the name of a priest or governor. The distribution of these

seals reaches from Mizpah in the north to Jericho in the east, to En-
gedi in the south and to Gezer in the west.

These were the borders of Judea at the beginning of the period of
the second Temple through the Persian period until 332 BCE. This
Yehud/Judea was part of the Persian empire as a province of the
Satrapy "Beyond the River" (i.e., the Euphrates)—an established
region of that empire. The Persian rulers recognized this defined
territory, with Jerusalem as its center, as a sacred region
administered by priests in accordance with the law of Moses.[24]

It should be noted here that some Jewish communities lived
outside this Judean province. Nehemiah 11:25-36 recognized
settlements in Kiriath-arba (Hebron), the Negeb, the Shephelah (in
the Lachish area), and the "Plain of Ono" (south of Bnai Brak).

Implications About Sanctity of the Land in Light of the Halakhic Record

A focused look at a map of the State of Israel today—including the
West Bank, Gaza and the Golan Heights—combined with the biblical
and extra-biblical geographical data outlined above, will yield ready
and clear responses to the various *halakhic* questions posed at the
beginning of this essay. It will also yield a number of other startling
summations.

A methodological suggestion: the reader take the map of the
geography of the Israelite occupation of the land in Joshua's time
and superimpose it on the map of modern Israel. After that,
superimpose the map of the geography of Israel's occupation in
Ezra's time. Then, in turn, ask yourself this question: In light of
Jewish law concerning the sanctification of place in *Eretz Yisrael*,
what is the status of various specific places in Israel today, and hence
what are the answers to the questions of Jewish law posed? Also ask:
What other implications about the land of Israel today are indicated?

The maps and geographical data will speak for themselves. Here we confine ourselves to a few observations about some of the striking—startling—details that emerge from this examination.

1) *Gaza and the Golan Heights clearly do not fall within the purview of "holy" land.* Perhaps more startling is the inaccuracy of the persistent assumption about the presumed status of "Samaria," which is facilely coupled with Judea in the various debates and discussions about the sanctity of the land. For example, Shechem/ Nablus, Elon Moreh, Shilo, Gilgal—*all within "Samaria": biblically revered and originally sanctified according to Jewish law to be sure, these locales do not, in fact, fit into the* halakhic *context of territorial* kedusha.

2) There are profound ironies in this examination. Some locales that clearly have a hallowed place in Jewish history and memory do not have "sanctified" status in Jewish law. *Of the four holy cities to which Jews came with greatest frequency (Jerusalem, Safed, Hebron, Tiberias), only Jerusalem and Hebron were sanctified by biblical events.* The other two became hallowed by later religious circumstances. When Jews began to return to the land in the 18th century, they settled in Safed and Tiberias and imbued them with powerful religious energy that radiates to this day. Shall Safed and Tiberias be dismissed from the category of "holy" because the classical *halakha* does not deal with them as such?

3) Yet another striking irony: the State of Israel today encompasses far more territory than Jewish law validates as sanctified. For example, the whole of Galilee, the entire coastal area from Nahariya to Acco, from Haifa to Netanya, from Tel Aviv to Ashdod and Ashkelon to Gaza, as well as the bulk of the Negev from Sde Boker clear down to Eilat on the Gulf of Aquaba. *Shall these areas be deemed religiously or otherwise status-less because the* halakha *confers no "sanctity" on them?*

The Rabbinic Perspective and the Needs of Our Time

As we have seen, a number of implications from our analysis of traditional *halakhic* data have led us to a set of startling (and for many, disturbing) conclusions concerning what is, and what is not, holy land in our time. However, since the context of our analysis is the religious one, we cannot evade the perspective of Jewish law, which is central to the religion of the Jewish people and its national enterprise.

Normative Judaism has always been a total entity covering all aspects of individual, collective, and national rules of conduct. It does not recognize a distinction between secular and religious law. It unites the people of Israel with the religion of Israel and the land of Israel. Rabbi Abraham Isaac Kook, Israel's pre-statehood chief rabbi, invoked this unity of nationality and religion in order to justify their cooperation:

> It is a great error to be insensitive to the distinctive unity of the Jewish spirit, to imagine that the Divine stuff which uniquely characterizes Israel is comparable to the spiritual content of all the other national civilizations. This error is the source of the attempt to sever the national from the religious elements of Judaism. Such a division would falsify both our nationalism and our religion, for every element of thought, emotion, and idealism that is present in the Jewish people belongs to an indivisible entity, and all together make up its specific character.[25]

In light of the changed world in which we find ourselves, this is precisely why Jewish law with regard to the definition of land-holiness and hence its status today needs revision—adaptation to new conditions—within the framework of the *halakhic* system itself. Such an effort would be in keeping with the very nature of that system, which has always adapted principle to circumstance.

Indeed, the circumstances of our time with regard to the condition of the Jewish people and the land of Israel have undergone major changes, radically different from that of traditional rabbinic times centuries ago: migrations, wars, national movements, political alliances, demography—and, alas, the Holocaust.   This all has impacted the land of Israel, its borders and the destiny of its people and status in the world.

The early pioneers whose sacrifice and toil reclaimed barren land were driven unconsciously yet inevitably by the religious yearnings of the Jewish people throughout the millennia.   In their zeal, they struck roots in the malaria-infested swamps and dry stretches of arid land.   Their brothers centuries before infused the land with mystic character by their incoming presence.   In our time these pathbreakers built the idealistic yet practical *kibbutzim*. They built new towns and bigger cities all over the land. They secured their status in the land with their blood during several wars.   They welcomed their weary and deeply hurt kinsmen who survived the catastrophe of the 1930s and 1940s.

Halakha and New Conditions

How does the traditional *halakha* that formulated notions about the sanctity of land centuries before our radically changed world speak to these new circumstances? The rabbinic authorities of our time must do so lest the system of Jewish law waft into the air of irrelevance. It would seem astonishing to question the "holiness" of Tel Aviv, Haifa, Eilat, let alone Safed and Tiberias, and therefore their legitimacy as integral to the state of Israel based on Jewish law.

The Jewish system of law has been and remains a central element in Judaism, the Jewish people and its national life. It is for this reason that the *halakha* must be honestly and accurately read; yes, it deserves our respect; it must have a vote but not a veto for our time if it remains fixed. Because of the system's status in Jewish life, it is all the more reason why it must be creatively updated and courageously adapted to the geopolitical, national and humane realities of a modern state whose task it is to help assure that the people of Israel—both in the homeland and in the diaspora—lives.

THE USE—AND MISUSE—OF BIBLICAL AND RABBINIC DATA ABOUT THE LAND

How the *Halakha* is used in interpreting issues and events pertaining to the Land of Israel is discussed in Chapter Eleven, "The Land as 'Holy Land'," and in Supplement III, "The Land of Israel: What is 'Holy Land' and What is Not." The following amplifies this issue further in the context of a specific event.

———

Yigal Amir, Prime Minister Yitzhak Rabin's assassin, was no lone gunman. He was not a deranged person but a sane, even thoughtful, right-wing religious hard-liner. He was a diligent student of biblical and rabbinic texts and traditions, and he was a loyal disciple of his rabbinic mentors. His action, he said, comes straight from a specific reading of the religion of Israel, and, according to this reading, the taking of Rabin's life was done in the name of God, the Bible, and of *halakha* (Jewish law).

In the Bible, according to Amir, the land of Israel was promised by God to the Jewish people forever, starting with *Avraham Avinu* (the patriarch Abraham); the Bible records that the Israelites could not live in peace under the same roof with the non-Israelites; the *halakha* holds that the entire land is holy and holy land cannot be given away. "Maybe God acted with me," said a defiant Yigal Amir, the assassin. "My goal was to awaken the Israeli people to the fact that a Palestinian state is being created here with an army of terrorists. According to the *halakha*, the moment a Jew turns over his people and land to the enemy, he must be killed. I have studied Jewish law all my life, and I have all of the information."

Amir's presumed knowledge of God's will and his overconfident take on the *halakhic* information are so painful and shameful precisely because they represent a dreadful distortion of the biblical and halakhic perspectives on the land of Israel as a religious category. Let me explain.

• *The Promise Misread*

Yes, indeed, the land of Israel was promised to the biblical patriarchs and to their descendants, and the promise is a regular refrain throughout the biblical literature. Yes, this promise has been a permanent fixture in the mindset of the Jewish people throughout its history. And yes, the promise does confer legitimacy for the claim of that people on the land of Israel.[1] However, this does not mean that the promise can be so easily interpreted to segue directly to legitimizing taking the life of the established leader of the State of Israel, a human being fashioned in the image of God.

The rabbis would never allow such a view, let alone act on it. The Mishna emphasizes the ultimate and supreme value of a single person, and the implications beyond that person for a larger realm:

לְפִיכָךְ נִבְרָא אָדָם יְחִידִי לְלַמֶּדְךָ שֶׁכָּל הַמְאַבֵּד נֶפֶשׁ אַחַת מִיִּשְׂרָאֵל
מַעֲלֶה עָלָיו הַכָּתוּב כְּאִלּוּ אִבֵּד עוֹלָם מָלֵא וְכָל הַמְקַיֵּם נֶפֶשׁ אַחַת
מִיִּשְׂרָאֵל מַעֲלֶה עָלָיו הַכָּתוּב כְּאִלּוּ קִיֵּם עוֹלָם מָלֵא

For this reason was man created alone: to teach you that whoever destroys a single soul of Israel ["Israel" is absent from some texts] scripture imputes guilt to him as though he had destroyed a whole world; and whoever preserves a single soul of Israel, scripture ascribes merit to him as though he had preserved a whole world.

This dictum flows from the event recorded in the Bible of Cain's slaying his brother, Abel. In Gen. 4:10 God says to Cain:

מֶה עָשִׂיתָ קוֹל דְּמֵי אָחִיךָ צֹעֲקִים אֵלַי מִן הָאֲדָמָה
What have you done! The *bloods* of your brother cry to me.

Note that the word used is *bloods* in the plural; thus the Mishna infers that Cain shed not only Abel's blood but also the דְּם זַרְעוֹתָיו, "the blood of his (potential) descendants."[2]

Yitzhak Rabin was the leader of his people who, in the *Sturm und Drang* of the practical affairs of state, had to make difficult decisions, choices which keep the very promises to Israel's ancestors in the realm of reality. They are often wrenching choices, frequently made unwillingly, yet necessary for the safety and security of the people in her land. This was Rabin's larger "world."

Thus to have shed the blood of Yitzhak Rabin was not only to take the life of a single human being, an act in defiance of Jewish law (which Amir claimed to have studied all his life), but also to endanger and seriously stain the name of Rabin's "world," that of his people and country.

To make claims, therefore, about what a leader of a nation may or may not do on the basis of God's promises in scripture, while leaving out the authoritative rabbinic caveats, is to seriously distort the normative Jewish stance on the matter.

Tzom Gedaliah

The rabbinic stance on a matter such as this is further indicated by its establishment of a special fast day to commemorate the assassination of a Jewish leader in ancient times. It considers such an act vile, so much so that each year the third day of the Hebrew month of *Tishre* is designated a fast day during which Jews mourn the assassination of Gedaliah ben Ahikam. Down through the generations the Jewish calendar reminds Jews to observe *Tzom Gedaliah*, "The Fast of Gedaliah," in order to express deep disdain for the dastardly act of murder of a Jewish leader at the hands of a super Jewish zealot.

In the period following the dismembering of Judah by the Babylonians in 586 BCE and exile of the Jews to Egypt and elsewhere, Gedaliah, a respected leader among the Jewish remnant in the land, was appointed by the Babylonian king to be governor of Judah. Gedaliah was conciliatory in his approach to his people's adversary, an approach shared by the highly influencial prophet Jeremiah. The governor was sympathetic and supportive of Jewish needs and reassured other Jewish leaders and his people in general of his positive intentions on behalf of their welfare.

Because of his position and conciliatory approach, however, he was regarded by a coterie of Jewish zealots as a Babylonian puppet and traitor to the Jewish cause. These zealots considered cooperation with the enemy anathema. As the antagonism peaked, the leader of the zealots, Ishmael ben Netaniah, struck down Gedaliah in cold blood along with fellow Judeans and the Babylonian soldiers stationed in the area. As a result, out of fear of Babylonian reprisal, the Jewish remnant fled to Eygpt and the land of Israel became denuded of Jews and in ruins.[3]

The assassin in biblical times, as in our time, no doubt felt he was doing God's work in bringing down the leader of his people. Surely he considered himself a fervent patriot intending to strike a blow for the Jewish cause. In such circumstances the "deluded" leader of his own people would have to be eliminated, the voice of accommodation silenced. And if murder was called for, so be it.

The rabbinic response to such a stance, to this violent act, was and is clear. A sense of revulsion is proclaimed year after year after year via *Tzom Gedaliah*. Jews mourn the murder of one Jew by another in the name of "patriotism."

• *Living With Others*

To claim, on the basis of scripture, that to live in the land with non-Jews is impossible is another serious distortion. The biblical account itself portrays the relationship between the Israelite and Canaanite populations. A careful reading of the texts shows clearly and unequivocally that the Israelites never supplanted the native

Canaanites, that throughout biblical history – from the 13th century BCE down to the exile in the sixth century BCE – Israelites and Canaanites lived side by side in many of the major towns and villages throughout the country.

Martin Noth points out that at the time of Israel's settlement in Canaan, she was able to gain a footing in the land without turning out the older Canaanite inhabitants from their properties. The first chapter of Judges states repeatedly that the Canaanites persisted in dwelling in their places. For example, verse 21 states: "But the people of Benjamin did not drive out the Jebusites who dwelt in Jerusalem; so the Jebusites have dwelt with the people of Benjamin in Jerusalem to this day," i.e. to at least 800 BCE, probably later. A bevy of other texts document this actual situation.[4]

Concerning the subsequent period of the monarchies, Noth stresses that the native inhabitants, though under the general hegemony of the Israelite leaders, retained their social and political structures, and that their economic, cultural and religious lives remained fundamentally intact. "The Canaanites remained in the land," says Noth, "and generally speaking, were able to continue unimpeded with their own way of life and with their possessions undiminished."

This era was the "heyday" of Israelite history – the time of Kings and Prophets, of economic prosperity, of high Israelite culture, and of religious creativity – and this all occurred at the very time when the two populations lived with each other. To be sure, significant conflict and tension existed between the two groups during this period; but they did not have to destroy one another to flourish.

• *The Halakha on Holiness*

To invoke the *halakha* as validation of the Jewish people's sole right to *all* the land of Israel as "holy" is another blatant distortion of Jewish law. The rabbis of the Talmud established criteria for the "holiness" of the land. The tractates *Yevamot* 82b, *Hagiga* 3b and

Hulin 7a define the notion. The Talmudic principle is *kedusha rishonah kidshah le-sha-atah ve-lo kidshah le-atid lavo,* which basically means that the first sanctification (in the days of Joshua) was meant for "its time" and was not permanent. Joshua's sanctification of the land was temporary in nature and was abrogated upon destruction of the first Temple in 586 BCE and subsequent exile because he came into possession of the land through conquest. (The biblical book of Joshua details the conquest of the land of Canaan by the Israelites who had left Egypt.)

By contrast, the second part of this principle is *kidshah le-sha-atah ve-kidshah le-atid lavo,* which means that the sanctification was for its time and permanent. Ezra's sanctification of the land was permanent because he came into possession of the land not by conquest but through a peaceful return of the exiles from Babylonia. (The biblical book of Ezra 2:1-34 and Nehemiah 3:1-32 and 7:6-38 detail this process of settlement.)

According to Maimonides in his *The Laws of the Temple* 6:16, this rabbinic principle is the definitive *halakha.*[5]

The point of this analysis is this: Ezra and his relatively small group of followers settled in what was at the time the province of Judea. It was bounded by En Gedi at the shore of the Dead Sea, continued west to Azeka, northward to Gezer, eastward to Bethel and Jericho, then south to the northernmost point of the Dead Sea, which constituted the eastern boundary, and at the point the sea reaches En Gedi the boundary comes full circle. A look on page 58 in the Macmillan Bible Atlas shows clearly the locale of Ezra's settlement— the limited province of Judea as outlined above.

Thus Jewish law is clear in defining the sanctity of the land as requiring *both* elements of the above principle: possession of the land by conquest and non-conquest. Joshua's conquest was necessary for sanctification and holds for that section of land occupied by Ezra peacefully. And since most of the land conquered by Joshua was not in fact occupied by the Ezra returnees, that land—a good portion of the land of Israel today—is not, by definition, "holy" in accordance with Jewish law.

It is, therefore, a fundamental misrepresentation of the traditional *halakha* itself, as it exists today, to claim that Jewish law commands the refusal to relinquish any part of the land of Israel (outside of Judea, which is today part of the West Bank) on the ground that this land is "holy." Such refusal is most assuredly not the requirement of the *halakha*.

I have argued elsewhere in this book (see conclusion of Supplement III, "The Land of Israel: What is 'Holy' Land and What is Not: The Rabbinic Perspective") that the traditional *halakha* defining the sanctity of the land needs updating in light of new conditions brought on by our time. In the meantime, however, this *halakha* with regard to the land's sanctity remains operative in our time, and is the basis for Amir's serious distortions.

Conclusion

Aside from the separate moral issue of shedding the blood of another human being, it is apparent that Yigal Amir's position cannot be upheld. His claim that God, the Bible, and the *halakha* legitimized the slaying of the leader of the State of Israel is a distortion of the religion of Israel.

SUPPLEMENT V

THE JEWISH PEOPLE AND THE LAND OF ISRAEL:
A UNION FOR SERVICE TO HUMANKIND

Eretz Yisrael is an indispensable theological component of Jewish existence. This is validated by our literature, which has linked the land with Israel's covenant and with its messianic aspirations. It is a central tenet in our *Tanakh*, and a continuous principle in our subsequent literature. With all of its reservations about political sovereignty, Pharisaic Judaism conceived of the land as indispensable for the fulfillment of Israel's covenant with God. Upon that sacred stage were to be enacted the sacred obligations of the community.[1]

In the early part of the movie *Gandhi*, we witness the oppression of the Hindus in South Africa, and how Mahatma Gandhi, in his early career as an attorney, led the struggle of his fellow Hindus for some measure of freedom in that country.

As I watched that part of the film, I thought of the famous open letter written by Martin Buber in 1939 to Gandhi. The letter was a reply to the Indian leader who had written an article questioning the validity of the Jewish claim to Palestine. He had compared the situation of the Arabs there to that of the Hindus of South Africa. He then accused the Jews of seeking to support their cry for a national home by citing ancient promises, of "seeking a sanction in the Bible."

Buber responded that there was far more to this than quotations from scripture. The history of the Jewish people, her purpose for being, her destined role in the world were involved here. What was decisive, said Buber, was not the promise of the land to Israel, but the demand, the obligations whose fulfillment were bound up with the land, with the existence of a free and distinct Jewish community in Palestine. For the Bible tells us, and our innermost knowledge testifies to it, that once, more than 3,000 years ago, Israel's entry into this land took place, with the consciousness of a mission, to set up a just way of life through the generations of the Jewish people. And, Buber went on, this role Israel is to play in the world—as a model, as a moral conscience—obtains today even as it did in ancient times.[2]

Israel's Role in the World

Now, a bit more specifically: What is this role of Israel's, and how is it bound up with its land? Let me examine Martin Buber's perspective, which, I am persuaded, the normative Jewish religious tradition embraced.

Deuteronomy 7:6 puts it this way: "For you are a people holy to the Lord your God (*ki am kadosh ata lashem elohecha)*; the Lord your God has chosen you to be a people for his own treasured possession (*am segula*)." These phrases indicate Israel's understanding of herself as having a unique attachment to God. Anything *holy* is that which has been separated off for the service of the Transcendent. Such was Israel, for it was through her that God had determined to manifest Himself to the world (Exodus 19:5-6) and it was through Israel that the nations of the earth would be blessed (Genesis 12:1-3).

To hear this in more contemporary terms, listen to what Leo Baeck, the heroic leader of German Jewry, said in the midst of the dreadful darkness of the Nazi era: "Judaism is the decision to be the great exception for the sake of God, to be the great difference, because God commands it."

The Jewish people, according to this perspective, is, as Isaiah taught, to be a "light unto the nations," demonstrating criteria for right and wrong, an example to the world of what justice, love and humanity ought to be.

The Jewish people is to be the great difference in order to demonstrate that not only individual life (such as that of a Jew in the Diaspora), but also life in the collective sense must be infused with ethical consciousness—that politics, economics, military policy, international relations, must all be seen in their moral dimensions.

The Need For a State

These corporate aspects of life, by definition, require the context of a state in which the people control the entire social apparatus, and thus has the materials which she seeks to fashion in the image of her ideals. As A.D. Gordon, the early apostle of manual labor in Palestine, wrote: "We the Jewish people were the first to proclaim that man is created in the image of God. We must go further and say: the *nation* must be created in the image of God."

And this is why the Jewish people must have a land of her own. For again: in order for her role in the world to even be a possibility, to be acted out in a real way, this people has to be rooted in a particular place. Land is the indispensable setting in which ideals might be lived, where a conviction-driven people is confronted by hard realities, and thus is forced to grapple with the challenges that come from the conflict between utopian ideals and the stubborn facts of life.

Maurice Samuel has articulated this convergence of task and place this way:

> The poignant and indestructible longing of the Jews for the Holy Land was far more than an extraordinary vitality of nostalgia, more also than an equally indestructible hope of escape from physical vagabondage, insecurity, and humiliation. It was the will to continue the search first incorporated in the land, in its heroes and topography. Through those men, among those scenes, *the attempt had begun to create a moral standard for all mankind, and the history of that attempt is the essential history of the Jewish people*. All its other achievements, however

impressive they may be, are incidental. And wherever else
Jews might settle, even in large numbers, and perhaps
permanently, *the land was an indispensable instrument
for the continuation of the attempt.*[3]

Indeed, without concrete nationhood, without a specific space,
without an earthly place on which to seek to act out her ideals, the
idea of Israel having a mission would be without the concrete means
with which to pursue it.

I have no easy answers to the real issues that divide Jew and Arab
today. But I do know that this land, in the perspective of normative
Jewish thought, is inextricably interwoven with the special
understanding that the land of Israel and the children of Israel have
been brought together to serve.

SUPPLEMENT VI

WHAT BINDS DIASPORA JEWRY TO ISRAEL?

The issue of the Jewish people's "exile," its being dispersed throughout the world, has been a fundamental theological preoccupation in this book. In our own time with the establishment of the State of Israel, the vexing question about the relationship between the State and Jewry living outside the State has been everpresent. What follows is this author's view of the issue.

We have all heard countless talks about the proverbial *matzav*, "the current situation," with regard to the problems, needs, etc., of the State of Israel. One such talk has stood out in my mind over the years.

The speaker, a local lay leader, had just returned from a United Jewish Appeal Mission in Israel. He movingly described his thoughts regarding the Jewish State: the courage and confidence of the Israelis in the face of constant hostility...his feelings of deep attachment to the Jewish people as he experienced new immigrants from India arriving at Ben Gurion Airport...how stimulated to renewal he was after visiting the Yad Vashem memorial in Jerusalem commemorating the Holocaust...America's obligation to support Israel because she is our only ally and the outpost of democracy in the Middle East...the military and economic problems and needs of the State requiring American Jews to give of their substance as never before.

As I listened to this clearly impressive presentation, I was a bit troubled. Something important was missing.

I was troubled because of recent conversations I've had with rabbinic colleagues who tell me of comments made by some in their congregations about Israel today. These are comments I, too, have heard in one form or another.

A Puzzling Condition

Indeed, some in our midst are puzzled. Accustomed as they are to the religious focus on Judaism in America, they say they do not understand the nature of the attachment of diaspora Jews to Israel. It is basically a secular state, they point out, most of whose people are either predominantly non-religious or indifferent to religious practice; non-religious military men like Moshe Dayan, Yitzhak Rabin and Ariel Sharon have been its culture heroes. Yet more, they observe, American Jews appear to be so deeply involved with Israel, with its political, military, economic and social problems with a passion that seems to rival their devotion to America. Why is this so, our interlocuters demand to know. And what does this mean about the character of the attachment of the American Jew to the State of Israel and its people?

An Exchange

These conversations rankled as I listened to our UJA speaker. They renewed old issues, past debates, involved rationalizing about the connection of the Jewish people in the diaspora with the State of Israel. And so, while I'm aware that this is a complex issue and that understanding the essential nature of "Jewishness" and of the Jewish people is hardly an easy task, I was moved to ask our UJA friend two "socratic" questions:

If a skeptical Jew listening to your speech this morning claimed afterward that you sounded like an Israeli national living in another country, how would you respond?

He answered, "I see no problem or conflict at all. As an American, I feel it is in America's best strategic and political interests to support Israel. Remember, Israel is the only democracy in the Middle East."

I asked further, "What if it was not in America's best interests (certainly a possibility) to support Israel? And what if another democracy in the Middle East emerges that is in conflict with Israel?"

His response was quite clear: "I am a Jew."

A "Straw Man"?

An unfair question? A non-politic answer? Maybe. The UJA speaker set up as a straw man whose response was unique to him? I think not.

The frankness of both question and answer uncovers a real issue. Some time ago, prominent Frenchmen openly accused French Jews of dual loyalty; the aftermath of Pompidou's visit to the United States elicited a major story in TIME magazine entitled, "Is There a Jewish Foreign Policy?" Moshe Dayan once bluntly acknowledged the problem in a speech in England.

Is it not a problem when some Jews appear unclear about the nature of their relationship to the country in which they live? Is it not unsettling when loyalty to America is juxtaposed with loyalty to another country? Do we not play into the hands of hostile others with confused thinking on the subject?

I contend that many Diaspora Jews themselves contribute significantly to our problems in the world. Unaware of the true nature of the relationship between Israel and the Diaspora, we often undermine the moral and legitimate basis for our loyalty to the Jewish State.

We are not bound to Israel by racial ties. Any visitor to the state will attest to the multiplicity of races and colors in the Jewish population.

We are not bound to Israel by national ties. All Jews do not live in or share a common territory, a single government to which we owe allegiance, an everyday language common to all of us.

We are not even bound to Israel by cultural ties. The increasing interest of American Jews in Israeli art, dance, music, etc., is only a hobby – a good and enriching interest, but a hobby nevertheless. The dominant culture of America is our own culture.

The "Capital" of Ancestors

It is, of course, true that since the emancipation Jewish "people-hood" has taken on determinative meaning as a way to define Jewish identity for many Jews. But this is a phenomenon of our people living off the "capital" our predecessors deposited in the Jewish memory bank, as it were. We all enjoy the "interest" that capital provides without being conscious or even caring about how those resources came to be deposited into our mindset and value system. Indeed, the source of our peoplehood was that transcendent experience at the foot of Mount Sinai that welded a group of rough-hewn clans and fugitives from oppression into a people whose fundamental character was stamped and molded, then, and ever after.

The Tie That Binds

What this means is that what Jews everywhere share is a common faith. The basic "glue" then which binds the diaspora Jew to the Israeli Jew, the Jewish people outside the land with the Jewish people inside the land, Jewry with the State of Israel itself, is the *religion* that is shared in common. This is not necessarily a settled set of dogma or beliefs, or rigorous adherence to traditional ritual, but a sharing of basic attitudes and action symbols rooted in the faith of Israel.

Diaspora and Israeli Jews are bound together because they were either born into or converted into the faith of Judaism. We have inherited the belief that the Jewish people has a unique relationship to the Sovereign of the Universe, that our task is to know the will of God as truly as possible, to live by that will and to proclaim the principles of justice and morality to others. A Jewish State is indispensable to the concretization of this purpose; and Jewish "action" in the Diaspora on behalf of Israel – politics, philanthropy, education, welfare and defense work are all powered by and give meaning to this fundamentally religious purpose.

According to the Bible, God's promise to the Patriarchs, to Abraham, Isaac and Jacob, was that their seed would inherit the land of Canaan (Genesis 15:13-17; Genesis 26:3-5; Genesis 38:9-11). All the great prophets foretold the restoration of Israel to its homeland, including the establishment of Jewish rulers in a Jewish state, in concrete form in the real world of the here and now. (Hosea 3:5; Amos 9:3-13; Isaiah 11:11-16; Jeremiah 31:14-16; Ezekial 37:15-28; Isaiah 54:1-8; Isaiah 60:1)

An Organic Bond

Passages such as these, which can be multiplied, may be evaluated differently from various theological positions. But their historical significance is undeniable; they are indicative of the organic bond between the Jewish people and the Land of Israel, antedating the Holocaust and the Balfour declaration by millennia. It is no wonder that during the Mandatory period, when the British government set up innumerable royal commissions in order to find a "respectable" formula for contravening it's promise to "facilitate the establishment of a national home for the Jewish people in Palestine," Dr. Chaim Weizmann declared: "You imagine that the Mandate is our Bible. It is the Bible that is our Mandate."

The hope for the re-establishment of Jewish sovereignty in the "Promised Land" has been a basic element of the Jewish religion for nineteen centuries. Throughout the period of *galut*, the Jewish tradition employed every resource of ceremony and prayer, every occasion, personal or collective, to remind the Jew of his link to the Land of Israel. For example, *rites de passage* from the cradle to the grave—at birth, marriage and death—were accompanied by expressions of fervent hope not only for a "spiritual" return to Zion, but a "political" restoration as well, the re-establishment of a Jewish commonwealth in the Land of Israel.

There is, of course, so much more to be said about this subject from the religious, historical and political points of view. None of it, in my view, can gainsay the fundamental notion about the essence of what binds Jews in America and elsewhere in the diaspora to the State of Israel: the faith of Israel and the history-drenched tenets of the Jewish religion that have nurtured the Jewish people everywhere through the ages and into our own time.

RELIGION AND STATE: THE ONGOING TENSION

From the analyses in this book, it has become clear that the biblical/rabbinic notion about the insepara- bility of religion from nationhood is a fundamental premise. The following deals with this subject in context of the modern era.

Martin Buber has pointed out the difference between "religiosity" and "religion." The former connotes the essential spiritual content of a faith community while the latter indicates its formal organization. Religiosity is man's sense of wonder and spiritual creativity while religion embraces the customs and teachings that are handed down as binding to future generations. Religiosity represents freedom to choose while religion calls for conformity. Buber spells out the crucial and highly consequential differences between these two phenomena. [1]

In our time, the issue of the relationship between religiosity as a general spiritual force in the life of the people in the land of Israel versus organized religion (or, as we designate it here, "the religious establishment") as integral to the governing bodies of the State of Israel is a vital and controversial one. To this issue we turn our attention.

Maurice Samuel some seventy-five years ago already alluded to the differences between the religious establishment and the nascent state indicating that Jewish nationalism at the time never became a purely secular and purely rational phenomenon. It rejected the dogmatic aspect of religion in nationalism, but retained its psychological aspect.

The enthusiasm for the rebuilding of the Jewish homeland was, among Jewish nationalists of the secular type, a religious emotion. Thus the two currents drew together—a secular nationalism psychologically religious, and a religious nationalism psychologically secular.[2]

While Samuel's analysis touched on a crucial condition, I believe it more accurate to describe the two currents not as having drawn together but, rather, having functioned side by side in genuine tension. James Diamond has pointed to this tension that has existed throughout the modern Zionist era. "The sensitive spot, the 'Achilles heel' of Zionism," he tells us, "is its undefinedness, its inherent lack of clarity about whether its goals are secular or religious." This tension between the secular and religious establishments is at the heart of the Zionist enterprise and the lack of clarity and the contradictions arising from it have been a perennial problem for the State both before and after its founding.[3]

Theocracy Affirmed

One of the basic perspectives that emerges from scripture is that the government of a state functions as a theocracy. That is to say that on its land religion governs *all* facets of life—political, economic, social, military, cultural, etc. This is the biblical view in a direct worldly sense, and the rabbinic view in most pre-modern eras in the long stream of history. This perspective cannot be gainsaid on the one hand, and on the other, is what the reader of Jewish tradition would expect.

In the recent past there were those who morphed this notion into a firm partnership in keeping with the longstanding tradition. They formulated the idea this way: "The Land of Israel without the Torah is like a body without a soul." Israel, they contend, cannot simply function as a secular state; she cannot take authentic shape without the religious component at the very heart of her being. Maurice Samuel saw the religious and secular currents drawn together in his day—and traditional religionists view them as inextricably interwoven in our day.

Thus the rise to prominence and significant power and influence of a fundamentalist religious ideology and political program in contemporary Israel. Based on the biblical tradition and the various messianic events in Jewish history—from the Maccabean uprising to the Bar Kochba rebellion to the Sabbatai Zvi and Frankist movements—the contemporary fundamentalists are crystal clear in their objective. Ian Lustick has encapsulated it this way:

> ...Zionism and the State of Israel are central factors in the long-awaited process of redemption. In their minds this will eventually entail the return of all Jews to the Land of Israel, extension of Jewish rule over the entirety of the Promised Land, reestablishment of the legal dominance of the *halacha*, reconstruction of the Temple in Jerusalem, and the appearance of the Messiah.[4]

This "platform" has been fueled with special emphasis due to the euphoria evoked by the Six Day War, combined with the personal charisma and stimulating ideology of Rabbi Abraham Isaac Kook and his son Rabbi Zvi Yehudah, both of whom firmly connected the religious tradition of the past to the present era. The extent to which this fundamentalism has penetrated the mindset of contemporary Israel's governing leadership can be discerned by the following incident. A student at Merkaz Harav, the Yeshiva established by Rav Kook senior and later presided over by his son Zvi Yehudah until his death in 1982, describes an "audience" Zvi Yehudah granted to Menachem Begin shortly after the latter's victory in the 1977 parliamentary elections:

> When Begin was chosen as Prime Minister he came to visit Tzvi Yehudah as if to Canossa, as if this man, Tzvi Yehudah, was God's representative. Suddenly the Prime Minister kneels and bows before Tzvi Yehudah. Imagine for yourself what all the students standing there and watching this surrealistic scene were thinking. I'll never

forget it. I felt that my heart was bursting within me.
What greater empirical proof could there be that his
fantasies and imaginings were indeed reality? You could
see for yourself that instead of treating him as if he were
crazy, people looked upon him as upon something holy.
Everything he said or did became something holy as well.[5]

Theocracy Negated

Many religious modernists, *including the author of this book*,
view this matter differently. They consider democratic nations and
institutions a desideratum of contemporary life, with the separation
of Church and State as a blessing for it makes for a free, open and
inclusive society, one that embraces all its people who share a variety
of religious views.

Though religious guidelines are, of course, indispensable
elements of a society, religious modernists cannot accept the
condition of a modern State of Israel as a theocracy in literal continuity with the Jewish historical past. Religious fundamentalists (and
we would add, many other fervent traditional religionists as well) are,
as noted, uncompromising in their political, governmental and
personal life positions. They view all facets of life, not just the
sacramental, as integral to national life. They view these as commanded by a theological system that is rooted in transcendent
authority. This stance, which is the source of intolerance of the views
and ways of others, can and does lead to inevitable and unavoidable
conflict, dissension and disarray. If allowed to have its way, it would
vitiate the ways of democracy—a condition contrary to its invaluable
principles and to the best interests of the State and of Jews throughout the diaspora.

Based on the above observations—the views of the traditional
religionists on the one hand, and the modern religionists on the
other, we pose these questions:

- In continuity with Jewish history and with the long-established religious tradition that has preserved the Jewish people intact throughout the centuries, should the religious establishment in our day be an integral part, politically and otherwise, of the governing body of the State of Israel?

- Alternatively, should the religious establishment, as such, function apart from the governing bodies of the State, that is, adhere to the practice of separation of Church and State? Concurrent with such separation, however, should essential "religiosity," without coercive powers, seek to become a potent force in Israeli society, nurturing moral and humane action and sharpening awareness of transcendence in its midst? Is Martin Buber's notion of religiosity really but an inchoate, impractical aspiration?

SYNOPSIS OF THE FINDINGS IN THIS WORK
AN INTERVIEW

While teaching in the Bible Department and serving as Dean of Continuing Education at the University of Judaism, I completed my doctoral work on the theology of the land. Yehudah Lev, the editor of the University's publication *Direction,* interviewed me on the subject in an effort to discern the essence of the work for accessibility to the general public.

Yehudah Lev began:

The claim of the Jewish people to the land of Israel is long established—and long challenged. Most Jews, asked to explain their relationship with the actual physical territory of Israel, will offer some vague reference to God's promise or to historical right.

Even the Bible presents some difficulties in this regard since it suggests different and sometimes contradictory explanations. When you add to these the confusions that accompany conflicting theological and political perceptions, you end up with claims and counterclaims that would try the patience and stamina of the most patient and stamina-strong of people.

Yet, Rabbi Jack Shechter, the University of Judaism's Dean of Continuing Education and a member of the Bible faculty, has stepped forth into the ideological quicksand that surrounds the entire question of the relationship between God, the Jewish People, and the land of Israel, in a doctoral dissertation just completed, titled "The Theology of the Land in Deuteronomy." Rabbi Shechter will soon be receiving his Ph.D. in Biblical Studies from the University of Pittsburgh.

Recently, Rabbi Shechter met with the editor of *Direction* to discuss some of the implications of his findings.

Lev: Have you produced a definitive explanation for the Jewish claim to the Land of Israel?

Shechter: I do think that the theological perspective about the land in Deuteronomy represents the dominant biblical view. However, there are other theologies about the land in the Pentateuch itself, in the prophetic literature, in the Writings, and in the biblical histories. There are, of course, the later rabbinic perspectives. And there are those in modern times who claim the land on nonreligious bases. These are important caveats when one attempts to link the contemporary situation with traditional perspectives.

What I can say is that in Deuteronomy the land of Israel is promised by God as a gift and via an oath to the Jewish people forever. It is an unconditional promise, not dependent upon Israel's behavior or the vicissitudes of history. This is clear from the covenant made with Abraham and his progency and is a central theme in biblical literature.

At the same time, Deuteronomy integrates into the picture the covenant entered into at Mount Sinai with declares, in effect, that the land is Israel's under certain conditions. I make the point that, according to Deuteronomy, though the promise is unconditional, its fulfillment, Israel's actual living on the land, does depend upon her behavior and the substance of her faith.

Lev: Isn't the Sinaitic covenant depicted in Deuteronomy the Ten Commandments?

Shechter: The Ten Commandments are, of course, the foundation, but there are in Deuteronomy a whole series of additional laws. These are specific laws, involving moral and ethical attitudes and civic behavior, which the Israelites were required to observe so that they might be entitled to live on the land. For example, there is the dictum which begins, "Honor your father and your mother..." and concludes, "...in order that your days may be prolonged on the land which the Lord your God gives you." God has indeed given Israel the land via His firm oath and as His gracious gift, but to actually possess it, to stay on it, the Israelites were required to do what the Bible indicates they were to do.

Lev: Who determines whether or not the people of Israel is carrying out these injunctions, and on what basis are these judgments made?

Shechter: There are recognized authorities and criteria for these. During different stages in the biblical period it was the judges, the Levites, or the priests who were entrusted with the responsibility for interpreting and applying biblical law. The prophets pronounced resounding judgments on the people; they said a great deal when they condemned Israel for sin and immorality and social injustice. The very fact that the prophetic writings were canonized, became integral to the synagogue service, remain to this day central to the entire world of ethics, indicates that they were accepted as authorities for making such judgments.

Of course, the prophets often met with hostility and opposition in their own day, but they were always taken very seriously. So were the words and actions of the judges, priests and Levites in their time. And so were the criteria upon which they based what they said and did as the accepted leaders and authorities.

Later, the determinations were made by the duly constituted rabbinic authorities of their times. Jewish life has always had recognized authorities who made judgments, and these judgments were made for the most part on the basis of commonly accepted criteria. I realize, of course, that when it comes to moral and ethical and ritual decision-making on the personal and corporate levels there are a lot of shadings and it becomes a very difficult business. But in principle the authorities and the criteria were always there.

Lev: There are other interpretations found in the Bible. Are they in conflict with your findings?

Shechter: Yes, there are and they do. But first let me review
Deuteronomy's viewpoint. The land of Israel is a *holy land* not
because it has an inherent property of holiness but, rather, because
the people aspire to be a *goy kadosh*, a holy people, on this land.
Israel, as a partner with God in a covenant, is to be a blessing to the
nations of the world, is to be an example, is to be a vehicle through
which God transmits His message to the world. The land is the place
where this happens. It is the indispensable instrumentality through
which Israel as a nation is able to carry out its task of developing
model patterns of living in the political, military and economic
realms, as well as in the non-corporate, strictly ritual and personal
ones. Only in the land can this people function fully as a *holy people*
where all of life, not just aspects of it, however vital, can be suffused
with a consciousness of the Divine. This is the land's special role and
function and is what makes it, according to Deuteronomy, *holy*.

Now there is another theology in the Bible which views the land
as being holy because God, Himself, as it were, dwells in it. It is His
holy abode, the place of His dwelling, the sanctuary of the Lord.
There are many references in biblical literature in which God, while
ruling over all the earth, has chosen one specific place, the land of
Israel, and in particular Mount Zion, as the place of His dwelling.

The Polemic

I argue that Deuteronomy was polemicizing against this concept
because this kind of localizing of the Divine Presence suggests a
lessening of God's universality. Yehezkel Kaufmann points out that
one of the reasons for Deuteronomy's emphasis on the centralization
of worship in Jerusalem was to avoid worship by the Israelites at
specific *holy cult* places throughout the country. For this implied that
the Deity dwelled in Shilo, or in Gilgal, or in Bethel, or in Shechem–a
pagan-like concept that God could be visited especially or only in
specific geographical locations. The idea that land itself in general
and specific sites in particular were *holy* savored strongly of natural
sanctity, which was rooted in the mythological mindset of the pagan
world.

Deuteronomy resists that perspective. It emphasizes that the sacredness of space is based upon history, upon God's will and action in time, rather than the naturalistic concept. The land is *holy* not because it has any inherent quality or property derived from God's own presence on or in it, but because Israel and God have a special relationship, because the people Israel as a distinct nation has a mission to perform on that land, because the land is the instrument through which that role can be implemented in the world.

Lev: To what extent do Christian theologians agree or disagree with your thesis?

Shechter: Their theological perspective on this matter is different. Christians tend to emphasize the purely theological elements and to omit the national and ethnic ones which are so much a part of the Jewish religious experience. They look at the relationship between God and Israel and say that that special relationship is sufficient. They do not give credence to the Hebrew Bible's belief that the land is an indispensable element in the relationship between God and Israel. They study the Hebrew bible as a guide for their Christianity; it is not for them the final, definitive word.

The church regards itself as universal, as transcending land and place, not dependent on one particular physical site as means to the fulfillment of religious ends. But for Jews the land is central and indispensable to the whole mission of the people of Israel in the world. To sever the land and nationhood from the religion of Israel is, for the Jew, to distort and misrepresent a basic tenet of biblical theology.

I need to add here that what I just said about the Christian outlook is a broad generalization. There are many serious Christian bible scholars and theologians today, including my Pittsburgh mentors, who accept the Hebrew bible on its own terms without seeking to mold it in a Christian image.

Lev: If the land is so central, how was the Jewish people able to survive 1,900 years of living in a Diaspora while the land belonged to others?

Shechter: Once it is established that the people Israel has a covenant with God, then that special relationship itself makes it possible to live at least a partial Jewish life—the ritual, personal, internal group aspects—without the land. The covenant with Abraham was made outside the land, before Abraham actually settled in it himself, and some 400 years before his descendants lived there in significant numbers. The Sinai covenant with all its laws was established in the desert before Israel entered Canaan. Religiously, therefore, there is a basis for the people living in relationship with God without her territory.

However, in normative Judaism, being without the land is an abnormality. It was always regarded as something temporary. It was an aberrant situation that had to be corrected. It was indicative of Israel's incompleteness. It is significant that Judaism never developed a theology which affirmed and legitimized a full Jewish life without the land.

In the theological perspective, the Jewish people which lives outside her territory is living *in exile* and is not a complete, fully authentic people, for without a land this people cannot be a nation able to fully carry out its mission to be a blessing to the world. The basic assumption of the Jewish people in exile has always been that if she is faithful to God, to the precepts and practices of her religion, she will return to the land God promised her—a never-rescinded, eternal promise, an irrevocable right and a permanent possibility.

QUESTIONS FOR THE
CONTEMPORARY SITUATION

What Do the Theological Materials in This Work Mean for Our Time? A Set of Questions.

My grandfather, Pinchas Schechter, taught me a lesson I have never forgotten. He cited a talmudic passage in the tractate *Sanhedrin* (106b): רבותא למבעי בעיי. "Is there any benefit in asking questions?" Yes, there is, he said: "Yankel, on the tip of the tongue lies the entire world. Ask and ask again and you will find answers."

Once when I was 15 years old, he applied this dictum to a concrete situation. He was sending me to the offices of the Hebrew Immigrant Aid Society (HIAS) to fetch the documents he needed for relatives of ours to immigrate to America from Milan, Italy. I didn't know how to get to the HIAS office. To which problem my grandfather said in his native Yiddish: "Yankel, on the tip of the tongue lies the entire world. Ask."

THE QUESTIONS

Palestine has the size of a county and
the problems of a continent.
Arthur Koestler, *Promise and Fulfillment*

Preliminaries

I believe it would be an evasion to assume the stance that the
material of this book does not contain implications of all kinds,
major and minor, for the contemporary situation in the Middle East,
that this discussion does not impinge significantly on the attitudes
and aspirations of the peoples and nations in that area today. Surely
the content of this work is connected to those around the world
whose lives—religiously and historically, culturally and emotionally—
remain affected by the situation in the Middle East section of the
globe.

In limited areas in the main body of this book as well as in some
of the supplements, I have ventured into contemporary territory
from a personal standpoint in an effort to locate linkages with the
work's basic materials. However, I recognize that this kind of effort
is a difficult, hazardous and controversial one in a book designed to
illumine life and thought and place in the distant past. What I do in
what follows, therefore, is to pose a series of basic questions that
appear to flow from the results of this research. These questions are
designed to suggest avenues for further exploration. In this way, the
reader can decide—or not decide—for him/herself on possible
linkages to the contemporary situation.

Words of Caution

Before proceeding, notes of caution must be introduced. I would
suggest that whoever would seek to find implications for, or venture
applications to, the life and thought of peoples and nations and
religions today on the basis of the materials here, keep in mind these
caveats:

First, I believe that the theological perspective about the land in Deuteronomy and the major prophets, as depicted in this book, constitute a dominant biblical view on the subject of the promise of the land and its "holiness." The rabbinical era perspective, as described, reinforces this contention since it adumbrates in significant measure the Deuteronomic view; this is also the case with regard to major facets of the modern perspective. In our opinion, therefore, Deuteronomy, the prophets, the rabbis and leading modernists, taken together, constitute the normative Judaic outlook down through the ages.

However, what must be borne in mind is that, as I have pointed out, Deuteronomy itself also contains another perspective on the land, and other biblical sources harbor a different view on the subject. Hence, a comprehensive biblical picture on the subject would have to include the differing Deuteronomic perspective, the non-Deuteronomic Pentateuch, the biblical *Ketuvim* (writings), as well as the prophets not discussed by me. Yet more: the Christian and Muslim communities have their own distinctive theological perspectives on the matter. They, too, have claims that they base on history and religious writings—though, we would note, without the incomparable tenacious passion and persistence evidenced by Jewry through the centuries. This being so, how does one decide, and who decides, which point of view at which particular time in history is definitive and authoritative, and hence allows for action based on that view?

Second, my depiction of the notion of the land in the modern period contends that there is, for the most part, basic continuity with the religious perspectives of Deuteronomy, the prophets and the rabbis—this serving as the "template" for the modernists. However, this is not true of all the leading modernists. There are many today who operate from purely historical and/or "secular" premises with regard to the issues of the contemporary situation. The "theological," or "religious," assumptions of the biblical and rabbinic tradition are simply not the basis for the thought and action of many leaders and movements in modern times. This fact must be carefully kept in mind because much confusion and misunderstanding often stems, not only from varying interpretations and readings of shared premises, but simply from varying viewpoints stemming from different starting-premises altogether.

The above cautionary considerations must necessarily be borne in mind in order to be able to make informed, responsible, and undogmatic claims about contemporary life and thought based upon the experience of the past.

With these caveats in mind, the following are a set of questions that appear to emerge from the materials we have explicated in this volume...

The Questions

I. *Boundaries*
When the *halakhic* tradition establishes which areas of the land are sanctified and which are not, it thereby designates the sanctified areas as ones in which religious law applies and the non-sanctified areas in which religious law does not apply. (See Supplement III, "The Land of Israel: What is 'Holy' Land and What Is Not").

Question:
- What pertinence, if any, does the above geographical land entity have to the debate about the contemporary State of Israel's halakhically defined boundaries, e.g., the West Bank, Jerusalem, the Golan Heights, the Gaza Strip, the Sinai Peninsula?

II. *Relationship With "Others"*
Deuteronomy projects Israel's relatively clear-cut relationship

with "the nations" in the land of Canaan: displacement and separation in order to establish her own distinctive identity. (See Chapter Ten , "Israel and the 'Nations' in the Land").

Questions:
- What pertinence does that claim and action have vis-à-vis the manner in which *other* nations and religions have acquired *their* territories—and the treatment of those whom *they* dispossessed?

- When is war a legitimate means of achieving a nation's ends? How do we know that?

III. *"Holy" to Whom?*

In this book, we have posited the notion that the land of Israel is a "holy land" because of Israel's history upon it and because on that land she feels obligated to strive to act so as to live up to God's summons of her to be a "holy people." (See Chapter Eleven ,"The Land as 'Holy Land'").

Question:
- In what sense is the land "holy" for Christians and Muslims? How specifically do they differ from Jews in this regard?

IV. *Jerusalem*

The centralization of worship "in the place He will choose" is a basic emphasis in Deuteronomy. Though the name Jerusalem is, of course, never used in the book, it is manifest that Jerusalem is "the place He will choose." Further, Jerusalem was the religious and political capitol of the northern and southern kingdoms of Israel and Judah during significant stages of the biblical period. (See Chapter Eleven, "The History").

Question:

- What should Jerusalem's role be today? A religious center primarily or the capitol of a political state only? If both: is such feasible in the modern world?

V. *People or Nation?*

Deuteronomy speaks of Israel as a "holy people to God" (*am kadosh la-adonai*). Israel is also referred to as a "holy nation" (*goy kadosh*). (See Chapter Three, "Ronald Clements,," and note #3 to the chapter.)

Question:

- In referring to Jews today—those living in and out of the State of Israel—are they members of a "people" (an *am*) or of a "nation" (a *goy*)? Is there a distinction between the two terms? If so, what is it?

VI. *Religious Norms: Feasible?*

Scripture expects the affairs of a nation to be conducted in accordance with moral/ethical/religious norms. (See Supplement V, "The Jewish People and the Land of Israel: A Union For Service to Mankind.")

Questions:

- Does such a view apply to the State of Israel today, in continuity with this spiritual tradition? Is it a practical, reachable requirement? Is Israel to be judged for shortcomings regarding these requirements? And who is to judge?

- If scripture's expectations of moral/ethical/religious requirements does apply to the State of Israel today, is she the only nation so obliged and so judged? Are faithful Muslims and Christians who accept the moral/ethical/ religious norms of the biblical/Koranic traditions similarly obliged to live by their norms and obliged to judge the affairs of *their* nations in accordance with *their* scriptural criteria? Assuming they accept such obligations, do they, in fact, do so with the same emphasis and passion that they, along with Jews themselves, employ with regard to the people and State of Israel today?

VII. *The Land as a Means*

In the Deuteronomic perspective, the land is the basic instrumentality through which Israel can fulfill her role and function in the world. (See "Synopsis of Findings.") Israel Friedlander has articulated this notion in contemporary terms:

> The land is not an end in itself, an agency for political aggrandizement and the injustice and oppression that goes with it, but it is a means to an end, the physical vessel for spiritual content, the material agency for the consummation of the great ideals of justice and righteousness....[1]

Questions:
- Can Jews in the diaspora, without the instrument of land, fulfill such a role and function in the world?

- How does one account for the people of Israel surviving as a distinct entity for two millennia *without* the land?

VIII. *Statehood and Religion*

We have pointed out in this work that the land of Israel is a holy land because the people of Israel is a "holy people", which is to say that the *Jewish enterprise is fundamentally a religious one.*

Questions:
- Because of the fundamentally religious nature of the Jewish

enterprise as indicated, we pose this question: Could this be the reason for the opposition to the very idea of a distinctive secular Jewish state on the part of prominent contemporary Jewish intellectuals? To assist in considering this question, we quote Yoram Hazony:

> When the idea of establishing a sovereign state for the Jewish people was made the goal of the Zionist Organization, it was greeted by many Jewish intellectuals as an abomination. Thinkers such as Hermann Cohen and Franz Rosenzweig—and later Martin Buber, Gershom Scholem, Hannah Arendt, Albert Einstein, and Hans Kohn—all opposed the idea of a Jewish state.

> And for much the same reason: all of them argued that *the Jewish people was* in *its essence an achievement of the spirit* which would be degraded and corrupted *like all other nations,* the moment it was harnessed to tanks and explosives, politics and intrigues and bureaucracy. No state should be a Jewish one so that *the Jewish people as a whole and Judaism as a faith could be retained in perfect purity as an ideal.* [2]

In light of the above, would the Jewish people not be considered a disembodied spirit if detached from the real world of landedness?

To assist in considering this question, we quote Louis Ginsberg:

> The great expounders of the universalistic element in Judaism, the Prophets, were at the same time the staunchest *upholders* of Jewish nationalism. Not as if nationalism belongs to the essence of Jewish religion, but because it is necessary for its existence. Breath is not a part of man, it comes to us from without, yet no one can live

without breathing. Nationalism is the air in which the Jew breathes.

> Those among us who rest in a vague ethical monotheism, deprived of organic contact with the past, are idle dreamers. As well hope that an uprooted tree might flourish. For there can be no Judaism without Jews, and there can be no Jews without the bond of a common love for the past of our people, of a common belief in its future. In Judaism, religion and history are inseparably woven; the one draws nutriment from the other.[3]

- Has exile from a concrete homeland been considered by classical Judaism an abnormality, an evisceration of a fundamental element of the nature of the Jewish enterprise?

- Is landedness indeed but a peril, a snare, yet also a home, a promise for natural growth and blessing?

For additional exploration of this issue, see Supplement VII, "Religion and State: The Ongoing Tension."

IX. *Evangelicals and Israel*

As we know, in our time, the Christian evangelical domain, for the most part, is a fervent supporter of the State of Israel. We know, as well, that this powerful support is based on a carefully worked out theological scheme concerning the messianic age, the "Millennium," as evangelical Christians designate it. The following summarizes the formulation of this perspective by John Walvoord, a leading conservative evangelical theologian:

The trials of the Jewish people stem from the basic conflict between divine purpose and "satanic" opposition. The very fact that God selected Israel as a special means of divine revelation is what makes her the object of harsh attack. Scripture has predicted and depicted Israel's dreadful suffering; however, God will redeem this people and re-establish it on the Promised Land. This, for Christians, is a firmly held belief and accounts for the fervent support for the State of Israel in our time; it is God's will. (The italics are mine in what follows):

> This return of Israel to her ancient land and the establishment of the State of Israel is the first step in a sequence of events that will culminate in the messiah's millennial kingdom on earth. The present return of Israel is the prelude and will be followed by the dark hour of their suffering in the great tribulation.
>
> *Heartrending as it may be to contemplate, the people of Israel who are returning to their ancient land are placing themselves within the vortex of this future whirlwind that will destroy the majority of those living in the land of Palestine. The searching and refining fire of divine judgment will produce in Israel that which is not there now—an attitude of true repentance and eager anticipation of the coming of the Messiah.* The tribulation period will then be followed by Israel's days of glory in the millennium marked by her new faith (John Walvoord in his *Israel and Prophecy*, p. 113).

Questions:
- How ought the leaders of the State of Israel, Jews in the diaspora, as well as non-evangelical Christians react to this theological thought line?

On one hand, the powerful political evangelical support for the State of Israel is a major plus for the state's security and well-being. Worry about the millennium can wait till it arrives!

On the other hand, this theology, of necessity, projects suffering for the Jewish people and its ultimate demise as a distinct people with a faith independent of Christianity—this because of its resistance to belief in Jesus as the messiah. Hence, should even beneficial support of Israel be welcome?

X. *Evangelicals vis-à-vis Jews, Muslims, Hindus*

According to evangelical thinkers, the millennial age not only affirms that the messiah will reign from Mount Zion, but that all nations of the world will come under his reign, which requires faith and acceptance of him. *This includes all peoples, all languages, all cultures everywhere on God's planet* (Walvoord, p. 120). Clearly, this notion encompasses the many millions of Muslims, Hindus and other non-Christian faith communities who eschew such faith and acceptance.

Questions:

- Why is it that evangelical calls to faith in the Christian messiah is not nearly as emphatic toward Muslims and Hindus as it is to Jews?

- If such weak emphasis on outreach to Muslims and Hindus in contrast to Jews is, indeed, the case, is this only because Jews are specifically cited in scripture as a special element in the Christian millennial process? Or is it because, in contrast to Muslims and Hindus, Jews are miniscule in number, hence more vulnerable and reachable? Or is it because an aggressive outreach to Muslims and Hindus would not be tolerated and/or because their massive numbers as candidates for another faith would be but a remote possibility and hence not a practical undertaking?

XI. *Selective Salvation*

The millennium will be characterized by justice and righteousness and universal peace, according to evangelical thought. At the same time, non-believers will be purged out of the millennium at its very beginning, and hence not beneficiaries of its blessings (Walvoord, pp. 122-123).

Questions:

- How are religionists to think about such selective entitlement to the blessings of a future world?

- While many Christians, of course, have not embraced the evangelical millennial construct with regard to the State of Israel and the Jewish people, the resistance of Jews to accepting the central Christian doctrine of belief in Jesus as the messiah remains for them theologically problematic. For non-evangelical Christians, therefore, do not Jews remain without salvation even as evangelicals believe?[4]

XII. *Israel and Exile*

The Zion-intoxicated poet of medieval times, Yehudah Halevi, delivered himself of this passionate plea: "Zion, won't you ask about the well-being of thy prisoners?"

Clearly, the poet was referring to his fellow Jews living throughout the diaspora, a condition he considered as exile, an unfortunate condition of those living outside the Land of Israel.

Question:

- Assuming that "exile" (*galut*) defines the condition of Jews (the dominant view as per scripture and the rabbis), should "exile" continue to define the condition of Jews outside the State of Israel in our time?

XIII. *The Relationship Between Israel and Diaspora Jewry*

Gershom Scholem in his *Israel and the Diaspora* poses the following...

Questions:

- "Is Israel, created by the forces of the Jewish people and out of the condition of the Diaspora, destined to detach itself once and for all from that condition and to lead a new life as a new nation with a new rootedness in the events of the recent years?"

- "Or are we rather dealing with a whole whose parts are mutually dependent on each other, where the isolation of one part, no matter how crucial a link or constituent, must lead to the destruction of the whole?"

Note: For a discussion about the link between Jews inside and outside the land, see Supplement VI.

XIV. *The Land as the Natural Environment*

Much has been written about man's responsibility for the natural environment based on the scriptural sources, especially on the kinds of materials delineated in this book. Issues such as pollution of our air and water, ravaging our natural resources, overpopulation, and the indiscriminate exploitation of the land—these have been interpreted in detailed theological categories.[5] For our purposes here I include but one set of questions that appear to flow from the text of this book.

In Deuteronomy land is a home, a place of rest, a place of vast possibility.

Questions:

- How does this outlook speak to problems in modern society caused by rootlessness and great mobility wherein people are detached from their places of origin?

- How does the Deuteronomic notion about land speak to the contemporary condition of many for whom land in general is an abstraction rather than a physical reality in their lives?

- How does the idea of "home" help define the identity of individuals and groups?

- What are the implications of this outlook on land for peoples' responsibility toward the land in particular, and the natural environment in general?

NOTES

BIBLIOGRAPHY

INDEX OF AUTHORS CITED

ABOUT THE AUTHOR

NOTES

PART ONE

INTRODUCTION AND "ROAD MAP"

1. See Chapter 6, "The Land in Talmudic and Medieval Periods," and Chapter 7, "The Land in the Modern Period."

2. For an analysis of Deuteronomy as the central biblical text about the land, see Arnold Eisen, *Galut: Modern Jewish Reflections on Homelessness and Homecoming*, Chapter 2, "Imagining Home: Deuteronomy," pp. 19-34.

CHAPTER ONE

THE PROMISED LAND AS GIFT

1. The following are the texts that speak about the Promised Land as gift: 5:16, 5:28, 6:10-11, 6:23, 7:13, 8:10, 9:4-6, 9:23, 10:11, 11:9, 11:17, 11:21, 11:31, 12:1, 12:9, 15:4, 15:7, 16:20, 17:14, 18:9, 19:1-2, 19:8, 19:10, 19:14, 20:16, 21:1, 21:23, 24:4, 25:15, 25:19, 26:1-11, 26:15.

2. Albrecht Alt, "The God of the Fathers," *Essays in Old Testament History and Religion*, p. 84. For detailed discussion of the origin of the promise concept, see Alt, ibid., p. 3 ff; R. E. Clements, *Abraham and David*, pp. 15-22; W. Zimmerli, "Promise and Fulfillment" in *Essays in Old Testament Hermeneutics*, pp. 89 f; M. Noth, *A History of Pentateuchal Traditions*, p. 54 ff.

3. *The "Covenant Between the Pieces": Very Old?*

A close reading of the full text of the "Covenant Between the Pieces" (Genesis 15:17-21) reveals this passage embedded in it: "...Know well that your offspring shall be strangers in a land not theirs, and they shall be enslaved and oppressed four hundred years; but I will execute judgment on the nation they shall serve, and in the end they shall go free with great wealth." This appears to be a veiled reference to the later experiences of the Israelites in Egypt some five hundred years later than Abram's time. According to the accepted view of modern biblical scholarship, this covenant incident was incorporated in the "J" (Yahwist) document, one of the book of Genesis' basic sources, which document was compiled during the period of Kings David and Solomon, i.e., the mid-10th century BCE from earlier oral and written materials. This would suggest a much later period than that of Abraham, i.e., ca 1800 BCE for the provenance of the "Covenant Between the Pieces" vision. However, Albrecht Alt claims this text and the experiences it portrays is very old and indeed its provenance in the era of Abraham. He does so by separating out the promise of the land to Abraham from the Egyptian allusion claiming thereby the "Between the Pieces" element to be of hoary antiquity. This claim is based on the assumption that the vision as we have it is based on much older oral and written sources from which the "Between the Pieces" derive. (See Alt, "God of the Fathers" article mentioned above. Also Martin Noth in his *A History of Pentateuchal Traditions*, pp. 54-58.)

4. *Responses, Not Conditions Accepted:* As pointed out later in this chapter, some of the references in the contexts of these covenants to Abraham's positive actions are *responses* to the covenant promises, and *not conditions accepted* for their being vouchsafed to him. For example, Abraham is to "walk in My ways and be blameless," God declares (Gen. 17:1). Circumcision as a "sign" of the covenant (Gen. 17:10). "Abraham believed in the Lord and He [God] counted it for him for righteousness" (Gen. 15:6). This covenant in its three basic forms were originally and subsequently always unconditional.

5. For this exposition of the land promise by the J source, see G. von Rad, "The Promised Land and YHWH's Land" in *The Problem of the Hexateuch and Other Essays*, pp. 82-84.

6. This is a key Deuteronomic text that emphasizes the notion of the land as a gift. It is contained in the Ceremony of the First Fruits, which has come to be labeled a credo. Note the following analysis of this passage by Leah Shechter:

The Ceremony of the First Fruits: Meaning Embedded in Its Structure (Deut. 26:1-11)

In verses 5-9 a credo was recited in a cultic setting when the first fruits of the harvest were offered:

> A wandering Aramean was my father; and he went down into Egypt and sojourned there, few in number; and there he became a nation, great, mighty and populous. And the Egyptians treated us harshly, and afflicted us, and laid upon us hard bondage. Then we cried to the Lord the God of our fathers, and the Lord heard our voice, and saw our affliction, our toil and our oppression. And the Lord brought us out of Egypt with a mighty hand and an outstretched arm, with great terror, with signs and wonders. And He brought us into this place and gave us this land, a land flowing with milk and honey. And behold, now I bring the first of the fruit of the ground, which Thou, O Lord, hast given me.

Close examination of both the language and structure of this credo reveals stress on the importance of the notion of the land as the gift of God. In the passage containing instructions and the credo itself the God of history and the Giver of the land is mentioned fourteen times as if to emphasize that He is one and the same. Fourteen as a mulitple of seven connotes perfection and consummation, which is what the gift of land means for Israel (see Chapter Two for the symbolism of the number seven in scripture).

Further, the literary structure of the credo suggests the preeminent importance of the land gift. The credo is structured into three main groupings based on the use of verbs. There are three sets of actions followed by a response or reaction, as follows:

Action 1

... A wandering Aramean was my father
... And he went down into Egypt
... And he sojourned there, few in number

Reaction 1

...   And he became there a nation, great, mighty, and populous

Action 2

...   And the Egyptians treated us harshly
...   And they afflicted us
...   And laid upon us hard labor

Reaction 2

...   And we cried to the Lord, the God of our fathers

Action 3

...   And the Lord heard our voice
...   And He saw our affliction, our toil and our oppression
...   And the Lord brought us out of Egypt

Reaction 3

...   And He brought us to this place

Culminating Reaction

...   And He gave us this land, a land flowing with milk and honey.

With Reaction 3, "And He brought us to this place," the symmetry of the credo is completed. But this is not its final statement, which in fact is: "And He gave us this land, a land flowing with milk and honey." Structurally, this statement stands by itself. It is not only that the gift of land is the "grand finale" of the saving history contextually, but structurally it gains for itself special recognition. It is not only "and He brought us to this place," but also "and He gave us this land...," which is the concluding statement. The "bringing" follows the regular flow of the structural pattern; the "giving" is set into relief. God's gift of land is thus proclaimed the gift par excellence—part of the saving history, to be sure, but on a level all its own.

7. John Walvoord, *Israel in Prophecy*, p. 43.

8. Moshe Weinfeld, *Deuteronomy and the Deuteronomic School*, p. 74f.

See also his "The Covenant of Grant in the Old Testament and in the Ancient Near East," JAOS 90 (1970).

Inconsistent Scholarship: Harry Orlinsky takes issue with the notion of the Abrahamic covenant being illuminated by two ancient Near Eastern treaties, it being of the "grant" type versus the "vassal" type, and thus represents a gift from master to servant without conditions. So, too, the Abrahamic covenant: master (God) grants a pact to servant (Israel) without stipulations for reciprocity. Orlinsky writes the following:

"Whether the biblical concept of the covenant between God and Israel derived from the Mesopotamian concept of the suzerain treaty— and in which period and milieu—or not, is not relevant to this study. I have never been persuaded by the arguments for the Mesopotamian suzerain origin for the nature of the biblical concept.... While the discovery of parallels elsewhere in the Near East to various aspects of the biblical covenant, including that of terminology, is a useful scholarly pursuit, more care should first be taken to determine the precise nature of the biblical covenant; moreover, sight should not be lost of the important fact that parallels in societies that are much the same, in this case agricultural-commercial, do not automatically indicate borrowing and dependence" (*The Land of Israel: Jewish Perspectives*, pp. 56-57).

Yet this is perilously close to what Orlinsky himself does when making the case for the Hebrew root *ntn* signifying not simply to "give" but to "assign, deed, transfer, convey." He contends that this term was used as a legal real estate term to indicate transfer of ownership of or title to a piece of property. He then proceeds to buttress his contention by citing Near Eastern parallels extensively: Egyptian sources that contain a corresponding term *yhv* in Aramaic real estate documents of the Jewish community at Elephantine.

I wonder how one is to understand this inconsistency.

9. *Unearned Gift and Human Action:* This notion of Israel's own action in taking possession of the land is derived from the Deuteronomic texts. In several passages that contain the idea of the promised land as gift, note the following linguistic pattern: The Lord (הֹ' נֹתֵן לְךָ) gives/

gave (לָכֶם) you/them (לָהֶם) land (אֲדָמָה / אֶרֶץ) to possess (לְרִשְׁתָּהּ). What is the purpose of the additional words "to possess" here? Without "to possess" the clause already has the basic terms needed to convey the content of the idea, of (a) giver, (b) recipient, (c) object. Thus this basic pattern would be sufficient unto itself to express the notion of gift. In addition, however, we find the concept of "possession" linked to gift by means of the word ירש in various forms. Further, the word most associated with dispossessing the native peoples is the same word (ירש) used to depict possession of the land. *Israel is able to take possession because by her own initiative she dispossesses the seven nations living in it* (7:1). And so, from Deuteronomy's language there emerges a connection between the notion of an unearned gift and the human action envisioned to actualize it.

10. See P. Miller on this idea, "The Gift of God," *Interpretation*, 23 (1969), p. 455.

11. An elaboration of the Holy War genre in Deuteronomy is seen in Joshua 1-12. The stereotyped mode of expression goes something like this: God has given Jericho into your hands (Joshua 6:2); there is a miracle during the battle that tilts events in Israel's favor (10;12-13, cf. Judges 5:20-21); the enemy becomes confused and bewildered (Joshua 8:21); cities are put to the ban (Joshua 11:12, 20). On the subject of Holy War see G. von Rad, *Der Heilige Krieg in Alten Israel*; see also Leah Shechter, "Holy War: History of a Tradition," in *The Day of the Lord in Jeremiah*, pp, 28-42.

12. See Josh. 23:14 for the Deuteronomist's assertion that "not one word from all the good words that the Lord your God has spoken to you has failed; everything has come to pass for you; not one thing failed to be realized."

13. See G. von Rad, *Deuteronomy*, p. 25.

14. For additional indications of Baal worship in Israel, see Hosea. 11:2; Jer. 2:20, 12:16, 19:5; Judges 2:13, 6:25, 28:30; I Kg. 16:32; II Kg. 10:19, 26, 27.

15. H. E. von Waldow in his "Israel and Her Land," p. 496, points out the great impact of this perception when he says, "This concept made the Lord so far superior to Baal that over the centuries Baal disappeared and the God of the Old Testament became the God of two world religions." M. Sweeney in a personal note.

16. The phrase "From Thee unto Thine" is the beginning of a sacrificial formula among worshippers in the present-day Middle East. See M. Buber, *On Zion*, p. 5.

CHAPTER TWO

THE PROMISED LAND AS OATH

1. Ronald Clements, *Abraham and David*, p. 64.

2. The following are the texts that speak of the land in terms of a divine oath to the patriarchs: 6:10, 6:18, 6:23, 7:13, 8:1, 9:5, 10:11, 11:9, 11:21, 19:8, 26:3, 26:15. For a full technical exposition of these texts, see Jack Shechter dissertation *The Theology of the Land in Deuteronomy*, pp. 18-24.

3. For amplifying information on the subject of "oath" in the Bible see Sheldon Blank, "The Curse, Blasphemy, the Spell, and the Oath," *HUCA* 23/1 (1950-51), pp. 73-95; Manfred Lehmann, "Biblical Oaths," *ZAW* 81 (1969), pp. 74-92; "Oaths," *Interpreters Dictionary of the Bible*, Vol. 3, pp. 575-577.

The Meaning of "Seven": The Bible has two words for "to swear"-- שבע and אלה. "Seven" is from the same root as "swear" and means "to come under the influence of seven things." The word signifies wholeness, completion; the number is the embodiment of things perfect, of awe-inspiring Divine power. Hence, whatever is inspired by the sevenness of the world amounts to wholeness. Likewise, the oath that appeals to Divine powers as expressed in the number seven, שֶׁבַע is thus rendered whole. And so when a person takes an oath, he asserts his integrity by associating himself with the number seven, which symbolizes wholeness with God. With regard to the second word for "swear," אלה, which literally means "curse," the two words (שבע/אלה) often appear together (Numbers 5:21, I Kings 8:31, II Chronicles 6:22, Nehemiah 10:30). Thus the force of the oath is enhanced by adding a curse on the vower should truth be absent in his words.

4. Amos 6:8 and 8:7, Genesis 22:16; Exodus 32:13.

5. Marvin Sweeney has directed us to a more detailed account of this historical development. This account shows that strong Assyrian rule was indeed cast off in Josiah's time, and Egyptian rule took its place. The account in our text attests that this Egyptian rule was more laissez-faire than the former Assyrian rule insofar as Josiah's Judah and the northern Israel realm were concerned. Thus, this factor did allow Josiah to act as depicted in our text. On this see Miller/Hayes, *A History of Israel*, p. 391f.

6. Isaiah 9:7; Amos 3:3-8; Habakuk 2:3.

Transition Stages in Life: The belief in the dangers inherent in an in-between stage where an action has begun but has not yet been completed is alluded to by G. von Rad concerning the laws of military release (Deut. 20:5-8). A man who has built a house but has not yet dedicated it; a man who planted a vineyard but has not yet tasted its fruit; a man who betrothed a woman but had not yet consummated the planned marriage—these all were released from military service. While on the surface these laws are motivated by humane considerations, they actually originated out of fear. According to ancient beliefs, anyone involved in inaugurating an activity and not completing it was threatened to an unusual degree by demons (see von Rad, *Deuteronomy*, p. 132).

In anthropological studies much has been said about the anxieties associated with transition stages, whether these are the normal life crisis points such as birth, puberty, marriage, death, or particular events such as going to war or planting a new crop. In these situations, one of the functions of religion is to provide the rites and rituals that facilitate, ease, help to satisfactorily negotiate the transition from these dangerous, anxiety-producing states. See on this Victor Turner, "Betwixt and Between" The Liminal Period in Rites of Passage," in *Proceedings of the American Ethnological Society* (1964), pp 4-20; Arnold von Gennep, *The Rites of Passage* (Routledge and Kegan Paul, 1960); Eliot Chappel and Carleton Coon, *Principles of Anthropology* (Henry Holt & Co., 1942).

It is especially interesting to note how Robert Cohn interprets the wilderness narrative in the Bible in terms of this "betwixt and between" category, i.e., the Israelites' condition after leaving Egypt and not yet in the Promised Land. (See Cohn's *The Shape of Sacred Space*, Chapter Two: "Liminality in the Wilderness").

7. *The Deuteronomic texts indicating the inclusive embrace of the oath detailed:*

- 10:11 = "to give to them," i.e., *the patriarchs*
- 11:9 = "to give to them and to their children," i.e., to *the patriarchs and latter's descendants*
- 11:21 = "to give to them, as long as the heavens are above the earth," i.e., *to patriarchs forever*
- 6:10 = "to give to you," i.e., *Moses generation*
- 7:13 = "to give to you," i.e., *Moses generation*
- 19:8 = "and gives you," i.e., *Moses generation*
- 6:23 = "to give to us," i.e., *Moses' generation and Josiah's generation*
- 26:3 = "to give to us," i.e., *Moses' generation and Josiah's generation*
- 26:15 = "you have given us," i.e., *Moses' generation and Josiah's generation*

8. J. Pedersen, *Israel: Its Life and Culture*, pp. 474-479.

9. Levenson, *Sinai and Zion*, p. 38.

10. G. von Rad, *Old Testament Theology*, Vol. II, p. 104 f.

11. G. von Rad, "The Promised Land and Yahweh's Land," in *The Problem of the Hexateuch*, pp. 79-93.

12. Pritchard, *ANET*, p. 68 f.

13. For this data see Walther Zimmerli, "Promise and Fulfillment," in *Essays in Old Testament Hermeneutics*, pp. 95-96.

14. See Chapter Eleven for detailed discussion of this issue: the mythic/cultic versus historic notion of land.

CHAPTER THREE

THE LAND AND THE LAW

1. *Laws as norm for life in the land*—11:31-32, 12:1, 12:8-11, 17:14-15, 19:1-2, 19:8-10, 21:1-2, 25:19, 26:1-2.

2. *Laws* associated *with the land*—5:16, 15:1-6, 16:18-20, 17:14-20, 18:9-15, 19:1-13, 21:1-9, 21:22-23, 23:20-21, 24:1-4, 25:13-16.

3. *Land laws*—14:22-29, 16:9-12, 16:13-15, 18:3-5, 19:14, 22:9, 22:10, 23:25-26, 24:19-22, 25:4, 26:1-4, 26:12-15.

4. *Law as* condition—5:16, 5:28-30, 6:1-3, 6:16-19, 8:1, 8:6-10, 11:8-9, 11:13-17, 11:18-21, 11:22-25, 15:1-6, 16:18-20, 18:9-15, 19:8-9, 21:22-23, 23:20-21, 24:1-4, 25:13-16, 26:12-15.

5. *Against Mingling Dissimilar Things:* An example of but one of the laws to which the people were to adhere is the proscription of mingling dissimilar physical elements. Preserving the singularity of different natural species is part of the Divine plan and to blur the distinctions intended is to disrespect that plan. Examples: "A woman shall not wear man's clothing" (22:5); "you shall not sow your vineyard with two kinds of seed"; "you shall not plow with an ox and an ass together"; "you shall not wear mingled stuff, wool and linen together" (22:9-11). The purpose of these laws is to teach that God has made distinctions in the natural and human world and it is wrong for man to try to obliterate them by the process of intermixing. Each species is designed to be distinct; each has its own unique characteristics. This is a principle visibly impressed by the Creator of the world of nature and is not to be thwarted by man. See Walther Eichrodt, *Theology of the Old Testament*, Vol. 2, pp. 118-119.

According to G. von Rad in his *Deuteronomy*, p. 141, the prohibition against the mingling of dissimilar things strikes at age-old magic customs which endangered the purity of the religion of the Lord. For example, the ordinance against men and women wearing clothing of the opposite sex was in reaction to a cultic practice of masquerading in clothing of the opposite sex before the goddess Astarte. This we learn from a later source, Lucian of Samosata of Antioch in Asia Minor, a prominent theologian of the third century C.E., who studied the roots of biblical practice.

6. See Marvin Sweeney, *King Josiah of Judah*, pp. 150-158, for a detailed description of Deuteronomy's concern for the disadvantaged.

7. See Martin Noth, *The Laws of the Pentateuch*, pp. 44-45. For further amplification of the cultic origins of Deuteronomy and its connection with the Sinai covenant, see G. von Rad, *The Problem of the Hexateuch*, pp. 26-33.

8. See Bernard Levinson, *Deuteronomy and the Hermeneutics of Legal Innovation, Chapter One*, for the clear link between Deuteronomy and the Covenant Code. See also P. C. Craige, *The Book of Deuteronomy*, who emphasizes Deuteronomy as the renewal of the Sinai covenant.

CHAPTER FOUR

THE INTEGRATION OF THE UNCONDITIONAL AND CONDITIONAL CONVENANTS

1. Walter Brueggeman describes the tension between these two covenants in his book *The Prophetic Imagination*.

2. *History of the Covenants: Sources.* This account is my own reconstruction based on the work of John Bright, *A History of Israel*, pp. 220-223, 227-296, 315-321; R. E. Clements, *Abraham and David*, pp. 61-68; W. D. Davies, *The Gospel and the Land*, pp. 15-20. For the emphasis on the notion of the unconditionality of the Davidic covenant, see Levenson, *Sinai and Zion*, pp. 101, 212-213, as well as George Mendenhall, *The Tenth Generation*, p. 87, and Walter Brueggeman, "The Epistemological Crisis in Israel's Two Histories (Jeremiah 9:22-23)," in *Israelite Wisdom*, Missoula: Scholars, 1978.

3. *The Puritans of New England:* In this connection, it is interesting to note Belden Lane's depiction of the predicament of the Puritans of New England—their impermanence as pilgrims while simultaneously yearning for rootedness in the new land—in terms of the Bible's covenants. On the one hand, the conditional Mosaic covenant suggested precariousness based on humans' non-adherence to the law; and on the other hand, there was the unconditional Abrahamic/Davidic covenant that suggested permanent rootedness based on God's irrevocable word. The question then was how the American Puritans were to conceive of their own covenant with God (*Landscapes of the Sacred*, p. 114).

4. "Divine Commitment and Human Obligation," *Interpretation*, 1964, pp. 13-14.

5. *Deuteronomy*, Interpreters' Bible II, pp. 403-404.

6. *The Problem of the Hexateuch,* p. 221.

7. *The History of Israel,* p. 221.

8. *Sinai and Zion,* pp. 45, 99, 211.

9. See #VI in the "Questions" section of this book for contemporary implications of the issue here discussed.

10. For Simon: "The Biblical Destinies—Conditional Promises," *Tradition*, Volume 17, No. 2, pp. 84-90.

For Kaplan: "Divine Promises—Conditional and Absolute," *Tradition*, Volume 18, No. 1, pp. 35-42.

CHAPTER FIVE

THE LAND IN THE PROPHETS AND THE WRITINGS

1. *Interpreter's Dictionary of the Bible,* Volume 3, p. 913.

2. Most scholars agree that Amos 9:11-15 could not have been spoken by Amos inasmuch as there is a reference here to "the fallen booth of David," i.e., the Jerusalem kingdom that fell with the destruction of Judah. During Amos' time the kingdom of Judah in the south had reached its zenith in terms of material wealth and well-being. It would not have been described as a "fallen booth."

3. W. D. Davies, *The Gospel and the Land,* p. 108; R. Clements, *Abraham and David,* pp. 66-68.

4. For further tracing of this construct, and its continuity in later history, see Chapters Six and Seven.

All other sources for this chapter are cited in the body of the text.

CHAPTER SIX

THE LAND IN TALMUDIC
AND MEDIEVAL PERIODS

1. In time, the rabbis established the principle of דִּינָא דְמַלְכוּתָא דִּינָא, "The law of the kingdom is the law," meaning that Jews were obligated to obey the laws of the land in which they lived.

2. *Orla*: Lev. 19:23. With regard to fruit trees, there is a rule that only fourth-year fruits are eligible for offerings.

Omer: Lev. 23:10. This refers to bundles of stalks bound together after reaping and brought to the priest.

Shmitta: Lev. 25:2. This is the law of the sabbatical year during which the land itself is to observe a rest from the planting cycle.

Peyah: Lev. 25:22. This law obligates the farmer not to cut the corners of the field but to leave that area for the poor and the stranger.

Shikhah: Lev. 23:22. The law that forbids the farmer from gleaning his field. This too should be left for the poor and the stranger.

Ma-aser: Deut. 14:22 ff. The law that obligates the farmer to set aside a tenth part of the yield of the field for the clergy. In addition, there are tithes such as *masser ani*, which is to be set aside for the Levite, the stranger, the orphan and the widow.

Bikkurim: Deut. 26:1 ff. This law pertains to the first fruits of the harvest, which the farmer was to bring to the Temple each year.

For a reliable set of sources dealing with the rabbinic notion of the land, see the following:

- "Eretz Yisrael" in *Encyclopedia Talmudica* (Vol. 3), pp. 1-68, or the Hebrew version published by *Hamerkaz Ha-olami shel Mizrachi*, "Eretz Yisrael," pp. 199-235.

- *Eretz Yisrael Ubyoteha* by Shmuel Zvi Herman (Yeshivat Ohel Yosef, Bnai Brak, 1984). This volume deals with both classical and modern issues pertaining to the land.

- W. D. Davies, *The Gospel and the Land*, pp. 54-74, and *The*

Territorial Imperative, pp. 100-110. These volumes provide a full and detailed roster of the classical rabbinic sources on the subject.

3. Rashi, *Commentary on Genesis*, 17:2.

4. Nachmanides, *Commentary on Leviticus*, 8;25 and 25:2.

5. David Kimchi, *Commentary on Isaiah*, 52:1 and 63:1.

6. Rashi, *Commentary on Genesis*, 1:1.

7. Michael Signer, "The Land in Medieval Literature," in Lawrence Hoffman, ed., *The Land of Israel*, p. 226.

8. *On Exile and Return: The Shekhina* In thinking further about the reason for God's presence, His *Shekhina*, going into exile with His people Israel, it is because of God's empathy that He went where His people went. Yet also those of Israel in exile who are genuinely faithful, on whom the *Shekhina* dwelt during their dispersion and who ascend to the Holy Land take this *Shekhina* with them. Thus they not only gather together the assembly of Israel, but also lead to the re-concentration of the *Shekhina* itself in the place.

9. Gershom Scholem, *Major Trends in Jewish Mysticism*, p. 261. See also Scholem's summary of Lurianic Kabbalah in chapter VII of his book. In this summary exposition I have followed the thought-line of J. Z. Smith in his *Map is Not Territory*, pp. 122-126.

10. See Scholem, ibid., p. 284. For the quote see *Sefer Halikutim*, 89:6. For a detailed discussion about the Kabbalah and the Land of Israel, see Moshe Idel, "The Land of Israel in the Medieval Kabbalah," in Lawrence Hoffman, ed., *The Land of Israel*, p. 170 ff.

11. Martin Buber, *Hasidism and Modern Man*, pp. 187-189 and his *Hasidim*, pp. 7-8. For details on how this notion of the lost sparks is experienced and enacted in ritual (e.g., Shabbat eve), see Gershom Scholem, *On the Kabbalah and Its Mysticism*, pp. 148-150.

12. Moshe Idel, "The Land of Israel in Medieval Kabbalah," in Lawrence Hoffman, ed., *The Land of Israel*, pp. 180-181.

CHAPTER SEVEN

THE LAND IN THE MODERN PERIOD

1. Mordecai Kaplan has emphasized avoidance of denigration of the diaspora. See his *A New Zionism*, pp. 19-22.

2. *The Martin Buber Reader*, ed. Asher Biemann, Palgrave/Macmillan, New York, NY, 2002, p. 129

3. *Siddur Hadash*, pp. 442-444. Though the English translation of the original Hebrew is an adaptation, it retains its essential meaning. It is interesting to note the longstanding Christian theological notion—since significantly altered due to the rise of the State of Israel—that the dispersion and suffering of the Jews in exile are punishment inflicted on them by God for the "sin" of having rejected Jesus.

4. Arthur Hertzberg, *The Zionist Idea*, p. 106.

5. Hertzberg, ibid., p. 112.

6. Hertzberg, ibid., p. 403.

7. Hertzberg, ibid., p. 420. For the essence of Rav Kook's emphasis on the centrality of the Land of Israel in the life of the Jewish people, for the religious and non-religious alike, see Bezalel Naor, "Eretz Yisrael," in *Kook-Orot*, pp. 89-95 and 209-210.

8. For this explication of Buber, see Ben Zion Bokser, *Jews, Judaism and the State of Israel*, pp. 47-48.

9. See Solomon Schechter, *Seminary Addresses*, pp. 91-104.

10. Arnold Eisen, *Modern Jewish Reflections on Homelessness and Homecoming*, p. 60.

11. Eisen, ibid., p. 66.

12. Hess, *Rome and Jerusalem*, pp. 43 and 55.

13. Hertzberg, ibid., pp. 184-185.

14. Hertzberg, ibid., p. 194.

15. Eisen, ibid., p. 60. For more on Herzl's emphasis on the traditional religious idea of the land of Israel as a state—this as a driving inspirational force of Zionism, see *Theodore Herzl* (edited by Ludwig Lewisohn), pp. 233-255.

16. Avi Ehrich, *Ancient Judaism*, p. 14.

17. Ahad Ha-am, *Complete Writings*, pp. 43-44.

18. Hertzberg, ibid., pp. 373-375.

19. Hertzberg, ibid., pp. 606-619.

PART TWO

CHAPTER EIGHT

THE LAND AS A GOOD LAND

1. The following are the texts that speak of the land as a good land: 6:3, 6:10-11, 6:18, 8:7-10, 9:6, 11:9, 11:10-12, 11:14-15, 11:17, 26:9, 26:15.

2. M. Eliade, "Sacred Space and Making the World Sacred," *The Sacred and the Profane*, pp. 20-65. See also Brevard Childs, "The Concept of Space," in *Myth and Reality in the Old Testament*, pp. 84-94, for an illuminating contrast between mythical and biblical space.

3. M. Eliade, op. cit., p. 30. For additional examples of this basic ancient idea see also Raphael Patai, *Man and Temple in Ancient Jewish Myth and Ritual*, pp. 105-113.

4. See John Bright, *A History of Israel*, p. 137 ff.

5. Flavius, Josephus, Antiquities *of the Jews*, Book 3, chapter 7:7. See also Jon Levenson in *Sinai and Zion*, pp. 122-127.

6. Eliade, op. cit., pp. 42-43.

7. See Weinfeld, Deuteronomy, pp. 246-50; A. S. Kopeland, "Temple Building, A Task for Gods and Kings," Or 32 (1963), pp. 56-62.

8. J. Pedersen, *Israel: Its Life and Culture*, p. 456; for the basic material in this section, see pp. 453-466.

9. For a useful summary of and expansion on the ideas alluded to here, see Jonathan Z. Smith, "Earth and Gods," *Map is Not Territory*, pp. 104-128.

10. Patrick Miller, "The Gift of God," *Interpretation* 23, p. 456.

11. R. Clements, *God's Chosen People*, p. 52.

12. G. von Rad, "The Promised Land and YHWH's Land in the Hexateuch," *The Problem of the Hexateuch and Other Essays*, p. 85; also E. von Waldow, "Israel and Her Land: Some Theological Reflections," *A Light Unto My Path*, pp. 493-496.

13. Y. Kaufmann, *The Religion of Israel*, pp. 288-290.

14. E. von Waldow, *A Light Unto My Path*, pp. 496-497.

CHAPTER NINE

THE LAND AS POSSIBILITY AND AS PERIL

1. I must acknowledge my indebtedness to Professor Walter Brueggemann for the basic thrust of this chapter, during which I have used some of his felicitous language. See his *The Land: Place as Gift, Promise, and Challenge in Biblical Faith.*.

2. Texts that, in one way or another, speak about the land as a home and place of rest: 7:1, 11:31, 12:9-10, 12:29, 15:4, 17:14, 19:1, 19:3, 19:10, 19:14, 21:23, 24:4, 25:19, 26:1.

Texts that speak in various ways about the land as a place of rest: Deut. 12:9-10, 19:10, 19:14, 21:23, 24:4, 25:19.

Texts that speak in various ways about the land as a locus for a good life: Deut. 5:16, 5:30, 6:3, 6:10-11, 7:13-15, 8:10, 11:9, 11:14, 11:21, 15:4, 16:15, 23:21, 25:15, 26:10-11.

3. See Pedersen on this in Chapter Eight.

4. See Eliade on this in Chapter Eight.

5. G. von Rad, *Old Testament Theology*, Vol. 1, p. 304.

6. G. von Rad, *The Problem of the Hexateuch*, p. 95

7. Because of the association of fertility with blessing, Pedersen suggests that the root *berekh* is connected with the Hebrew word for "knee" (*berekh*), which has been construed as a term for the abdominal region, the seat of the reproductive powers. So in Assyrian, *tarbit birki-ia*, which means "the seed of my knee," i.e., a son. Cf. Gen. 30:3, 50:23; Job 3:12. See Pedersen's *Israel*, I-II, p. 204 and note on p. 518. The first blessing given to the first male and female was to be fruitful and multiple (Gen. 1:22; cf. Gen. 15:5, 22:7, 28:14, 24:10; Proverbs 17:6; Psalm 127:4-5; Job 42:12-23). For an association of numerous progeny with defense from enemies, see Gen. 24:60, 61; Ps. 127:4, 5.

8. Deut. 28:21, 22, 27, 28, 35, in which the illnesses are enumerated. For a description of devastation wrought by a plague in an extra-biblical source, see "The Plague Prayer of Mursilis" in Pritchard's *ANET*, pp. 394-396.

9. G. von Rad, *Old Testament Theology*, p. 387 f.

10. *Life Expectancy:* According to Gen. 6:3 a person's allotted time was 120 years, while the Psalmist declares it to be 70 years and for the strong 80 years (Ps. 90:10). The ripe old age for Abraham was 175, for Isaac 180. L. Koehler in his *Der Hebraische Mensch* calculated the average life span of the kings of Judah to be approximately 45 years. When we realize that princes and kings were particularly well nourished and cared for, we would have to put the average person's life expectancy quite a bit lower.

11. Texts that speak in various ways about the land as peril: 6:10-15, 8:7-20, 9:1-6, 11:13-16, 12:29-30, 18:9-11.

12. The centrality of the law and the land as a dominant theme in Deuteronomy is discussed in Chapter Three.

13. *The theme of affluence leading to self-glorification and arrogance is widespread in scripture.* The affluent forget God (Prov. 30:9); they forsake God (Deut. 32:15); they rebel and cast away the law (Neh. 9:25); they lift up their heart (Hos. 13:6); they turn to other gods (Deut. 31:20); they are self-indulgent (Amos 6:1-6). Cf. Is. 25:11; Jer. 48:29; Prov. 29:23; Ezek. 29:3.

14. See Deut. 9:4 for a similar misinterpretation of power wherein Israel attributes possession of the land to her own righteousness. Note also the caution against self-reliance in connection with the laws for the king (Deut. 17:16 f.); the king is not to accumulate houses, women, silver and gold, which accumulation leads to arrogance: "that his heart may not be lifted up above his brethren."

15. *Worship of But One God:* The expression אֵל קַנָּא (a "jealous God") is found in the decalogue in conjunction with the proscription against worshipping other gods. Von Rad sees this "intolerant claim to exclusive worship" as something unique in the history of religion. He points out that in antiquity the cults left devotees a free hand to ensure blessings for themselves from the various gods available. In a temple, cultic gifts were often offered to other deities as well as to the god to whom the temple was dedicated—a situation that befell on occasion the temple of Solomon (II Kings 23:4). Further, behind the lists of unclean animals in Deut. 14:4 f. lies the cultic struggle in which animals used in alien cults were sacrally disqualified for Israel, which represents the final phase of the conflict with these cults. See G. von Rad, *Old Testament Theology*, Vol. 1, pp. 207-209.

16. W. Brueggemann, op cit., pp. 62-67.

CHAPTER TEN

ISRAEL AND THE "NATIONS" IN THE LAND

1. Additional texts in Deuteronomy that speak about the relationship of Israel to her neighbors in the land: 6:14-15, :18-19, 7:1-6, 7:14-16, 7:17-26, 8:19-20, 9:1-5, 11:23-25, 12:2-3, 12:9-10, 12:29-31, 15:6, 18:9-15, 19:1-3, 20:14b-18.

2. Martin Noth, *The History of Israel*, p. 141

3. For additional texts and a summary of the data on both sides of this issue, see a paper by Jack Shechter, "The Conquest of Palestine: Contrary Views in Light of the Literary and Archaeological Evidence" (Pittsburgh, 1970).

4. W. D. Davies, *The Territorial Dimension*, pp. 15-16.

5. *On a "Christian Witness" Concerning Nations Expropriating the Land of Others:* For a carefully documented analysis of Israel's relationship with the Canaanites in the land in the Hebrew bible, see Rolf Knierim's "Israel and the Nations in the Land of Palestine in the Old Testament" in *The Task of Old Testament Theology*, pp. 309-321.

Here is an example of the scholarly marshalling of biblical data which, in the author's view, points to the questionable actions of Israel in the context of her entry and occupation of the land. The moral view is invoked with emphasis in judging Israel negatively. The analysis then inevitably segues into the modern era with regard to the relationship between Jews and Arabs in Israel today. This all in the name not only of the Old Testament's testimony of justice and peace, but also of Christians today who walk in "the footsteps of Jesus Christ, the Lord." Indeed, Professor Knierim calls for a "Christian witness" to the presence of God in the affairs of *all* peoples of the world.

For the sake of consistency and in the name of the moral voice of Christianity on this issue—how nations other than Israel came into possession of their homelands—it would indeed be instructive to hear from Christian bible scholars how they relate Old and New Testament moral teachings to the ways in which Germany, Hungary, France, Norway, Australia and America came into being as homelands. Where and when does the world hear the voice of Christian witness that Professor Knierim calls for in these contexts? Where and when do we hear the "still small voice" or the not so still small voice of Jesus about the ways in which these nations came to be homelands of distinctive character?

6. See Avi Sagi, "The Punishment of Amalek in Jewish Tradition," Harvard Theological Review, Vol. 87, No. 3 (1994), pp. 323-346.

7. *Definition of "Nations":* "Seven nations" is the traditional term used in biblical scholarship, though a diversity exists among the twenty-six biblical passages enumerating the "nations" that inhabited Canaan before the formation of Israel. The number ranges from one to ten; the order exhibits great variation; the nations listed vary. We are not dealing here with Israel's relations with the foreign nations outside of Canaan such as the Edomites, Moabites, Ammonites and Arameans who lived along Canaan's eastern border, or with the Amalekites and Midianites in the southern desert region. Nor are we dealing with the traveling foreigner (נָכְרִי), resident alien (גֵּר) or sojourner (תּוֹשָׁב) who were absorbed into the dominant Israelite population and under its governance. What we are focusing on here is Israel's relationship to the nations (her neighbors) *in* the land.

8. The same perspective is adumbrated in I Kg. 14:24, 21:26; II Kg. 16:3, 17:8, 21:2, where a linkage between the abominable actions of the nations and the fact that God drove them out of the land is suggested.

9. *Child Sacrifice:* Anthony Phillips (*Cambridge Bible Commentary: Deuteronomy,* p. 125) indicates that the practice of child burning refers to the sacrifice to Moloch and was regarded as a type of magical practice. G. E. Wright (*Interpreters Bible: Deuteronomy,* p. 447) considers the practice a kind of "trial by ordeal of fire." S. R. Driver (*International Critical Commentary: Deuteronomy,* p. 222) indicates that child burning was not a form of idolatry but a superstition akin to divination and the other practices enumerated in Deut. 18:9-11.

10. See G. E. Wright, *Interpreters Bible: Deuteronomy,* pp. 446-447. For an illuminating discussion of the nature of divination in pagan religion, see Yehezkel Kaufmann, *The Religion of Israel,* pp. 42-52.

11. *For Pagan Thought and Practice—Sources:* The following are the works by Albright from which this description is culled: "The Role of the Canaanites in the History of Civilization," *The Bible and the Ancient Near East,* pp. 438-471—referred to henceforth as "BANE"; *YHWH and the Gods of Canaan,* pp. 110-152—referred to henceforth as "YGC"; *From the Stone Age to Christianity,* pp. 230-236—referred to henceforth as "FSAC." See *YGC,* pp. 198-207, where Albright takes direct issue with Y. Kaufmann's dissenting views on the issue of the nature of pagan religion, and *FSAC,* pp. 470-471; also R. de Vaux's *Ancient Israel,* pp. 441-446, who points out that Phoenician cultic practices, including child sacrifice, were in effect in the seventh and possibly sixth centuries BCE.

12. Y. Kaufmann, *The Religion of Israel,* p. 57, and Martin Noth in his

The History of Israel, p. 143. See also William La Sor, *Israel: A Biblical View*, pp. 41-42; for the relationship between myth and ritual, see Anthony Wallace, *Religion: An Anthropological View*, pp. 243-249, and Annemarie De Waal Malefijt, *Religion and Culture*, pp. 172-195.

13. M. Noth, *History of Israel*, p. 143

14. Nahum Sarna, *The Heritage of Biblical Israel*, p. 124 ff.

15. J. Pedersen, *Israel: Its Life and Culture*, pp. 474-479.

16. W. R. Smith, *The Religion of the Semites*, p. 29. See Durkheim, "Religion as a Collective Representation," Birnbaum/Lenzer, eds., *Sociology and Religion*, pp. 138-143. For an opposing view to that of Durkheim, Smith and Pedersen concerning the concept of a "collective soul" and of the sociological aspect of ancient faith, see Bronislaw Malinowski in *Sociology and Religion, op. cit., pp. 144-152.*

17. Levenson, *Sinai and Zion*, pp. 66-67.

18. Petuchowski in his *Zion Reconsidered*, pp. 80-81. For his inability to share this summation of the traditional notion, see pp. 84-87.)

For further discussion of Israel as a "Holy People," see Supplement V.

19. Martin Buber, *On Zion*, pp. 48-49.

20. Solomon Buber, ed., *Tanchuma, Bereshit II*; also Rashi, *Mikraot Gedolot, Bereshit* 1:1, quoting Midrash Rabbah, 1:1. See also Ps. 24:1, "The Earth is the Lord's...," the title of A. J. Heschel's book on the subject, and Ps. 50:12, Ex. 9:29 and Joshua 3:11-13. For data about this notion of God's ownership and control of the land (*not* His dwelling *in* it), see W. D. Davies, *The Gospel and the Land*, pp. 24-35.

21. Buber, ibid., p. 48-49.

22. W. D. Davies, op. cit., *The Territorial Dimension*. G. von Rad, "The Promised Land and YHWH's Land," in *The Problem of the Hexateuch*, pp. 85-89. See also A. Alt, "The God of the Fathers," *Essays in Old Testament History and Religion*, p. 71.

23. A. Alt, *The God of the Fathers*, p. 71.

24. Martin Buber, *On Zion*, p. 49.

CHAPTER ELEVEN

THE LAND AS "HOLY LAND"

1. Chapter Two.

2. Ronald Clements, *God's Chosen People*, pp. 12-13, 30-37, 50-58.

3. The same terminology depicting Israel's chosenness, i.e., עַם קָדוֹשׁ and עַם סְגֻלָּה , is used in Deut. 14:2, 21 and Deut. 26:17-19; the idea of Israel's special relationship to God is also found in Deut. 5:2-3 and 10:14-15; for the notion in other sources see Deut. 4:7-8, 4:12-14, 20, 27:9, 28:9; Gen. 12:1-3; Exodus 19:5-6, 22:31; Lev. 19:2; Num. 23:19-24; Amos 3:2.

4. Gerhard von Rad, *Old Testament Theology*, Volume 1, pp. 223-226.

5. Joseph Hertz, *The Pentateuch and Haftorahs*, p. 735.

6. G. E. Wright, *Deuteronomy*, Interpreters' Bible, Volume II, pp. 326-328.

7. Martin Buber, *On Zion*, p. 49.

8. Robert Wilken, *The Land Called Holy*, p. 265, note 42.

9. *We suggest another possible example of the notion of conferred holiness—a parallel experience to that of Moses at Horeb/Sinai, that of the prophet Elijah:*

In I Kings 19:5-12 the experience of the prophet Elijah with the Lord on Mount Horeb/Sinai has a striking similarity to that of Moses on that mountain. First in Exodus 3:5 Moses encounters a burning bush that is not being consumed. There he hears the voice of God, who commands: "Remove your sandals from your feet for the place *(hamakom)* on which you stand is holy ground *(admat kodesh hu)*. Later, Moses again experiences the Lord as he receives the Ten Commandments (Exodus 19:16-20:1-15). These encounters both directly (at the bush) and by implication (at commandment time) are what conferred sanctity on the mountain.

Elijah flees to the wilderness to escape the wrath of Queen Jezebel. The parallel of Elijah's experience with God to that of Moses at Mount Sinai/Horeb is manifest. First, Moses encounters God at a burning bush and first Elijah encounters God in his sleep under a "broom bush" (19:5-7). Moses neither eats nor drinks for forty days on the mountain (Ex. 34:28) and Elijah neither eats nor drinks for forty days as he walks to "the mountain of God, at Horeb" (19:8).   Moses "stands on the mountain" (Deut. 10:10) and Elijah is told to "stand on the mountain before God" (19:11). The Lord "passes by" Moses (Ex. 33:22) and "lo the Lord passed by" Elijah (19:11). The Lord came to Moses in "thunder and lightning and a dense cloud" (Ex. 19:16) and though Elijah experienced wind and earthquake and fire wherein God did not appear, the Lord did come to him in a *kol d'mama daka*, "a still small voice"—and as Moses had a "private audience" with the Lord (Exodus 20), so did Elijah (19:13-14).

The theophany depicted in I Kings is in response to Elijah's complaints about his people's backsliding and who have forsaken the covenant. No, proclaims the Lord, the covenant remains in force and "the voice" commands Elijah to leave his cave, return to society and do the Lord's work.

And so, we surmise that even as Moses' encounter with the Lord at Sinai/Horeb conferred sanctity on that mountain at that moment in time, so did the parallel experience of Elijah at his moment in time. (See Robert L. Cohn, *The Shape of Sacred Space*, pp. 53-54.)

Here the question inevitably arises: How could Sinai/Horeb, the mountain of Israel's transforming vision, come to be forgotten? Indeed, the site of Mount Sinai is unknown; its legacy has endured but the place from which it originated has long ago vanished from the consciousness of Israel. How is it possible that the encounter with the transcendent of the great Moses could not have rendered Sinai sacred for all time given the monumental consequence of that encounter?

Gunther Plaut responds to that question. It is possible, he says, that the failure of the Jewish tradition to preserve knowledge of the Sinai locale has its deeper reason. The Torah states expressly (Deut. 34:6) that the place of Moses' grave remains unknown, presumably in order that it not become a place of pilgrimage, and the person of the lawgiver the object of adulation or even adoration. "Similarly," Plaut avers, "had the locale of the *holy mountain* been firmly known in later centuries, Jerusalem and the Temple could never have become the center of Jewish life for they would have been inferior in *holiness to the sacred mountain.* Sinai thus became either by design or happenstance a concept rather than a place, its universal importance heightened by the vagueness of its site, its timelessness unfettered by an identifiable place" (Plaut in *The Torah: A Modern Commentary*, p. 520).

The above italics are those of this book's author. The implication of Plaut's comment is clear: *Sinai presumably did partake of sanctity but for strategic reasons the tradition blanketed it.*

Jon Levenson has also posed our question: How could the covenant theology attributed to Sinai be so pervasive in the developing religion of ancient Israel when the mountain itself ceased to play any role?

And Levenson responds that however much Deuteronomy and the texts written under its influence (such as I King 19) may wish to isolate the Sinaitic theophany from the continuing tradition, other texts made it evident that *an experience like that of Moses was still possible but on a different mountain.*

For example, such an experience is depicted in Psalm 97. Here, ,as in Exodus 19, the account of the Sinaitic theophany, the atmospheric phenomena and pyrotechnics are stressed, rather than played down, as in the experience of Elijah at Horeb/Sinai. Here we see again the cloud and the fire and the lightning (vv. 2-4), and we hear again the Lord's assumption of universal kingship and his humiliation and subjugation of other gods (vv. 6-9). We hear even of the divine decrees or "judgments" that are so important in the Sinaitic materials. *In Psalm 97, however, Sinai is not the focus, but a new mountain (v. 8). The traditions of the Lord's theophany, His earth-shattering apparition to man* (even, to some extent, His revelation of law) *have been transferred from Sinai to Zion. In short, Sinai has not so much been forgotten as absorbed.*

Levenson continues by pointing out that in the early poetry of Israel it is from Sinai that the Lord acts (Psalm 68:8-9); but in most of its passages it is not from Sinai that He comes, but from Zion: "From Zion, perfect in beauty, God shone forth. Our God came; He did not fail to act.

Before Him was a devouring fire; around Him it stormed fiercely"
(Psalm 50:2-3). The transfer of the motif from Sinai to Zion was now
complete, so that the Lord came to be designated no longer as "The One
of Sinai" but as "He who dwells on Mount Zion" (Isa. 8:18).

And then Levenson concludes, "More than merely the name of the
mountain abode of the Lord is involved in the change. Zion, unlike
Sinai, was a known site in Israel. *The transfer of the divine home from
Sinai to Zion meant that God was no longer seen as dwelling in an
extraterritorial no man's land, but within the borders of the Israelite
community" (Sinai and Zion*, pp. 90-91).

Again, the above italics are those of the author of this book. Clearly,
the implication of Levenson's comment appears to be that, for strategic
reasons, *Sinai's sanctity was transferred to Zion.*

10. Robert Wilken, *A Land Called Holy*, pp, 9-10.

11. Robert Cohn, *The Shape of Sacred Space*, pp. 64-65.

Sanctity by Historical Association: The principle that it is humans
in encounter with the transcendent that confers sanctity on a place—and
specifically on Israel's place—has also been articulated from the vantage
point of history.

Louis Jacobs, speaking to an assemblage of rabbis, asserted that
fundamentalists see *kedushah* (holiness) as residing in a quasi-physical
way in the soil. Yet the rabbis did grapple with the problem of God's
imminence versus His transcendence:

Professor Heschel speaks of Shabbat as a "Temple in time." And the
Land of Israel, theologically speaking, is the location of God in space. But
how can the infinite be confined to particular times or particular places?
Thus the Rabbis aver that God is indeed beyond space and time, but *He can
be found in these since humans who are finding him in space are
themselves space and time bound, and for them associations matter.*

There is the rabbinic passage in which the angels ask God: "When is
Rosh Hashanah?" and God replies, "Let us go down to see *when* the people
Israel celebrate Rosh Hashanah, for that day *is* Rosh Hashanah. *The same
applies to the location of God in space. He is everywhere and beyond all*

place, but by historical association Jews can find Him here (the Land of Israel) more than anywhere else (Proceedings of the Rabbinical Assembly, 1981, p. 59).

12. *Mishnah Kelim*, 1:6-9.

13. W. D. Davies, *The Gospel and the Land*, pp. 58-60.

14. Richard Sarason, "The Significance of the Land of Israel in the Mishnah," in Lawrence Hoffman, ed., *The Land of Israel*, pp. 116-117, 126.

On the conferral of sanctity on the land according to Jewish law: Yet another articulation of this notion from the standpoint of the *Halakhah* comes from a work by Sol Roth: As a result of the "Covenant Between the Parts" (Genesis 15:17-21), the ancient land of Canaan became the promised land. *It was subsequently invested, also by covenant, with sanctity: that is to say, the Jew became obligated to abide by the* mitzvoth ha-teluyot ba-aretz, *"the precepts that depend on the land."* In no other place can the Jew experience that (full) intimacy of involvement with the Divine Being that he can in the land he knows to be sacred (by virtue of his own obligatory "holy action," as it were, on the place).

Hence, the sanctity of both the people and the land is expressed in obligation. The people was invested with sanctity at Sinai when it accepted the Decalogue. *The land is sacred in the sense that it imposes obligations of the holy people which are not in force elsewhere.* The Holy Land directs a greater challenge to the Jew and inspires a deeper (and more comprehensive) response. Hence, the fulfillment by the Jew of his own spiritual potential and, simultaneously, his contribution to the well-being of mankind, ultimately depend on his presence on the land (*Halakhah and Politics*, pp. 27, 30).

For further discussion about the holiness of the land from an halakhic *perspective, see Supplements III and IV.*

15. Moshe Idel, "The Land of Israel in the Medieval Kabbalah," in ibid., p. 175.

16. Martin Buber, *On Zion*, p. 53.

17. *Yevamot* 82b, *Hagiga* 3b and *Hulin* 7a. For a full amplification of this rabbinic perspective, see Supplement III, "What is 'Holy' Land and What Is Not: The Rabbinic Perspective Amplified."

18. *The Laws of the Temple*, 6:16.

19. Jonathan Z. Smith, *Map Is Not Territory*, pp. 109-110.

20. *God-Israel-Land: An Organic Unit of Holiness:* Eberhard von Waldow, in a personal communication with the author, explicated the notion of the holiness of Israel's land via an original construct.

Throughout our Deuteronomic texts we are presented with a picture in which God, Israel and land are inexorably interwoven. They speak of the God of history having promised a specific place to the people of Israel. They speak of this collective Israel—a real people—in a special relationship to her God. And they speak of a concrete land as having been entered in the 13th century BCE. Thus here is a triangular relationship:

God

Israel   Land

No point can be left out. Without *God,* who by definition is "holy" (Leviticus 19:2), there would be no promise of a land. *Israel*, without the claim of her being an *Am Kadosh*, a "holy people" (Deuteronomy 14:2), would be without any special status or responsibility for the world. And *the land*, without its assignment to the people of God (Deuteronomy 8:10) as the arena for acting out God's laws and His purpose for her in the world, would be just another geographical area of no particular consequence. Thus the holiness of the land is an integral part of this triangular relationship. It is a "Holy Land."

21. Ben Zion Bokser, *Jews, Judaism and the State of Israel*, p. 45.

22. Louis Jacobs, *A Jewish Theology*, p. 282.

Human Sanctification of Place: Yet another example of the role of human beings in sanctifying a place—and specifically Israel's place—may possibly be illumined from a psychological perspective. Jay Gonen in his *Psychohistory of Zionism*, p. 18, says this:

The promise of a happy repossession of the motherland continued to keep Jewish hopes alive during centuries of exile and finally led to the third Zionade, which was implemented by modern Zionism. The returning Zionist sons were enflamed by a sacred zeal to fertilize Zion. *Hafrahat Hashmamot* or "making the desolate land bloom" was a major aspiration and a central slogan in the entire settlement effort.

The Israeli journalist and author Amos Elon drew attention to the interesting phenomenon in that the early Zionist settlers described their return to Zion not only in usual terms such as "homecoming" or "rebuilding" but also in stranger terms such as return to the "womb" of history or return to Zion the "betrothed." This led him to conclude that a "libidinous link with the soil" was taking place and that the old liturgical references to a mystical "betrothal" between Israel and the promised land was being given new personal and political meaning. Elon reported a statement by the old-guard Zionist leader Meir Yaari to his pioneer followers, in which he proclaimed that the land they tilled was their bride. Yaari compared the *halutzim* to a bridegroom who abandons himself in his bride's bosom or to the motherly womb of sanctifying earth.

23. See Harry Orlinsky, *The Biblical Concept of the Land of Israel*, pp. 52-53.

24. Harvey Cox, *The Secular City*, p. 19.

25. For a detailed exposition of the *Shekhina*, God's presence in special places on earth, found in pervasive form in biblical and rabbinic literature, see *Interpreters Dictionary of the Bible*, pp. 317-319.

26. Vince Scully, *The Earth, the Temple and the Gods*, Chapter One, p. 8, and Appendix One, p. 214.

The reason why certain locales—natural or manmade—suggest sanctity: To amplify Vincent Scully on this phenomenon, we include here the following item published in the *Los Angeles Times* on December 11, 1983, titled, "Scholar Theorizes on Pyramid Siting." It speaks of natural locales such as mountain peaks and manmade objects such as the ziggurats in the Bible's tower of Babel episode. These have regularly stimulated the human imagination to view them as points of connection with the transcendent. Hans Goedicke, the internationally known Egyptologist, reflected the notion in terms of the Egyptian pyramids. "They are the only buildings," he said, "that have never disappointed me. The pyramid is the most perfect monument you can build. The amazing thing is that when you stand in front of it and look up toward the peak, it gives you the illusion of a road leading to the infinite."

27. René Dubos, *A God Within*, p. 118.

28. See *Los Angeles Times*, April 5, 1984, p. 8.

Johan Reinhard continued documenting worship on high places: Mountain deity worship also affected the famous Inca legacy of Machu Picchu. *All the peaks in view were considered sacred by the Incas and are still revered by their Peruvian descendants today.*

The sacred *inti huatana* stone, long thought to be a sort of sundial, stands in the center of the complex surrounded by four sacred mountains. "I believe the stone had little to do with the sun," says Reinhard. "It probably represented, and was worshiped as, a major mountain deity in the region."

Present-day offerings to the mountain gods are made far beyond Machu Picchu. People in the Andes still sacrifice such things as coca leaves, grain, textiles and llamas to the deities. Just as in Inca times, ceremonies include ritual drinking and communal meals, followed by dancing and singing. Llama is a popular main course when it's used as part of the offering.

Human sacrifices may also still take place. In 1942 and 1945, children reportedly were sacrificed in Peru to prevent a drought. Villagers in the central part of the country still talk about human sacrifices from time to time, especially when a major tunnel or road that might anger the gods is being built.

On various summits, Reinhard has found grain, textiles and coca leaves used in Inca rituals. But the most unusual things he found were small human-like statues fashioned from Pacific Ocean sea shells and outfitted with perfectly woven textile clothing. The Incas valued the red and white shells more than gold and considered them indispensable in ceremonies calling for rain.

Most impressive were the ruins of buildings and altar platforms on many of the peaks, some with walls five feet thick and 16 feet long. On Chile's Llullaillaco, at 22,057 feet one of the highest volcanoes and archaeological sites on earth, Reinhard found stone buildings, collapsed roofing, bits of ceramics, pieces of textile, firewood and a sacrificial altar. To build the altar on top of the Las Tortolas in Chile, Reinhard estimates that at least 4,000 baskets of gravel had to be carted 1,500 feet. Priests and their assistants were probably responsible for the building and maintenance of the lofty sites. They regularly scaled peaks more than 20,000 feet high in leather sandals.

29. *Los Angeles Times*, November 10, 2009, p. 20.

Some details in the above report about the Kenyan "Home of God":

It's no surprise that Kenya's earliest settlers revered Mount Kenya. Shrouded in mist and covered year-round with a blinding carpet of snow, the mountain inspired awe and legend from every tribe that laid eyes on it... Scholars date the oral traditions surrounding Mt. Kenya back as far as 500 years, when tribes such as the Kikuyu and Meru arrived in the region. Life and worship centered on the mountain. They prayed facing Mt. Kenya and oriented their homes toward the peak. Sacrificial animals were positioned to face the mountain before slaughter.

When he was a boy, said retired Catholic priest Joaquim Gitonga, 76, everyone here in the village of Muranga marveled at the mysterious source of Mt. Kenya's white tips. Living on the equator, no one in the village had any concept of ice or snow, so they assumed the brilliant white peaks were a sign of the mountain's divine nature.

Though how much of Mt. Kenya's forest cover was lost is unclear, a 1999 Kenya Wildlife Service survey observed nearly 20,000 acres of freshly logged terrain. Today around the base of Mt. Kenya, stumps are nearly as common as trees. "This is a sin against God," said John Irungu, a local farmer who helps maintain a shrine where the first Kikuyus were believed to have settled.

...During a months-long period of drought, a sacrificial goat was led to a bed of leaves at one of the shrines. One of the elders sang a prayer and the worshippers raised their hands toward the mountain. Before slaughter, the animal's head was gently positioned toward the mountain as a local prophetess in a multicolored head scarf predicted quick success. "It will rain," she said. "That I know. God is in this place."

As the service ended and worshippers drifted back to their homes, the sky was clear and blue. Weeks later, worshipers were still waiting for rain, and for God, their eyes turned hopefully toward the distant peak.

30. "Laborers Discover Ancient Temple Site," in *Los Angeles Times*, April 17, 1983.

31. Levenson, *Sinai and Zion*, pp. 138-141.

32. Levenson, ibid., pp. 111.

33. G. von Rad, *Old Testament Theology*, p. 184.

34. Ruth Goodhill, *The Wisdom of Heschel*, p. 240

35. Belden Lane, *Landscapes of the Sacred*, p. 28. Walter Harrelson adds that Israelite holy places were holy only "in virtue of the deeds of salvation associated with them." See his *From Fertility Cult to Worship*, p. 36.

36. *Shlomo Avineri in his The Making of Modern Judaism, pp. 25-26.*

37. Von Rad, *The Problem of the Hexateuch*, p. 68f. For Levenson on Kaufmann, see his *Sinai and Zion*, p. 111.

38. Louis Jacobs, *A Jewish* Theology, pp. 58-59.

39. *In* A Pilgrimmage to Palestine, *pp. 26-27, Harry Emerson Fosdick, depicts the land through the lens of history:*

The Holy Land's unique allurement lies in its antiquity. *Palestine is the home of history.* Acre, for example, ten miles north of Haifa on the seacoast, is a poor, shriveled town today with few visible reminders of its ancient glory, but *what ghosts walk its narrow streets and sail its choked-up harbor!* To these walls the Hebrew tribesmen came and here one of the tribes twelve centuries ago was unable to dislodge the town's natives: "Asher did not drive out the inhabitants of Acco" (Judges 1:31).

Here walks the shade of Sennacherib, who seized the city before he marched on Jerusalem in Isaiah's day, and here came Alexander the Great conquering the world. From the heights a few miles to the north Jesus must have looked upon the town—called Prolemais in Roman times—and perhaps he came here when he repaired to the coasts of Tyre and Sidon. Paul walked these streets, tarrying here a day with his fellow Christians, and before the second century was gone a Christian bishop had here is seat.

Then came the Moslems, in 638 A.D., within six years of Mohammed's death; and when, centuries afterward, the crusaders drove them out, Acre was for long their capital, the center of bloody sieges and hairbreadth escapes. Here Richard the Lion-Hearted is said to have slain five thousand Moslem captives whose ransom was not quickly paid; here Saint Francis of Assisi prayed; here Napoleon Bonaparte turned back baffled from the walls.

Was there ever such a summary of history as Palestine affords? He who sees the land without eyes to see the long, astounding play that has been staged upon it has not really seen the land at all.

40. A. J. Heschel, *Israel: An Echo of Eternity*, pp. 60-67.

41. Mark Smith has shown how the collective memory of land, cathedral and court stamp a people's notion about the character of those places. See his "Collective Memory and Amnesia in the Bible" in *The Memoirs of God*, pp. 131-152.

42. Belden Lane, *Landscapes of the Sacred*, p. 191.

SUPPLEMENTS

SUPPLEMENT I

THE LAND: WHAT GEOGRAPHICAL ENTITY?

1. The geographical data used here is based primarily on the work of Yohanan Aharoni, *The Land of the Bible: A Historical Geography* (Westminster Press, 1967), pp. 58-72; for supplementary and confirming data see "Palestine, Geography of," *Interpreters Dictionary of the Bible*, Vol. 3, p. 628. The map to assist in following the boundaries described here is reproduced from p. 64 of the Aharoni book.

For the complete picture as outlined, it is also necessary to use G. E. Wright and F. V. Filson, eds., *Westminster Historical Atlas of the Bible* (Westminster Press, 1956), pp. 41-42, 51-52; or L. H. Grollenberg, *Atlas of the Bible* (Thomas Nelson & Sons, 1956), pp. 59-60, 65-66; or Herbert May, ed., *Oxford Bible Atlas* (Oxford University Press, 1970), pp. 61-63; also Zaphenia Kallai, *Historical Geography of the Bible*, 1986. A map of the modern Middle East we found useful in the above survey was the one titled "Middle East," *The National Geographic Society*, September 1978.

2. On the point of Israel considering herself heir to the land of Canaan see Numbers 34:2, "...when you enter the land of Canaan this is the land that shall fall to you for an inheritance, the land of Canaan in its full extent." This passage also alludes to what is meant by "ideal borders."

3. See Joshua 13:1-2f. for the consciousness of territory ideally belonging to Israel but not yet taken: "...and there remains yet very much land to be possessed. This is the land that yet remains..." cf. Judg. 3:3.

SUPPLEMENT II

THE UNCONDITIONAL CHARACTER OF THE ABRAHAMIC COVENANT: CHALLENGE AND RESPONSE

References in body of text

SUPPLEMENT III

THE LAND OF ISRAEL: WHAT IS "HOLY" LAND AND WHAT IS NOT: THE RABBINIC PERSPECTIVE AMPLIFIED

1. *Ketubot* 110a/111b

2. *Sifra* on Deuteronomy 12:29

3. *Kebutot* 110b

4. *Avodah Zara* 19b and 20a

5. *Kiddushin* 37a

6. *Mishneh Torah*, Laws of Kings 5:9-10

7. *Yebamot* 82b

8. *Hagiga* 3b and *Hulin* 7a

9. *Laws of Voluntary Offerings* 1:5

10. The biblical book of Joshua details the story of the conquest

11. Ezra 2:1-34; Nehemiah 3:1-32, 7:6-38

12. *Hagiga* 3b

13. Maimonides, *Hilhot Terumot* 1:5; *Hagiga* 3b

14. *The Laws of the Temple* 6:16 and *The Laws of Voluntary Offerings* 1:5

15. For details of these views, see *Tradition*, Fall 1975, pp. 121-122

16. *Mekom Shmuel*, Monroe, NY 1988, No. 37

17. Psalms 105:44-45

18. *Yoma* 9b

19. *The Laws of the Temple* 6:16

20. For details of the above see Yohanan Aharoni, *The Land of the Bible: An Historical Geography*, pp. 58-72, and the map on page 64. For a summary of Aharoni on this subject, see Jack Shechter, *The Theology of the Land of Deuteronomy*, Doctoral Dissertation, University of Pittsburgh, 1981, pp. 11-15.

21. See *Macmillan Bible Atlas*, p. 58, the *Westminster Historical Atlas of the Bible*, p. 42, and the *Grollenberg Atlas of the Bible*, p. 59.

22. Ezra 2:1-34 and Nehemiah 3:1-32 and 7:6-38; *Macmillan Atlas*, p. 130.

23. For a map of the above see the *Macmillan Atlas*, p. 129.

24. For maps and details see *Macmillan Atlas*, p. 130; *Westminster*

Atlas, pp. 51, 56; *Grollenberg Atlas*, pp. 96, 100; and *Aharoni's Historical Geography*, pp. 356-365.

25. Arthur Hertzberg, *The Zionist Idea*, p. 425.

A strikingly similar emphasis came from the pen of Martin Buber: "Israel was and is a people and religious community in one, and it is this unity which enabled it to survive in an exile no other nation had to suffer, an exile which lasted much longer than the period of its independence. He who severs this bond severs the life of Israel" (*Israel and the World*, p. 249).

SUPPLEMENT IV

THE USE—AND MISUSE—OF BIBLICAL AND RABBINIC DATA ABOUT THE LAND

1. See Chapters One and Two in this book concerning the promise of the land as gift and oath.

2. Sanhedrin 37a.

3. For the account of the Gedaliah episode see II Kings 25:22-26 and the book of Jeremiah, chapters 40 and 41.

4. See Martin Noth, *The History of Israel*, pp. 141 and 193. For the additional texts that document the persistence of Canaanite life in the land, see Joshua 13:1-7, 15:13-19, 23:6-13; Deut. 7:22-23.

5. For a full exposition of this rabbinic stance, see Supplement III, "The Land of Israel: What is 'Holy' Land and What is Not: The Rabbinic Perspective."

SUPPLEMENT V

THE JEWISH PEOPLE AND THE LAND OF ISRAEL: A UNION FOR SERVICE TO HUMANKIND

1. David Polish, *Israel, Nation and People*, p. 89.

2. See Martin Buber, "The Land and Its Possessors," in *Israel and the World*, pp. 225-233.

3. See Maurice Samuel, *Light on Israel*, p. 19.

SUPPLEMENT VI

WHAT BINDS DIASPORA JEWRY TO ISRAEL?

References in body of text

SUPPLEMENT VII

RELIGION AND STATE: THE ONGOING TENSION

1. Martin Buber, *On Judaism*, pp. 80-81.

The Distinction Between Religiosity and Religion.

Note: When Buber speaks of the "unconditioned" he means God, that is, that which has not been acted upon, affected by outside forces of any kind. When he speaks of a person being "unconditioned," he similarly means that person has not been acted upon by outside forces, i.e., conditioned. Thus a human being has freedom, is unfettered, can choose for himself, can make a decision for the unconditioned, that is: God. Buber writes:

I say and mean: religiosity. I do not say and do not mean: religion.

Religiosity is a man's sense of wonder and adoration, an ever anew becoming, an ever anew articulation and formulation of his feeling that, transcending his conditioned being yet bursting from its very core, there is something that is unconditioned. Religiosity is his longing to establish a living communion with the unconditioned, his will to realize the unconditioned through his action, transposing it into the world of man.

Religion is the sum total of the customs and teachings articulated and formulated by the religiosity of a certain epoch in a people's life; its prescriptions and dogmas are rigidly determined and handed down as unalterably binding to all future generations, without regard for their newly developed religiosity, which seeks new forms. Religion is true so long as it is creative; but it is creative only so long as religiosity, accepting the yoke of the laws and doctrines, is able (often without even noticing it) to imbue them with new and incandescent meaning, so that they will seem to have been revealed to every generation anew, revealed today, thus answering men's very own needs, needs alien to their fathers. But once religious rites and dogmas have become so rigid that religiosity cannot move them or no longer wants to comply with them, religion becomes uncreative and therefore untrue.

Thus religiosity is the creative, religion the organizing, principle. Religiosity starts anew with every young person, shaken to his very core by the mystery; religion wants to force him into a system stabilized for all time. Religiosity means activity—the elemental entering-into-relation with the absolute; religion means passivity—an acceptance of the handed-down command. Religiosity has only one goal; religion several. Religiosity induces sons, who want to find their own God, to rebel against their fathers; religion induces fathers to reject their sons, who will not let their fathers' God be forced upon them. Religion means preservation; religiosity, renewal.

But whatever the way another people may find its salvation, to the Jewish people it will be disclosed only in the living force to which its peoplehood was ever bound, and through which it had its existence: not in religion but in its religiosity. The Baal Shem says: "We say 'God of Abraham, God of Isaac and God of Jacob'; we do not say 'God of Abraham, Isaac and Jacob,' so that you may be told: Isaac and Jacob did not rely on Abraham's tradition, but they themselves searched for the Divine."

2. Maurice Samuel, *On the Rim of the Wilderness*, p. 134.

3. James Diamond, *Homeland or Holy Land*, p. 5.

4. Ian Lustick, *For the Land and the Lord*, p. 29.

5. Ibid., p. 37.

SYNOPSIS OF FINDINGS IN THIS WORK

References in body of text

QUESTIONS FOR THE CONTEMPORARY SITUATION

1. Israel Friedlander, *Zionism and World Peace*, ZOA Pamphlet, 1919.

2. Yoram Hazony. *The Jewish State: The Struggle for Israel's Soul*, xxiv-xxv.

3. Louis Ginzberg, "Current Aspects of Judaism," *United Synagogue Review*, July 1923.

4. For a valuable set of statements regarding the theological commonalities and differences among Christians and Jews see Markus Barth's *Israel and the Church*.

5. *The Environment and Scripture*: A striking example of this concern for the environment in terms of scripture is a document adopted by a group of 70 Catholic bishops of a twelve-state area in middle America. The title of the document, *Strangers and Guests*, was taken from a verse in Leviticus 25:23 where God tells the Israelites that the land is His and that they dwell on it because of His goodness.

In the section titled "Stewardship of the Land," a theological/ ethical approach to land issues is proposed. With the Bible as base, ten "Principles of Land Stewardship" are offered:

1. The land is God's
2. People are God's stewards on the land.
3. The land's benefits are for everyone.
4. The land should be distributed equally.
5. The land should be conserved and restored.
6. Land use planning must consider social and environmental impacts.
7. Land use should be appropriate to land quality.
8. The land should provide a moderate livelihood.
9. The land's workers should be able to become the land's (civil) owners.
10. The land's mineral wealth should be shared.

John Hart in his *Spirit of the Earth*, pp. 122-127, proceeds to explicate how these principles are rooted in the biblical literature concerning the land and how they need to be implemented in concrete fashion in our day.

The following is a suggested set of resources dealing with religion and the environment:

- Harvey Cox, *The Secular City*, Chapter One, "The Biblical Sources of Secularization."

- René Dubos, *A God Within*, Chapter Two, "A Theology of the Earth," and Chapter Six, "The Persistence of Place."

- Frederick Elder, *Crisis in Eden*, Chapter Five, "Determinations: Biblical and Theological."

- Robert Gordis, *Congress Weekly* (April 1971), "Judaism and the Spoilation of Nature."

- John Hart, *The Spirit of the Earth: A Theology of the Land*, Chapter Two, "Mother Earth and God's Earth."

- Belden Lane, *Landscapes of the Sacred*, Chapter One, "Axioms For the Study of Sacred Place."

- Eric Rust, *Nature: Garden or Desert*, Chapter One, "The Biblical Approach to Nature."

- Vincent Scully, *The Earth, the Temple and the Gods*, Chapter One, "Landscape and Sanctuary."

BIBLIOGRAPHY

Ahad, Ha-am. *Complete Writings* (Hebrew). Tel Aviv: D'vir, 1965.

Aharoni, Yohanan. *The Land of the Bible: A Historical Geography*, trans. A. F. Rainey. Philadelphia: Westminster Press, 1967.

Albright, William F. *From the Stone Age to Christianity*. Baltimore: Johns Hopkins Press, 1957.

———. *The Biblical Period from Abraham to Ezra*. New York and Evaston: Harper and Row, 1963.

———. *YHWH and the Gods of Canaan*. New York: Doubleday & Co., 1968.

———. "The Role of the Canaanites in the History of Civilization," *The Bible and the Ancient Near East*, ed. G. Ernest Wright. New York: Doubleday & Co., pp. 438-471.

Alt, Albrecht. "The God of the Fathers," *Essays on Old Testament History and Religion*, trans. R. A. Wilson. New York: Doubleday & Co., 1968, pp. 1-86.

———. "The Settlement of the Israelites in Palestine, *Essays on Old Testament History and Religion*, trans. R. A. Wilson. New York: Doubleday & Co., 1968, pp. 176-221.

Anderson, Bernhard W. *Understanding the Old Testament*. Englewood Cliffs: Prentice Hall, 1966.

Anderson, George W. *A Critical Introduction to the Old Testament*. London: Gerald Duckworth & Co., 1972.

Angel, J. L. "Ecology and Population in the Eastern Mediterranean," *World Ecology*, No. 4, 1963.

Ardrey, Robert. *The Territorial Imperative*. New York: Atheneum, 1966.

Avineri, Shlomo. *The Making of Modern Zionism*. New York: Basic Books, 1986.

Baron, Salo W. *A Social and Religious History of the Jews*, Vol. 1. New York: Columbia University Press, 1952.

Barth, Markus. *Israel and the Church*. Virginia: John Knox Press, 1969.

———. "Israel and the Palestinians," *Jesus the Jew*. Atlanta: John Knox Press, 1978.

Bewer, J. A., Paton, L. B., and Dahl, G. "Symposium on Deuteronomy," *Journal of Biblical Literature*, 47 (1928), pp. 305-379.

Blank, Sheldon H. "The Curse, Blasphemy, the Spell and the Oath," *Hebrew Union College Annual*, 23/1 (1950-1951), pp. 73-95.

Bleich, J. David. "The Sanctity of the Liberated Territories," *Tradition: A Journal of Orthodox Jewish Thought*, Vol. 15, No. 3 (Fall 1975), pp. 119-135.

Bokser, Baruch. "Approaching Sacred Space." In *Harvard Theological Review*, 78 (1985).

Bokser, Ben Zion, ed. and intro. *Abraham Isaac Kook*. New York: Paulist Press, 1978.

———. *Jews, Judaism and the State of Israel*. New York: Herzl Press, 1973.

Botterweck, Johannes and Ringgren, Helme,r eds. *Theological Dictionary of the Old Testament*. Grand Rapids: William Eerdmans Publishing Co., 1977.

Bright, John. *A History of Israel*. Second edition. Philadelphia: Westminster Press, 1971.

Brueggemann, Walter. *The Prophetic Imagination*. Philadelphia: Fortress Press, 1978.

———. *The Land: Place as Gift, Promise, and Challenge in Biblical Faith*. Philadelphia: Fortress Press, 1977.

———. "Israel's Sense of Place in Jeremiah," *Rhetorical Criticism*. Pickwick Press, 1974.

———. "Weariness, Exile and Chaos," *Catholic Biblical Quarterly*, 34 (1972), pp. 19-38.

———. "Kingship and Chaos," *Catholic Biblical Quarterly*, 33 (1971), pp. 317-332.

Buber, Martin. *Israel and Palestine*, trans. S. Goodman. London: East and West Library, 1952 (republished as *On Zion*, Schocken Books, 1973).

———. *Israel and the World*. New York: Schocken Books, 1965.

———. *On Zion*. New York: Syracuse University Press.

Buber, Solomon, ed. *Midrash Tanchuma*. Wilna, 1885.

Buttrick, George A., ed. *The Interpreter's Bible*. New York and Nashville: Abingdon Press, 1962, Volume II, "The Book of Deuteronomy: Introduction and Exegesis," by G. Ernest Wright.

———. *The Interpreters Dictionary of the Bible*. New York and Nashville: Abingdon Press, 1962.

Campbell, Joseph. *The Mythic Image*. New Jersey: Princeton University Press, 1974.

Chapple, Eliot and Coon, Carleton. *Principles of Anthropology*. New York: Henry Holt & Co., 1942.

Charles, R. H., ed. *The Apocrypha and Pseudopigrapha of the Old Testament in English*. Oxford, 1913.

Childs, Brevard S. *Introduction to the Old Testament as Literature*. Philadelphia: Fortress Press, 1979.

———. *Myth and Reality in the Old Testament*. London: SCM Press, 1960.

Clements, Ronald E. *Abraham and David: Genesis XV and Its Meaning for Israelite Tradition*. Naperville: Alec Allenson, 1967.

———. *God's Chosen People: A Theological Interpretation of the Book of Deuteronomy*. Valley Forge: Judson Press, 1968.

———. *God and Temple*. Oxford, 1965.

———. *Abraham in History and Tradition*.

Cohn, Robert L. *The Shape of Sacred Space*. Chico: California Scholars Press, 1981.

———. "Mountains in the Biblical Cosmos." In *The Shape of Sacred Space*. Chico: California Scholars Press, 1981.

Cox, Harvey. *The Secular City.* New York: Macmillan, 1990.

Craigie, P. C. *The Book of Deuteronomy.* Grand Rapids, Mich.: William B. Eerdmans Publishing Company, 1976.

Cross, Frank M. "The Themes of the Book of Kings and the Deuteronomistic History." In *Canaanite Myth and Hebrew Epic.* Cambridge, Mass: Harvard University, 1973.

Cunliffe-Jones, Herbert. *Deuteronomy: Introduction and Commentary.* Torch, 1951.

Davies, W. D. *The Gospel and the Land: Early Christianity and Jewish Territorial Doctrine.* Berkeley and Los Angeles: University of California Press, 1974.

–––. *The Territorial Dimension.* Berkeley: University of California Press, 1982.

Diepold, Peter. *Israel's Land.* Berlin: Walter Kohlhammer, 1972.

De Vaux, Roland. *Ancient Israel: Its Life and Institutions*, trans. J. McHugh. New York: McGraw Hill, 1961.

–––. *Studies in Old Testament Sacrifice.* Cardiff: University of Wales Press, 1964.

Diamond, James. *The Homeland or Holy Land.* Indiana University Press, 1986.

Dorff, Elliot N., and Arthur Rosett. *A Living Tree: The Roots and Growth of Jewish Law.* Albany: State University of New York press, 1988.

Driver, S. R. *An Introduction to the Literature of the Old Testament.* New York: Meridian Books, 1956.

–––. *The International Critical Commentary* (on Deuteronomy). Edinburgh: T & T Clark, 1895.

Dubos, René. *A God Within.* New York: Charles Scribner's Sons, 1972.

Durkheim, Emile. "Religion as a Collective Representation," *Sociology and Religion*, ed. Birnbaum/Lenzer. Englewood: Prentice Hall, 1969, pp. 136-143.

Ehrlich, Ludwig E. *A Concise History of Israel.* New York and Evanston: Harper & Row, 1965.

Eichrodt, Walther. *Theology of the Old Testament*, Vols. I and II, trans. J. A. Baker. Philadelphia: Westminster Press, 1961-1967.

Eisen, Arnold M. *Modern Jewish Reflections on Homelessness and Homecoming*. Bloomington and Indianapolis: Indiana University Press, 1986.

Eissfeldt, Otto. *The Old Testament: An Introduction*, trans. Peter R. Ackroyd. New York and Evanston: Harper & Row, 1965.

Elder, Frederick. *Crisis in Eden*. Nashville: Abington Press, 1970.

Eliade, Mircea. *Images and Symbols*. New York: Sheed and Ward, 1969.

———. *Myths, Dreams and Mysteries*. New York and Evanston: Harper & Row, 1967.

———. *The Myth of the Eternal Return*. Princeton: Princeton University Press, 1965.

———. *Patterns in Comparative Religion*. New York: World Publishing Company, 1972.

———. *The Sacred and the Profane*. New York: Harcourt, Brace & World, 1959.

"Eretz Yisrael," *Encyclopedia Talmudica*, Vol. 3. Trans. David Klein, ed. Harry Friedman. Jerusalem: Zur-To Press, 1978, pp. 1-68.

Erlich, Avi. *Ancient Zionism: The Biblical Origins of the National Idea*. New York: The Free Press, 1995.

Finkelstein, Jacob J. *The Ox that Gored*. Transactions of the American Philosophical Society 71:2. Philadelphia: American Philosophical Society, 1981.

Finkelstein, Louis, ed. *Siphre on Deuteronomy*. New York: Jewish Theological Seminary of America, 1969.

Fohrer, Georg. "Deuteronomic Theology." In *History of Israelite Religion*. Nashville: Abington Press, 1972.

———. *Introduction to the Old Testament*, trans. David E. Green. Nashville and New York: Abingdon Press, 1968.

Fosdick, Harry Emerson. *A Pilgrimage to Palestine*. New York: Chautauqua Press, 1928.

Frazer, James. *The New Golden Bough*, ed. Theodor Gaster. New York: S. G. Phillips, Inc., 1959.

———. *Folk-Lore in the Old Testament*. Macmillan & Co., 1918.

Freedman, David Noel. "Divine Commitment and Human Obligation," *Interpretation* (October 1964), pp. 3-15.

Friedman, Richard E. *The Exile and Biblical Narrative: The Formation of the Deuteronomic and Priestly Works*. Chico, Calif.: Scholars Press, 1981.

Gaster, Theodor. *Myth, Legend and Custom in the Old Testament*. New York: Harper & Row, 1969.

———. *Thespis: Ritual Myth and Drama in the Ancient Near East*. Garden City: Anchor Books, 1961.

Glatt-Gilad, David. "The Deuteronomic Critique of Solomon: A Response to Marvin A. Sweeney." *Journal of Biblical Literature* 116 (1997).

Gonen, Jay. *A Psychohistory of Zionism*. New York: Mason/Charter, 1975.

Goodhill, Ruth, ed. *The Wisdom of Heschel*. New York: Farrar, Strauss and Giroux, 1975.

Gordon, S. L. *Tanakh*. (Commentary on the Pentateuch.) Tel Aviv, Israel. (Hebrew)

Gordis, Robert. "Judaism and the Spoliation of Nature," *Congress Weekly*. New York: April, 1971.

Gowan, Donald E. "Losing the Promised Land—The Old Testament Considers the Inconceivable," *From Faith to Faith*. Pickwick Press, 1979, pp. 247-268.

———. "Reflections on the Motive Clauses in Old Testament Law," *Pittsburgh Theological Monograph Series*. Pickwick Press, Vol. 33 (1981), pp. 111-127.

Grollenberg, L. H. *Atlas of the Bible*, trans. and ed. Joyce M. H. Reid and H. H. Rowley. London and Edinburgh: Thomas Nelson & Sons Ltd., 1963.

Grosvenor, Melville Bell, ed. *Everyday life in Bible Times*. Washington, D.C.: National Geographic Society, 1967.

Hanafi, Hassan. "Theology of Land: An Isamic Approach," *Israel: People, Land, State*. National Council of Churches Study Group, 1972.

Handy, R. T., Halkin, A. S., et al. "Zionism, Christianity and Judaism." Anti-Defamation League, 1975.

Harrelson, Walter. *From Fertility Cult to Worship*. New York: Doubleday and Co., 1970.

Hart, John. *The Spirit of the Earth: A Theology of the Land*. New York: Paulist Press, 1984.

Hazony, Yoram. *The Jewish State: The Struggle for Israel's Soul*. New York: Basic Books, 2001.

Hertz, Joseph H. *The Pentateuch and Haftorahs* (Deuteronomy). London: Soncino Press, 1964.

Hertzberg, Arthur. "Judaism and the Land of Israel." In *Being Jewish in America*. New York: Schoeken Books, 1979.

———. *The Zionist Idea*. New York: Meridian Press, 1960.

Heschel, Abraham Joshua. *Israel: An Echo of Eternity*. New York: Farrar, Straus and Giroux, 1969.

Hess, Moses. *Rome and Jerusalem*. New York: Bloch Publishing Company, 1945.

Hillers, Delbert R. *Covenant: The History of a Biblical Idea*. Baltimore: Johns Hopkins University Press, 1969.

Hoffman, Lawrence, ed. *The Land of Israel: Jewish Perspectives*. Indiana: University of Notre Dame Press, 1986.

Hooke, Samuel H., ed. *Myth and Ritual*. London: Oxford University Press, 1933.

Ibn, Ezra. *A Commentary on the Torah*. Edited by A. Weiser. 3 volumes. Jerusalem: Rav Kook Institute, 1977 (Hebrew).

Idel, Moshe. "The Land of Israel in Medieval Kabbalah." In Lawrence Hoffman, *The Land of Israel: Jewish Perspectives*. Indiana: University of Notre Dame Press, 1986.

Jacob, Edmond. *Theology of the Old Testament*. New York: Harper & Brothers, 1958.

Jacobs, Louis. In *Proceedings of the Rabbinical Assembly*. New York, 1981.

———. *A Jewish Theology*. New York: Behrman House, 1973.

Kaplan, Lawrence. "Divine Promises—Conditional and Absolute," *Tradition*, Vol. 18, No. 1 (Summer, 1979), pp. 35-42.

Kaplan, Mordecai M. *A New Zionism*. New York: Theodor Herzl Foundation, 1955.

Kaufmann, Yehezkel. *Toldot Ha-emunah Ha-yisraelit*. Jerusalem-Tel Aviv: Bialik Institute/Dvir Co. Ltd., 1937-1956 (Hebrew).

———. *The Religion of Israel*, translated and condensed by Moshe Greenberg. Chicago: University of Chicago Press, 1960.

Kimchi, David. *Commentary on Isaiah*.

Klein, Ralph W. *Israel in Exile: A Theological Interpretation*. Philadelphia: Fortress Press, 1979.

Knierim, Rolf P. "Israel and the Nations in the Land of Palestine in the Old Testament." In *The Task of Old Testament Theology*. Grand Rapids, Mich.: William B. Eerdmans Publishing Company, 1995.

Kook, Abraham Isaac. *Hazon Hageulah*. Jerusalem: *Agudah Lehotzaot Sifre Harayah Kook*, 1941 (Hebrew).

———. *Orot*. Jerusalem: Mosad Harav Kook, 1963 (Hebrew).

———. *Abraham Isaac Kook*. Translation and Introduction (of his key writings) by Ben Zion Bokser. New York, Ramsey, Toronto: Paulist Press, 1978.

Kuyper, L. "The Book of Deuteronomy," *Interpretation*, No. 6 (1952), pp. 321-340.

Lane, Belden C. *Landscapes of the Sacred*. New York: Paulist Press, 1988.

Lapp, Paul W. *Biblical Archaeology and History*. New York and Cleveland: World Publishing Company, 1969.

LaSor, William S. *Israel: A Biblical View*. Grand Rapids: William E. Eerdsman Publishing Company, 1976.

Lauterbach, Jacob Z., ed. *Mekilta de-Rabbi Ishmael.* Philadelphia: Jewish Publication Society, 1933.

Lehmann, Manfred R. "Biblical Oaths," *Zeitschrift Fur Die Alttestament-liche Wissenschaft,* 81 (1969), pp. 74-92.

Levenson, Jon D. *Sinai and Zion: An Entry Into the Jewish Bible.* Minneapolis: Winston Press, 1985.

Levinson, Bernard M. *Deuteronomy and the Hermeneutics of Legal Innovation.* New York/Oxford: Oxford University Press, 1997.

Lewisohn, Ludwig. *Israel.* New York: Boni and Liveright, 1925.

―――, Ed. *Theodor Herzl.* New York: 1955.

Lilburne, Geoffrey R. *A Sense of Place: A Christian Theology of the Land.* Nashville: Abingdon Press, 1989.

Lohfink, Norbert. *Die Landesverheissung.* Stuttgart: Katholisches Bibelwerk, 1967.

Lustick, Ian. "The Emergence of Jewish Fundamentalism." In *For the Land and the Lord.* New York: Council on Foreign Relations, 1988.

Malefijt, Annemarie de Waal. *Religion and Culture.* London: Macmillan Co., 1968.

Malinowski, Bronislaw. "The Public and the Individual Character of Religion," *Sociology and Religion,* ed. Birnbaum/Lenzer. Englewood: Prentice-Hall, 1969, pp. 144-158.

Manley, G. T. *The Book of the Law: Studies in the Date of Deuteronomy.* London, 1957.

May, Herbert, ed. *Oxford Bible Atlas.* London: Oxford University Press, 1970.

McCarthy, D. J. *Treaty and Covenant (Analecta Biblica 21A).* Rome: Biblical Institute Press, 1978.

McCarthy, D. J. *Old Testament Covenant.* Atlanta: John Knox Press, 1972.;

McCurley, Foster. "The Home of Deuteronomy Revisited" *A Light Unto My Path.* Philadelphia: Temple University Press, 1974.

Mendenhall, George E. "The Hebrew Conquest of Palestine," *Biblical*

Archaeologist 25 (1962), pp. 66-87 (reprinted in "Biblical Archaeologist Reader 3," Doubleday, 1970).

———. *The Tenth Generation*. Baltimore and London: Johns Hopkins University Press, 1973.

———. *Law and Covenant in Israel and the Ancient Near East*. Pittsburgh: The Biblical Colloquium, 1955.

Meyers, Carol. "The Roots of Restriction: Women in Early Israel," *Biblical Archaeologist*, Vol. 41 (Sept. 1978).

Milgrom, Jacob. "The Alleged 'Demythologization' and 'Secularization' in Deuteronomy." *Israel Exploration Journal* 23 91973), 156-61.

Miller, J. Maxwell, and John H. Hayes. *A History of Ancient Israel and Judah*. Philadelphia: Westminster, 1986.

Miller, Patrick D. "The Gift of God: The Deuteronomic Theology of the Land," *Interpretation* 23 (1969), pp. 451-465.

Montagu, Ashley. *Man and Aggression*. Second edition. New York: Oxford University Press, 1973.

Nachmanides, *Commentary on Leviticus*.

Naor, Bezalel. "Eretz Yisrael-The Land of Israel." In *Kook-Orot: The Annotated Translation of Rabbi Abraham Isaac Kook's Seminal Work*. London: Jason Aronson.

Neetzan, Yosef. *Toldot Eretz Yisrael: Yalkut M'korot*. New York: Torah Education Department, World Zionist Organization (Hebrew).

Nicholson, E. W. *Deuteronomy and Tradition*. Philadelphia: Fortress Press, 1967.

Noth, Martin. *The Old Testament World*, trans. Victor Gruhn. Philadelphia: Fortress Press, 1966.

———. *The History of Israel*, trans. from *Geshichte Israels*. New York and Evanston: Harper and Row, 1960.

———. *A History of Pentateuchal Traditions*, trans. Bernard Anderson. Englewood Cliffs: Prentice-Hall, 1972.

———. *The Laws in the Pentateuch and Other Essays*. Edinburgh and London: Oliver & Boyd, 1966.

Orlinsky, Harry. "The Biblical Concept of the Land of Israel." In Lawrence Hoffman, *The Land of Israel: Jewish Perspectives.* Indiana: University of Notre Dame Press, 1986.

Patai, Raphael. *Adam V'adamah: Man and Earth in Hebrew Custom, Belief and Legend.* Jerusalem: Hebrew University Press, 1942 (Hebrew).

———. *Man and Temple in Ancient Jewish Myth and Ritual.* New York: Ktav Publishing House, 1967.

Pedersen, Johannes. *Israel: Its Life and Culture,* Vols. I-II, III-IV. London: Oxford University Press, 1926 and 1940.

Petuchowski, Jakob J. *Zion Reconsidered.* New York: Twayne Publishers, 1966.

Phillips, Anthony. *The Cambridge Bible Commentary: Deuteronomy.* Cambridge: University Press, 1973.

Plaut, Gunther. *The Torah: A Modern Commentary.* Ne York: Union of American Hebrew Congregations, 1981.

Polish, David. *Israel—Nation and People.* Ktav Publishing House, 1975.

Polzin, Robert. *Moses and the Deuteronomist: A Literary Study of the Deuteronomic History.* New York: Seabury, 1980.

Pritchard, James B. *Ancient Near Eastern Texts Relating to the Old Testament.* Princeton: Princeton University Press, 1969.

Pythian-Adams, W. "The Origin and Evolution of Deuteronomy," *Christian Quarterly Review* 123 (1936-1937), pp. 215-247.

Rad, Gerhard von. *Old Testament Theology,* trans. D. M. G. Stalker, Vols. I and II. New York and Evanston: Harper & Row, 1962-1965.

———. *Studies in Deuteronomy.* Chicago: Henry Regnery Co., 1953.

———. *Deuteronomy: A Commentary,* trans. Dorothea Barton. Philadelphia: Westminster Press, 1966.

———. *Der Heilige Krieg im Alten Israel.* Gottingen: Vandenhoeck and Ruprecht, 1952.

–––. *The Problem of the Hexateuch and Other Essays*, trans. E. W. T. Dicken. New York: McGraw Hill, 1966.

Rashi. *Mikraot Gedolot*. Commentary on the Torah in Hebrew. New York: Pardes Publishing House, 5711.

–––. *Commentary on Genesis*.

Ramban (Nachmanides). *Mikraot Gedolot*. Commentary on the Torah in Hebrew. New York: Pardes Publishing House, 5711.

Reider, Joseph. *The Holy Scriptures: Deuteronomy* (with Commentary). Philadelphia: The Jewish Publication Society of America, 1948.

Religious Zionism: An Anthology. Jerusalem: 1975.

Roth, Sol. "Land." In *Halakhah and Politics: The Jewish Idea of a State*. New York: Yeshiva University Press, 1988.

Rubenstein, Richard L. "The Cave, the Rock, and the Tent." In *Morality and Eros*. New York: McGraw-Hill, 1970.

Rust, Eric C. *Nature—Garden or Desert: An Essay on Environmental Theology*. Waco, Texas: Word Books, 1971.

Samuel, Maurice. *Light on Israel*. New York: Alfred Knopf, 1968.

–––. *On the Rim of the Wilderness*. New York: Horace Liveright, 1931.

Sarason, Richard S. "The Significances of the Land of Israel in the Mishna." In Lawrence Hoffman, *The Land of Israel: Jewish Perspectives*. Indiana: University of Notre Dame Press, 1986.

Sarna, Nahum. *The Heritage of Biblical Israel*. New York: United Synagogue Commission on Jewish Education, 1964.

–––. *Understanding Genesis*. New York: McGraw Hill, 1966.

–––. *Exploring Exodus*. New York: Schocken Books, 1996.

Sauer, Alfred von Rohr. "Ecological Notes from the Old Testament," *A Light Unto the Nations*. Philadelphia: Temple University Press, 1974.

Schechter, Solomon. *Seminary Addresses and Other Papers*. New York: Jewish Theological Seminary, 1915.

Scholem, Gershom. *Major Trends in Jewish Mysticism*. New York: Schocken Books, 1946.

Schorr, Thomas (compiler). *Man's Relation to Land: Readings*. University of Pittsburgh, 1973.

Scully, Vincent. *The Earth, the Temple and the Gods*. New Haven: Yale University Press, 1979.

Seebass, H. "Der Erzvater Israel und die Einfuhrung der Jahweverehrung im Kanaan," *BZAW* 98. Berlin, 1966.

Segal, M. H. "The Book of Deuteronomy," *Jewish Quarterly Review* 48 (1957-1958), pp. 315-351.

Shechter, Jack. "The Conquest of Palestine: Contrary Views in Light of the Literary and Archaeological Evidence." Pittsburgh, 1970.

–––. "The Theology of the Land in Deuteronomy." Ann Arbor, Michigan: University Microfilms, 1981.

Shechter, Leah. *The Day of the Lord in Jeremiah*. Master of Theology Thesis. Pittsburgh Theological Seminary, 1975.

Simon, Uriel. "The Biblical Destinies—Conditional Promises," *Tradition*, Vol. 17, No. 2 (Fall 1978), pp. 84-90.

Smalley, Beryl. *The Study of the Bible in the Middle Ages*. Notre Dame, Indiana: University of Notre Dame Press, 1964.

Smith, Jonathan Z. "Earth and Gods," *Map is Not Territory*. Leiden: E. J. Brill, 1978, pp. 104-128.

Smith, Mark S. *The Memoirs of God: History, Memory and the Experience of the Divine in Ancient Israel*. Minneapolis: Fortress Press, 2004.

Smith, W. Robertson. *The Religion of the Semites*. New York: Meridian Library, 1956.

Sweeney, Marvin A. *King Josiah of Judah: The Last Messiah of Israel*. Oxford: Oxford University Press, 2001.

–––. "The Reconceptualization of the Davidic Covenant in Isaiah." In *Studies in the Book of Isaiah*, ed. M. Vervenne. Leuven: Peeters, 1997.

Tigay, Jeffrey H. *Deuteronomy: The JPS Torah Commentary*. Philadelphia: Jewish Publication Society, 5756-1996.

Tirosh, Yosef, ed. *Religious Zionism: An Anthology*. Jerusalem: World Zionist Organization, 5735-1975.

Turner, Victor. "Betwixt and Between: The Liminal Period in Rites de Passage," *Proceedings of the American Ethnological Society* (1964), pp. 4-20.

Van Seters, John. *Abraham in History and Tradition*. New Haven and London: Yale University Press, 1975.

von Gennep, Arnold. *The Rites of Passage*. Chicago: The University of Chicago Press, 1960.

von Rad, Gerhard. *Old Testament Theology* (two volumes). New York: Harper & Row, 1965.

———. *Deuteronomy*. Philadelphia: Westminster Press, 1966.

———. *The Problem of the Hexateuch*. New York: McGraw-Hill, 1966.

von Waldow, H. Eberhard. "Israel and Her Land: Some Theological Considerations," *A Light Unto the Nations*. Philadelphia: Temple University Press, 1974, pp. 493-508.

———. "Social Responsibility and Social Structure in Early Israel," *Catholic Biblical Quarterly*, 32 (1970), pp. 182-204.

Vriezen Theodorus. *An Outline of Old Testament Theology*. Newton, Mass.: Charles T. Branford Co., 1958.

Wallace, Anthony. *Religion: An Anthropological View*. New York: Random House, 1966.

Walvoord, John. *Israel in Prophecy*. Grand Rapids: Zondervan Publishing House, 1962.

———. *The Millennial Kingdom*. Grand Rapids: Zondervan Publishing House, 1959.

Weber, Hans Reudi. "The Promise of the Land," *Study Encounter* 7 (1971), pp. 1-16.

Weber, Max. *Ancient Judaism*. Glencoe: The Free Press, 1952.

Weil, Simone. *The Need for Roots*. New York: Harper and Row, 1971.

Weinfeld, Moshe. *The Promise of the Land: The Inheritance of the Land of Canaan by the Israelites*. Berkeley: University of California Press, 1993.

———. "The Loyalty Oath in the Ancient Near East." UF 8 (1976), 379-414.

———. *Deuteronomy and the Deuteronomic School*. London: Oxford University Press, 1972.

Weiser, Artur. *The Old Testament: Its Formation and Development*. Association Press, 1961.

Welch, Adam C. *The Code of Deuteronomy*. London, 1924.

———. *Deuteronomy: The Framework to the Code*. 1932.

Wellhausen, Julius. *Prolegomena to the History of Israel*. New York: Meridian, 1957.

Westermann, Claus. *The Promises to the Fathers*. Philadelphia: Fortress Press, 1980.

Wilken, Robert L. *The Land Called Holy*. New Haven and London: Yale University Press, 1992.

Wiseman, D. J. "The Vassal Treaties of Esarhaddon," *Iraq* 20 (1958), pp. 1-99.

———. "Abban and Alalah," *Journal of Cuneiform Studies* 12 (1958), pp. 126-147.

Wolff, Hans Walter. *Anthropology of the Old Testament*, trans. Margaret Kohl. Philadelphia: Fortress Press, 1973.

Wright, George Ernest. "The Book of Deuteronomy." Volume 2 of *The Interpreters Bible*. Nashville: Abingdon-Cokesbury, 1953.

Wright, George Ernest and Floyd Filson, eds. *Westminster Historical Atlas to the Bible* (revised edition). Philadelphia: Westminster Press, 1956.

———. *The Old Testament Against Its Enviornment*. London: SCM Press, 1950.

———. *God Who Acts*. London: SCM Press, 1952.

Yefet, S. *Emunot V'deot B'divray Ha-yamim*. Magnes Press (Hebrew).

Zimmerli, Walther. "Promise and Fulfillment," *Essays on Old Testament Hermeneutics*, ed. Claus Westermann. Atlanta: John Knox Press, 1971, pp. 89-122.

———. *Old Testament Theology in Outline*, trans. David E. Green. Atlanta: John Knox Press, 1978.

INDEX OF AUTHORS

ABOUT THE AUTHOR

Jack Shechter served as Associate Professor of Biblical Studies and Dean of Continuing Education at the University of Judaism (now the American Jewish University) for two decades. Prior to his tenure at the University of Judaism, he served as Executive Director of the New England Region of the United Synagogue of America, followed by a decade as the Rabbi of Congregation B'nai Israel in Pittsburgh. He was ordained at the Jewish Theological Seminary and received the Ph.D. in Biblical Studies from the University of Pittsburgh.

Breinigsville, PA USA
29 April 2010
237033BV00002B/1/P